IMAGES
of America

YARMOUTH

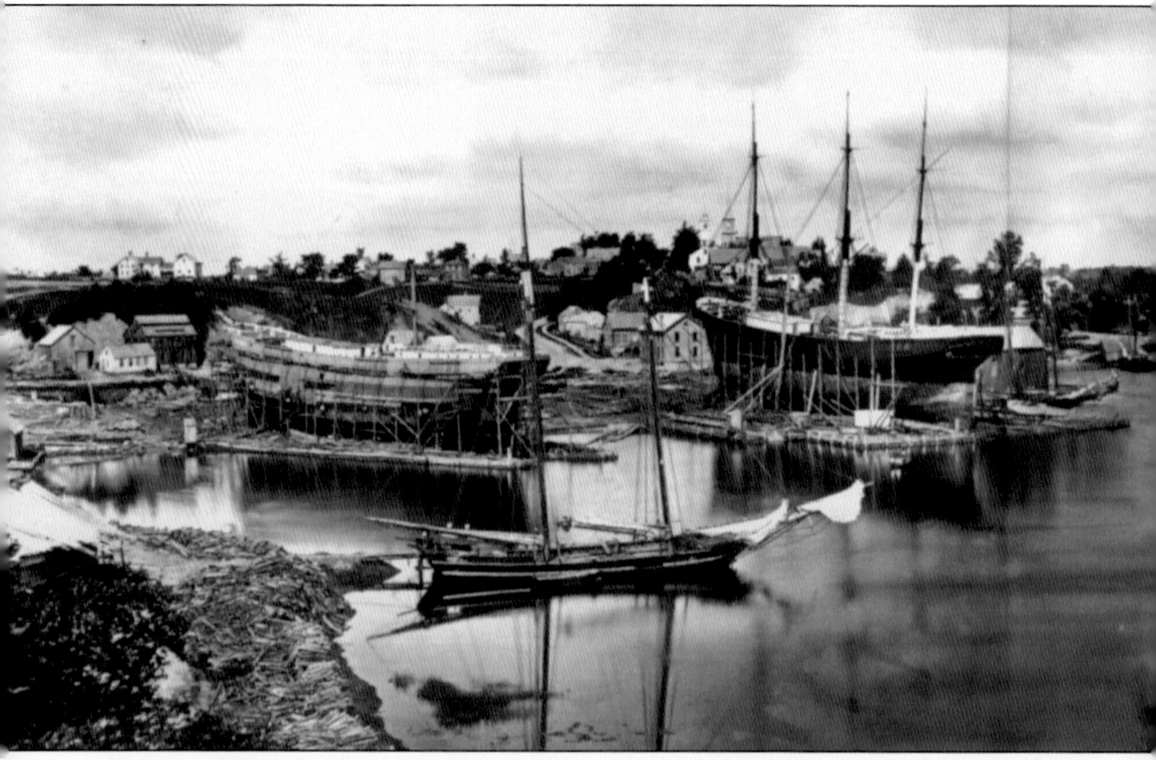

Between 1790 and 1890, Yarmouth's shipyards launched almost 300 vessels, bringing not only wealth to the community but also a sterling reputation for quality workmanship. This 1864 view of the harbor shows the westerly half of a famous panorama of the shipyards. In Lyman Walker's yard on the left, workmen are smoothing the hull of the *Eldorado* while the ship *Detroit* has already been painted and partially rigged in the Blanchard Brothers shipyard. Both vessels had long and successful careers hauling coal, guano, and grain around Cape Horn. (Collection of the Yarmouth Historical Society.)

On the cover: Mr. and Mrs. George Hammond and their cat entertain a nervous-looking Alex Twombly at their Yarmouth estate. As a draftsman at Hammond's Forest Paper Company, Twombly won favor when he drew up the plans for the couple's eccentric Camp Hammond, where this luncheon was held *c.* 1893. (Collection of Lois Rogers Lippincott.)

IMAGES
of America

YARMOUTH

Alan M. Hall

ARCADIA
PUBLISHING

ISBN 978-0-7385-0994-5

Published by Arcadia Publishing
Charleston, South Carolina

Printed in the United States of America

Library of Congress Catalog Card Number: 2001099151

For all general information contact Arcadia Publishing at:
Telephone 843-853-2070
Fax 843-853-0044
E-Mail sales@arcadiapublishing.com
For customer service and orders:
Toll-Free 1-888-313-2665

Visit us on the Internet at www.arcadiapublishing.com

To Martha, who always brings life and wisdom to the making of books.

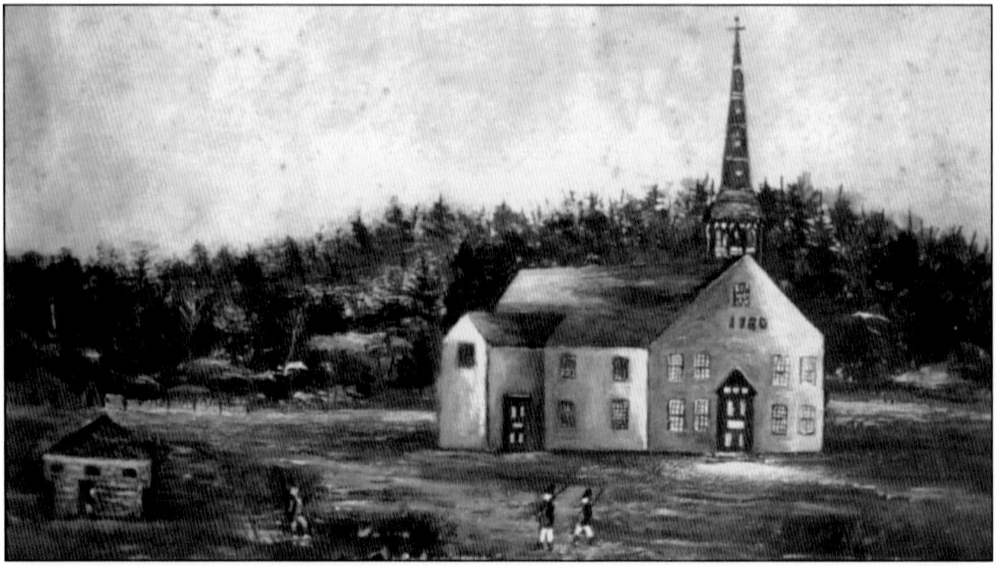

In 1729, Yarmouth's first meetinghouse was built near Wescustogo Hill on what is now Gilman Road. Because it was torn down in 1833, there are conflicting reports of what it looked like, resulting in this somewhat fanciful painting by George Allen. Yarmouth's early Calvinists fired one minister because he suggested that many people are worthy of salvation. Rev. Tristram Gilman was more to their liking when he declared in a sermon that Thomas Jefferson was the Antichrist. (Collection of the Yarmouth Historical Society.)

Contents

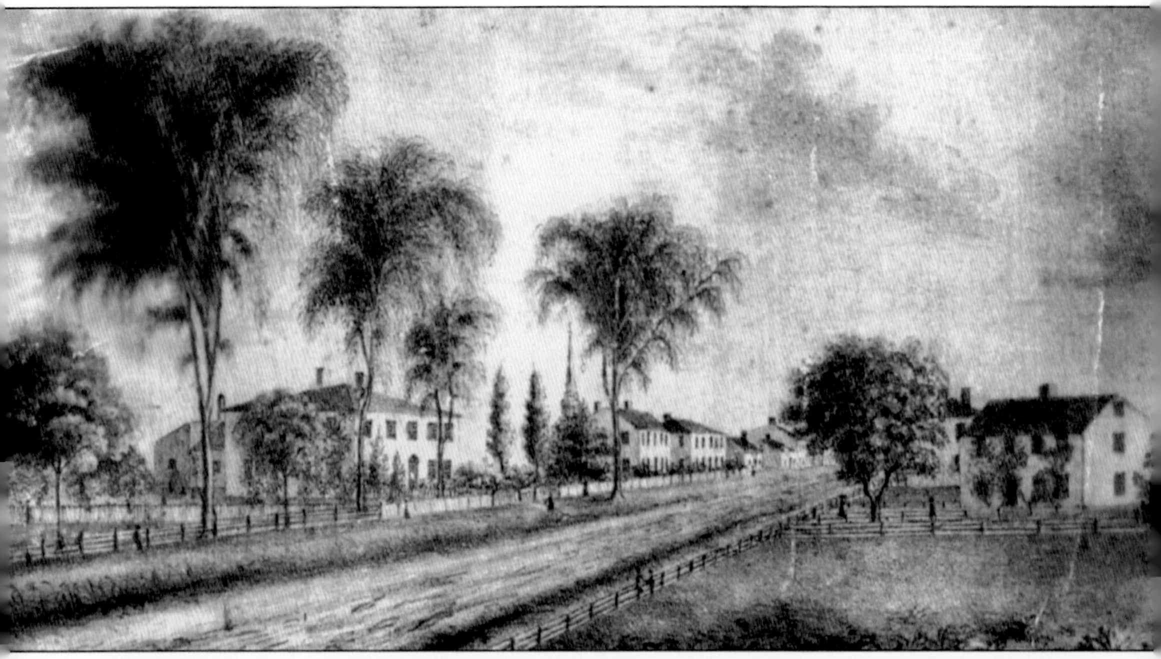

This drawing of the Upper Village may be the oldest Yarmouth street scene in existence. It was completed sometime between the 1837 renovation of the Baptist meetinghouse (center left) and the 1855 removal of the building on the right to construct Capt. S.C. Blanchard's house. The tiny store slightly to the right of the center of the picture is located where Center and Main Streets now intersect. Yarmouth's Catholic church now occupies the left side of this scene. This sketch was pasted inside the cover of a photograph album once owned by Walter B. Allen, a colorful local figure whose image appears several times in this book. (Collection of Lois Rogers Lippincott.)

Introduction

Nestled comfortably in a sheltered corner of Casco Bay, Yarmouth has always offered fertile soil, ample waterpower, a quiet harbor, and plenty of seafood. Although the recorded history of the area starts in the 17th century with the arrival of settlers such as William Royal and John Cousins, these early pioneers were driven away in a series of colonial wars. Permanent settlement began c. 1715, leading to the creation of a town called North Yarmouth that included all of the land and islands between Falmouth and Brunswick. Since Maine was then part of Massachusetts, the new town was named North Yarmouth because it was located north of the Yarmouth on Cape Cod.

As the land was divided and cleared for farms in the 18th century, settlers gradually pushed inland, particularly along the Royal River valley. By 1821, the towns of Harpswell, Freeport, and Cumberland had all broken away, leaving North Yarmouth as a long narrow strip stretching from the ocean to New Gloucester. The rich farms of the inland region around Walnut Hill produced abundant crops, while the two small villages near the harbor constructed mills, ships, and railroads. As conflicts arose between the northern and southern parts of town, the businessmen and sea captains engineered Yarmouth's secession from North Yarmouth in 1849. For simplicity's sake, this book will use the name Yarmouth for all events that occurred within the town's modern borders, even if they happened before 1849.

With the arrival of two railroads and a boom in shipbuilding, the new town of Yarmouth experienced rapid economic growth right after the Civil War. An extensive paper mill was constructed, the cotton mill was enlarged, and the stylish homes of sea captains and mill owners were erected along Main Street. When the era of wooden shipbuilding came to a close in 1890, the town became increasingly dependent upon its huge paper mill, the Forest Paper Company. At the same time, a real-estate boom developed as tourists and cottagers arrived by railroad and steamship to enjoy Yarmouth's coastal scenery. The new boardinghouses, cottages, and yachts all provided opportunities for seasonal employment and dramatically altered the traditional coastal lifestyle of farming and fishing.

In 1923, the paper mill abruptly closed, sending the town into an economic decline that was prolonged by the effects of the Great Depression. After World War II, Yarmouth started to recover, particularly when the new U.S. Route 1 brought more tourists to the community and simultaneously made it easier for local residents to commute to jobs in Portland. Yarmouth's transition into a suburban town was accelerated in the 1960s after Central Maine Power opened its new generating station on Cousins Island. Low taxes, good schools, and a new bridge to the town's major islands quickly turned the old town into a fashionable suburb. Yarmouth's renewed vitality and economic growth were symbolized not only by new public services, schools, and housing developments but also by the creation of the Clam Festival in 1965. By retaining traditions from firemen's musters and Old Home Week, the annual Clam Festival is oddly new and old at the same time, an appropriate symbol of Yarmouth's desire to hold on to its small-town heritage even as it rapidly grows and changes.

To tell this story, the photographs used here have been organized geographically, providing a tour through the different sections of Yarmouth as they existed from 50 to 100 years ago. The journey begins in the first chapter at the lower end of Main Street and moves inland before returning to the waterfront and Old Number Nine on the eastern side of Yarmouth. Chapters 6 through 8 are then approached thematically, showing images of civic spirit, work, and play. The concluding chapter returns to the tour by looking closely at Princes Point and the islands, but it also documents their shift from a traditional way of life into a summer colony.

Although the images in this book have not been presented in a chronological fashion, the captions of the photographs gradually introduce a number of colorful individuals and disclose useful themes that seem to recur in the town's history. For example, the traditions that are now associated with the Clam Festival appeared long before it began in 1965. To follow these themes and the lives of some of the people who wrestled with them, it is probably more rewarding to read this book from beginning to end rather than browsing randomly through it. Regardless of one's approach to them, the captions have been constructed around unusual facts and anecdotes in order to make the meaning of each photograph as engaging as the image it represents. An extensive bibliography has been included at the end of the book.

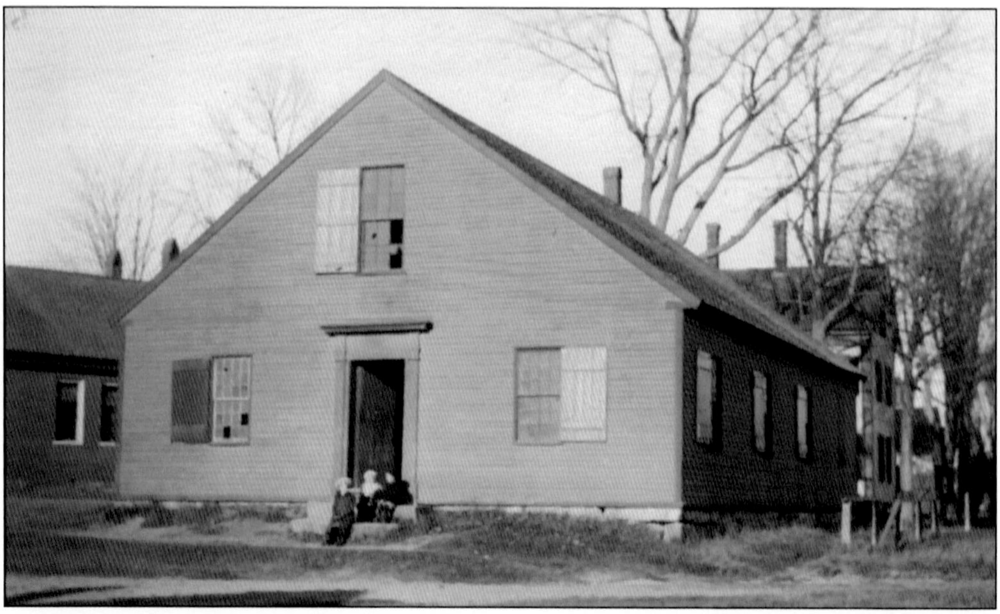

Located near the old brick schools at the intersection of West Main Street and Sligo Road, this large wooden building served as the town hall between 1833 and 1910. It was used primarily for town meetings, including the fierce debates in 1849 that led to Yarmouth's secession from North Yarmouth. (Collection of Chris Havey.)

One

THE LOWER FALLS

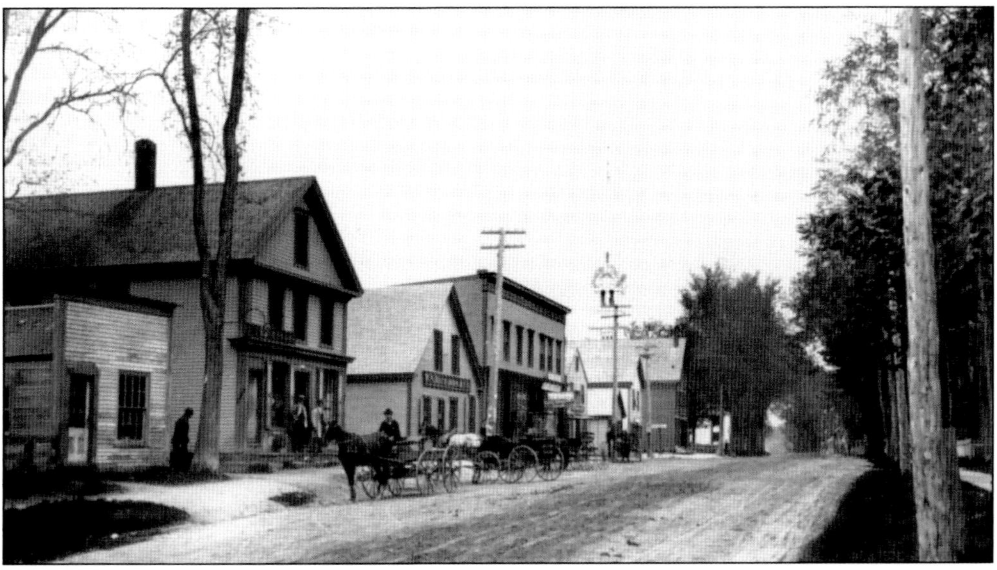

When the modern boundaries of Yarmouth were finally sorted out in 1849, the town was made up of two separate villages: the Corner, or Upper Village, which clustered around the intersection of Elm and Main Streets, and the Lower Falls, which stretched along Main Street from the waterfront to the present U.S. Route 1 overpass. By the 1860s, the shipyards, mills, stores, and warehouses at the Lower Falls had turned it into the wealthiest part of town. This influence can still be seen in its old commercial buildings and institutional landmarks such as North Yarmouth Academy and the First Parish Church. Although some of the smaller buildings have vanished, this *c.* 1888 view of lower Main Street is comfortably familiar. Goff's Hardware now occupies the flat-roofed Coombs Block. The brick building that was then Melville Merrill's drugstore still stands on the corner of Portland Street. Also, the steeple of the First Parish Church gracefully dominates the landscape. (Collection of the Yarmouth Historical Society.)

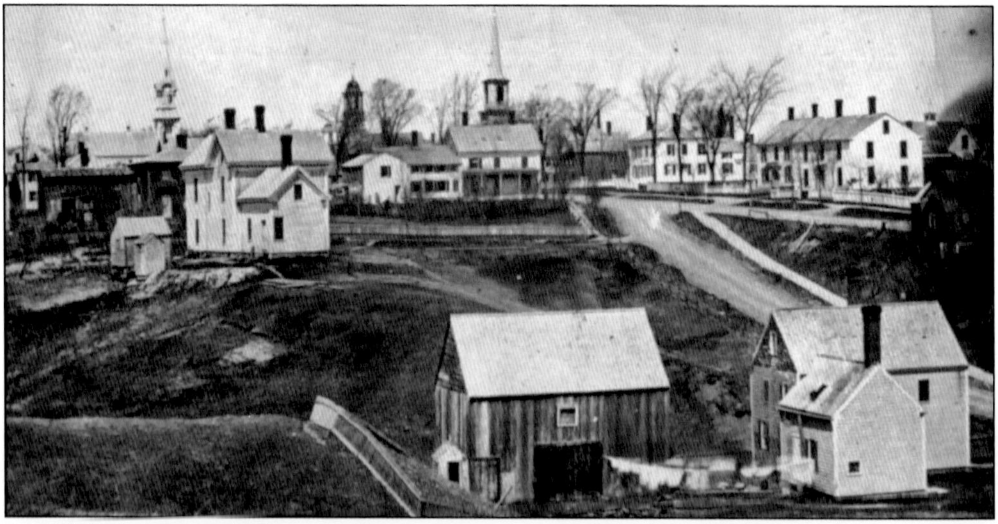

In 1874, the Lower Falls near the harbor was crowded with the homes of sea captains, merchants, and shipbuilders. From left to right, the church steeples are the First Parish, the old First Parish (called Old Sloop), and the Central Parish (now Unitarian). The large, white colonial home in the upper right belonged to Capt. J.W. Lawrence, while James Parsons's house is tucked beside it on the left. This photograph was taken from what is now the intersection of High Street and Rocky Hill Road. (Collection of Lois Rogers Lippincott.)

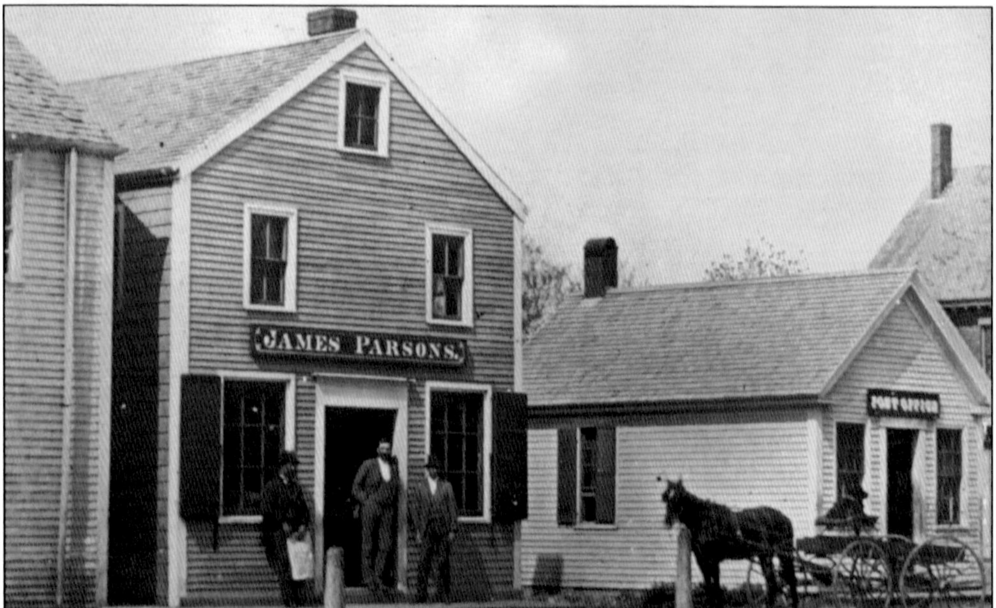

James Parsons was an Englishman who arrived in town *c.* 1860 and married a very wealthy local woman. His little grocery store had become a town institution by the mid-1870s, when this photograph was taken. Influential citizens would collect their mail next door from Lucy Groves and then hang around Parsons's store to discuss politics and keep alert for his constant barrage of practical jokes. When Lucy Groves was appointed postmaster in 1868, she became the first woman ever named or elected to an official position in the town of Yarmouth. (Collection of Lois Rogers Lippincott.)

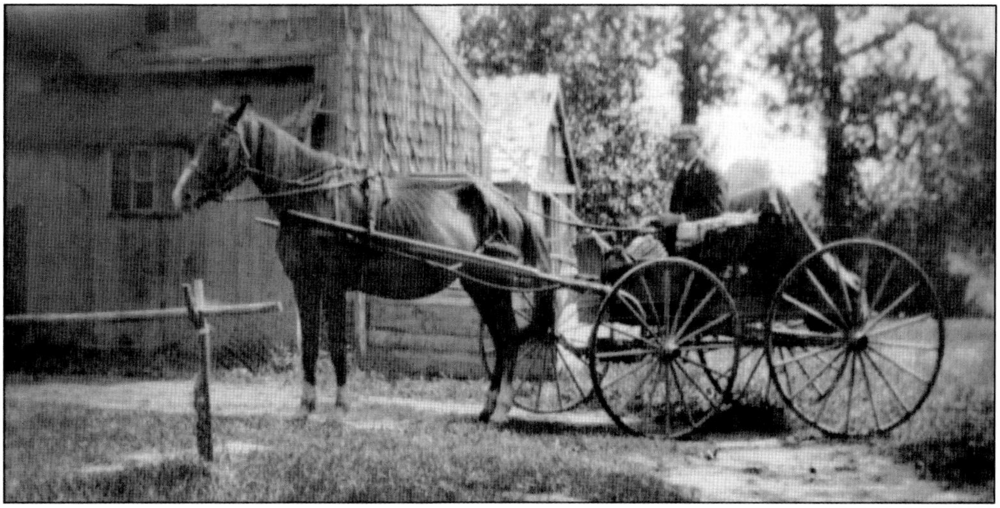

In 1903, the post office established a route in Yarmouth for the rural free delivery of mail and hired Joshua Drinkwater as the town's first letter carrier. Early in the morning, he would leave Princes Point, pick up the mail at the Lower Falls, and then deliver letters on the northern edge of town, including Sligo and Mountfort Roads. Around noon, he would pick up the afternoon sack of mail for the town's western and coastal farms. Every day, as he passed his farm on Princes Point Road, he would change horses and eat lunch with his wife. (Collection of Alfreda Drinkwater Thurston.)

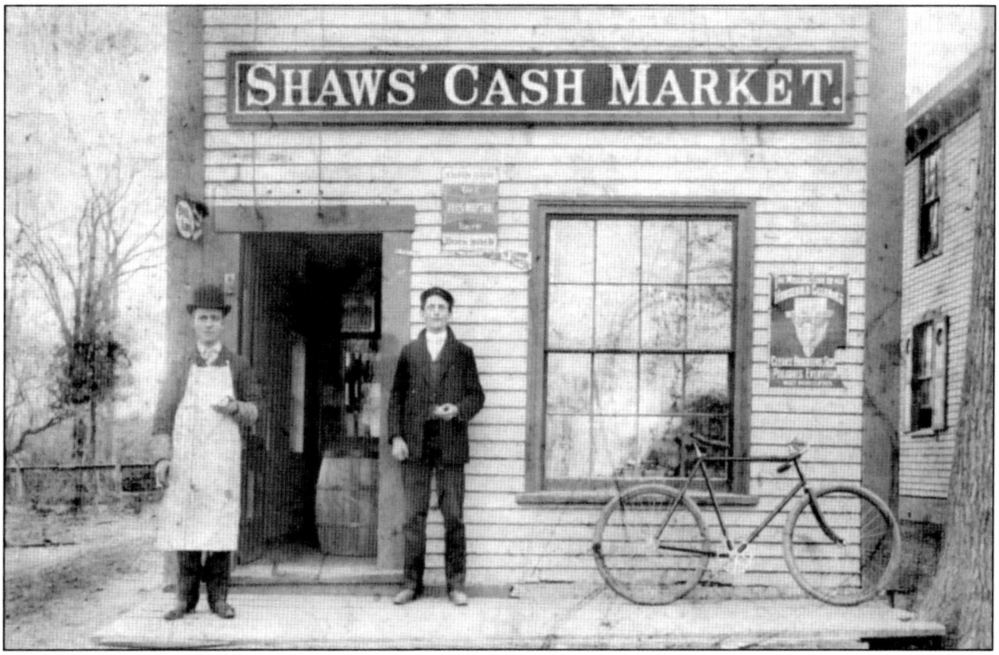

When Cornelius Shaw established this tiny grocery store on Main Street in 1899, his decision to make it a cash market was strikingly modern. Although he sold a variety of choice meats, vegetables, fruit, and eggs, he was breaking away from the tradition of general stores that carried everything and endlessly extended credit to their customers. The nattily attired clerk on the left is Robert Mansfield, and the bicycle belongs to the young customer on the right, 18-year-old Alfred Drinkwater. (Collection of the Yarmouth Historical Society.)

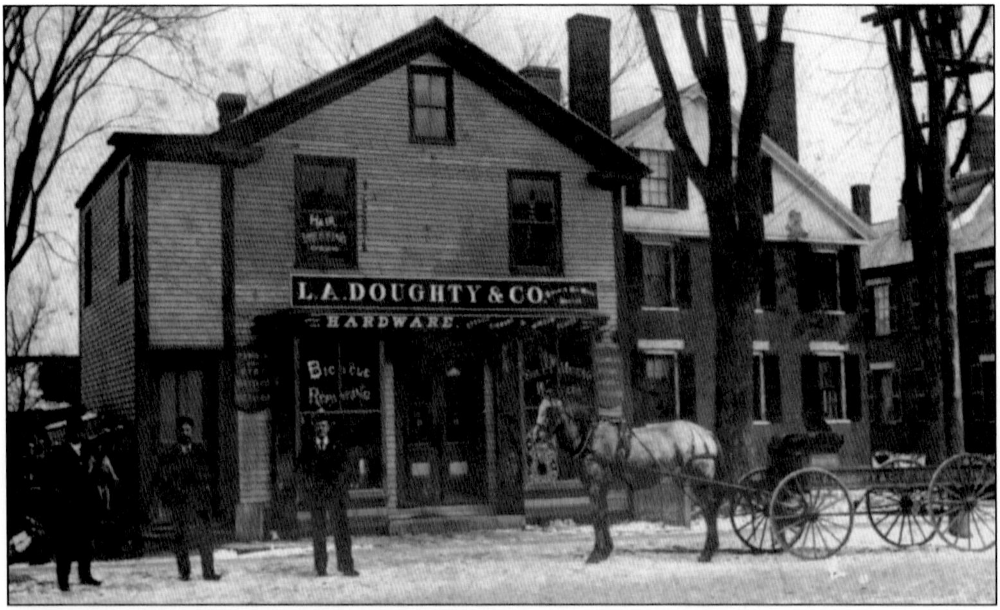

In the late 19th century, Leon Doughty's stove and hardware shop was located at 91 Main Street, across from Shaw's Market and next to the Unitarian parsonage. In the window of the second floor is a sign that advertises William Freeman's hairdressing salon. He was a member the small African American community that flourished in Yarmouth throughout the 19th century. (Collection of the Yarmouth Historical Society.)

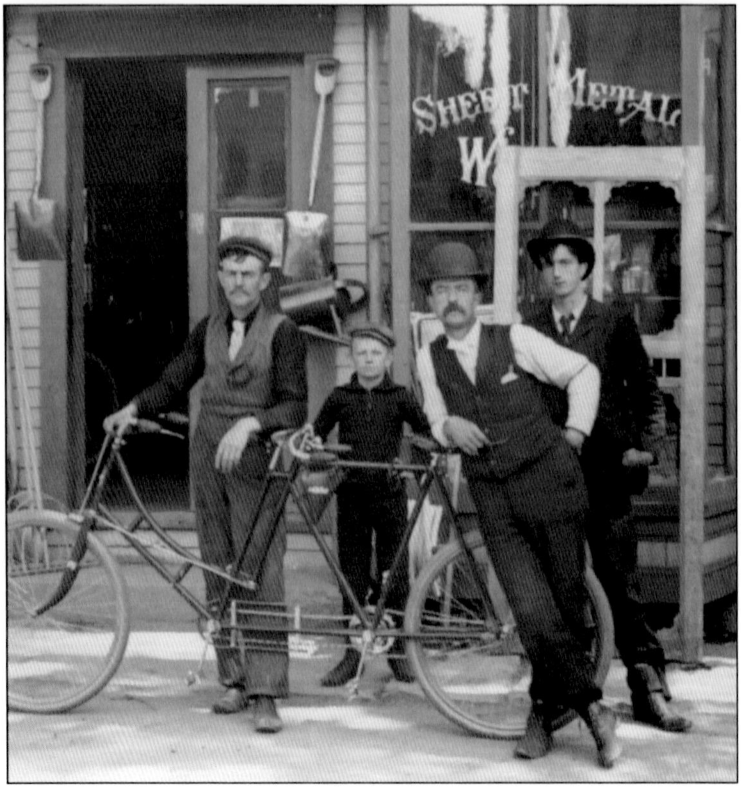

In addition to tinware, screen doors, and heating supplies, Doughty shrewdly added a full range of bicycles to his product line in the 1890s, when they suddenly became a popular fad. Later, he moved his store across the street into the space now occupied by Goff's hardware store. (Collection of the Yarmouth Historical Society.)

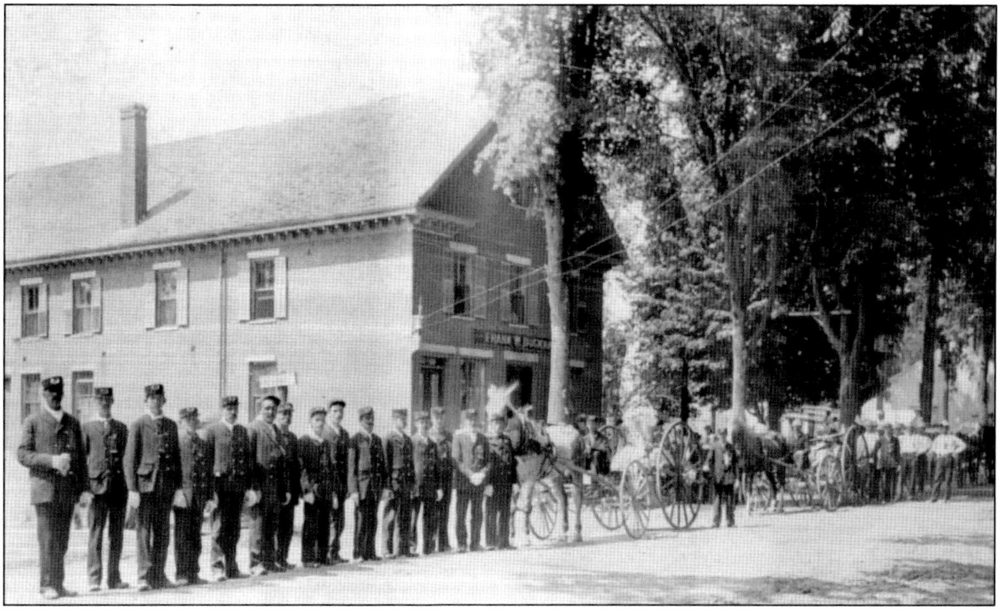

After the installation of fire hydrants in 1896, the town sponsored a grand firemen's muster with companies from all over the state and a parade that included more than 100 Civil War veterans. Hose reel races were held on the streets of the Lower Village to see which fire company was the fastest. The pharmacy sign for Frank Bucknam indicates that this particular muster was held two years later, in 1898. (Collection of Yarmouth Historical Society.)

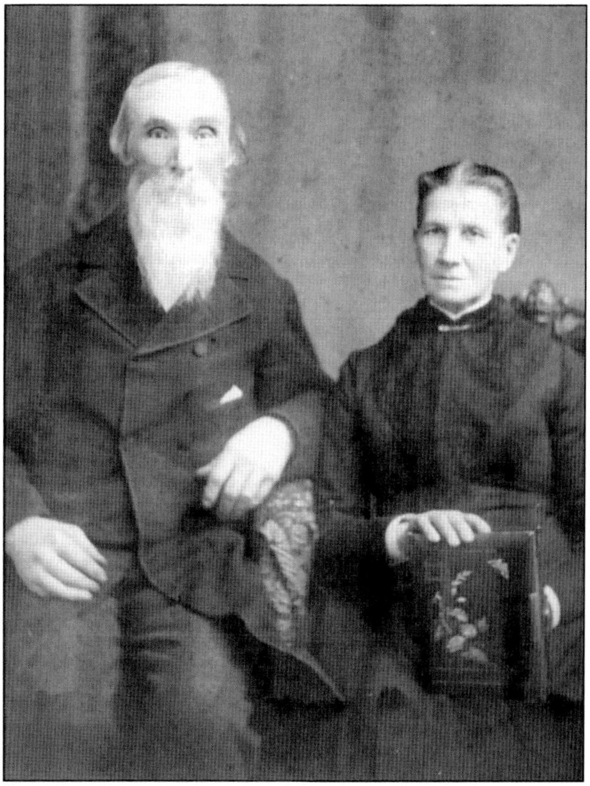

If the eyes of Rufus York seem a bit intense, this fervor served him well. In the 1860s and 1870s, York and his wife ran a general store in the old brick building on the corner of Portland Street. He also gained a local reputation as an evangelical preacher. Elder York reportedly had little difficulty convincing his customers that his limited stock of dry goods was exactly what they were looking for. (Collection of Lois Rogers Lippincott.)

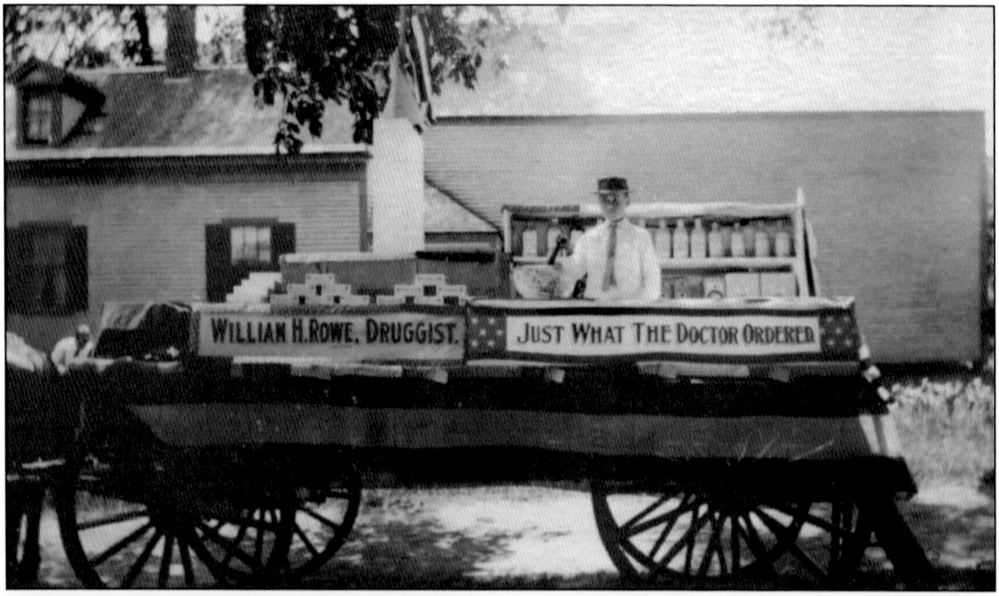

William Rowe was a trustworthy town official, a shrewd businessman, a quiet scholar, and a substitute minister. His pharmacy, with its old-fashioned soda fountain, was also the best place in the Lower Village to wait for a trolley car. To advertise his business, Rowe used this wagon in one of the Fourth of July parades *c.* 1912. Despite Rowe's gentle nature, he once fought off an armed robber who accosted Rowe on Main Street with a six-shooter. (Collection of Yarmouth Historical Society.)

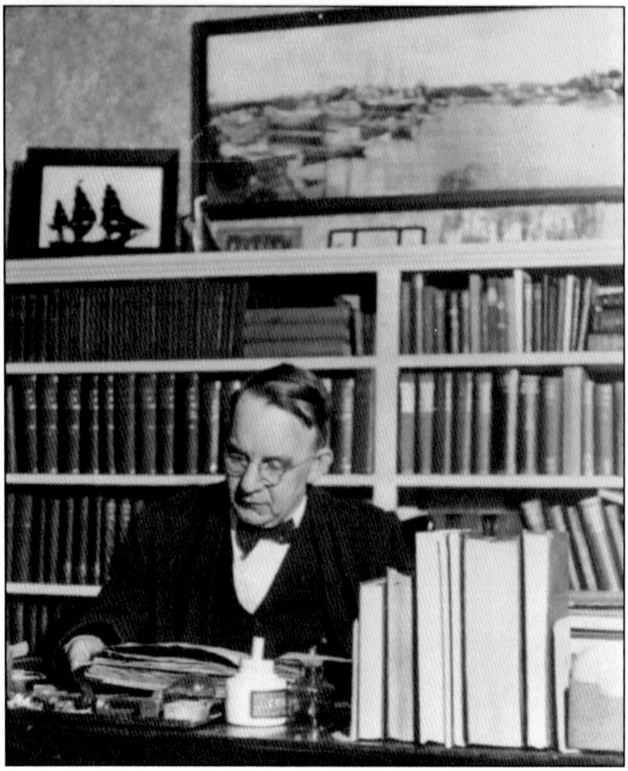

In 1923, William Rowe announced, "In the not too distant future we hope to publish a history of our grand old town." The project took 13 more years, but the book was so thorough that it is still in print. Born in Yarmouth in 1882, Rowe left Colby College to open his own pharmacy. After publishing four history books, serving 32 years as the town clerk, and serving two terms in the legislature, he was awarded an honorary degree from the University of Maine in 1940. (Collection of Yarmouth Historical Society.)

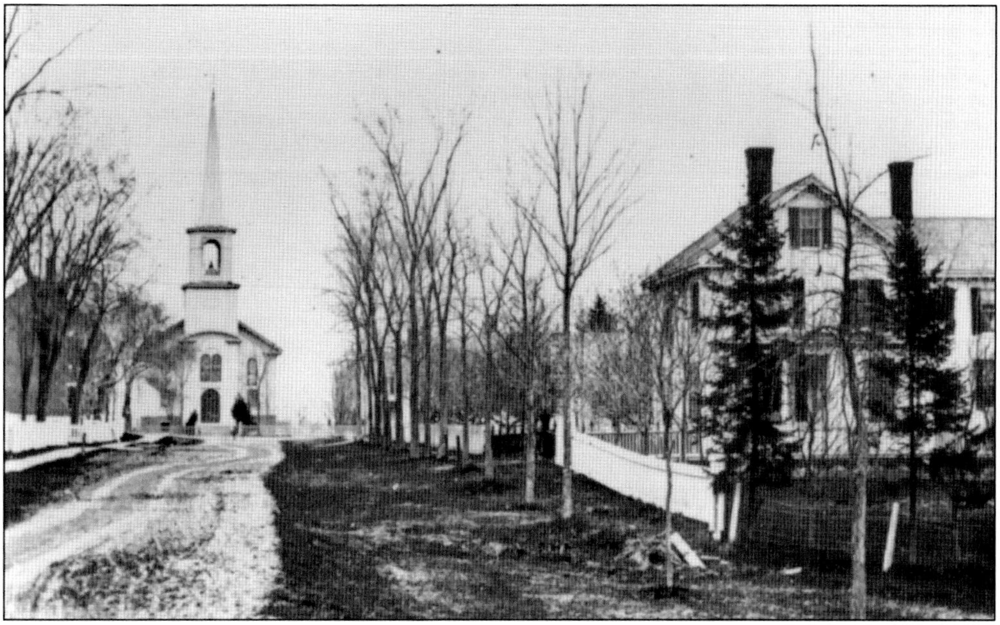

From this vantage point, Portland Street has changed very little since 1875. Capt. Henry Newton then owned the large house on the right. He commanded ships for the Blanchard family, and his success can be seen in the ornate iron fence in front of his home. The church at the end of the road was then being used by the Congregationalists of the Central Parish. On the left is Elder Rufus York's brick store, which was for many years William Rowe's pharmacy and residence. (Collection of the Maine Historic Preservation Commission.)

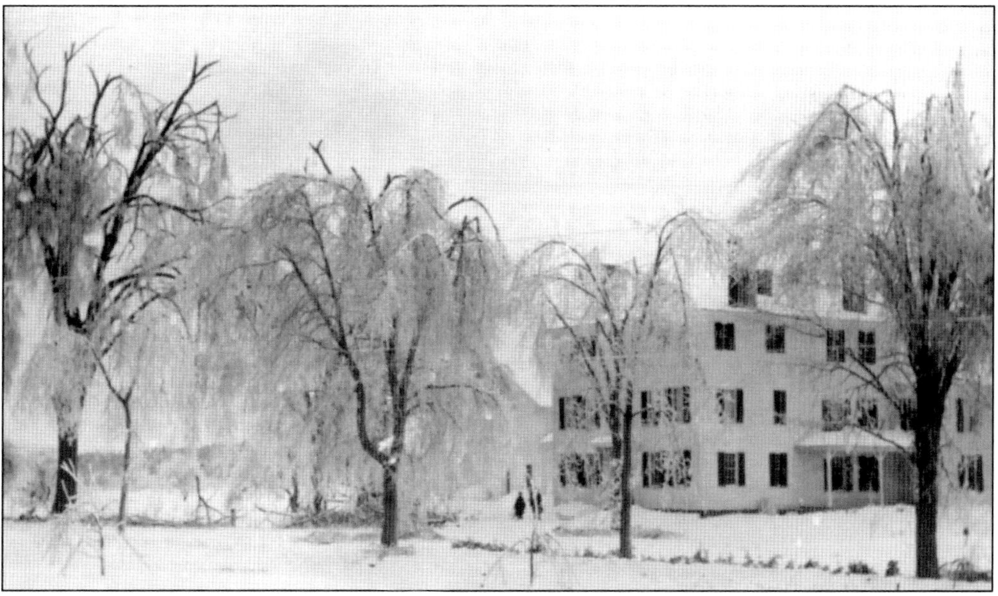

Charles Gooding captured many images of the spectacular ice storm of January 28, 1886, including this Portland Street photograph. The building is a tavern built in the Federal style by Col. Seth Mitchell c. 1810. Early in the 20th century, Ralph Redfern used the property for a dairy that became well known as Old Tavern Farm. It is currently used as an apartment house. (Collection of the Yarmouth Historical Society.)

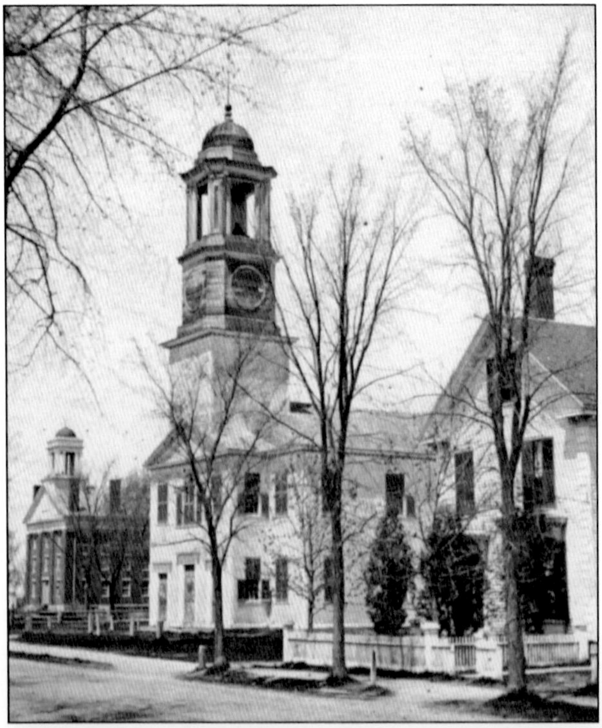

As Yarmouth's population shifted away from the coast, a meetinghouse war broke out in 1818 when the First Parish abandoned its original 1730 meetinghouse and built a new church on Main Street. Called the Old Sloop, the building served the parish until 1868. It was torn down 10 years later. In this view, to the right of the church is the home of one of Yarmouth's most prolific and successful shipbuilders, Edward J. Stubbs. It is now owned by the Vitalius family. (Collection of Alan M. Hall.)

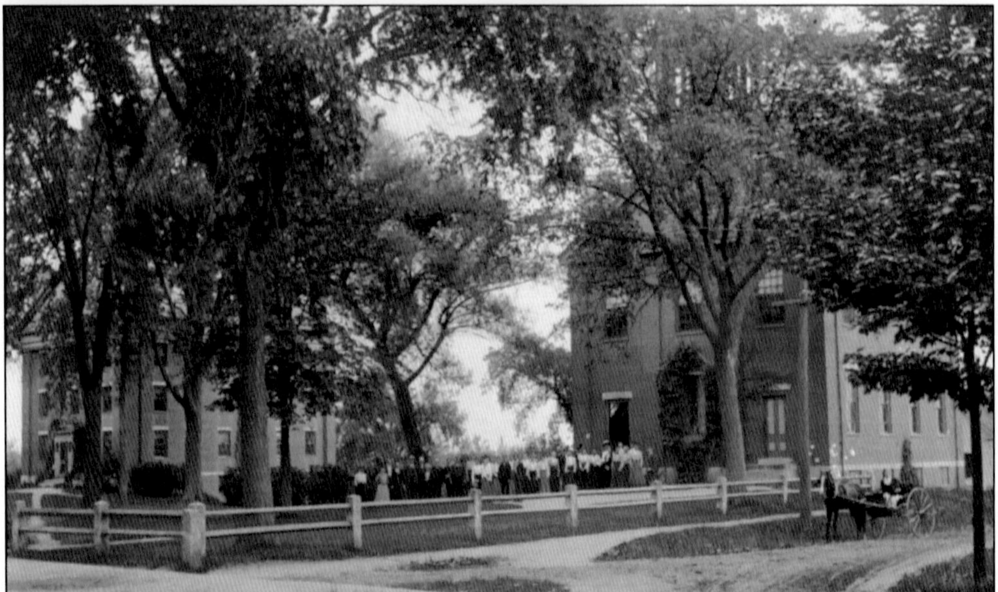

After a hesitant beginning early in the 19th century, North Yarmouth Academy earned an excellent reputation as a college preparatory school in the 1840s. Russell Hall and Academy Hall (right) both date from that period of rapid expansion. At the time of this photograph in the 1890s, the academy was trying to adjust to the creation of free public high schools in Maine. By the early 1930s, effective leadership and generous donations enabled the academy to expand into new facilities across the street. (Collection of Lois Rogers Lippincott.)

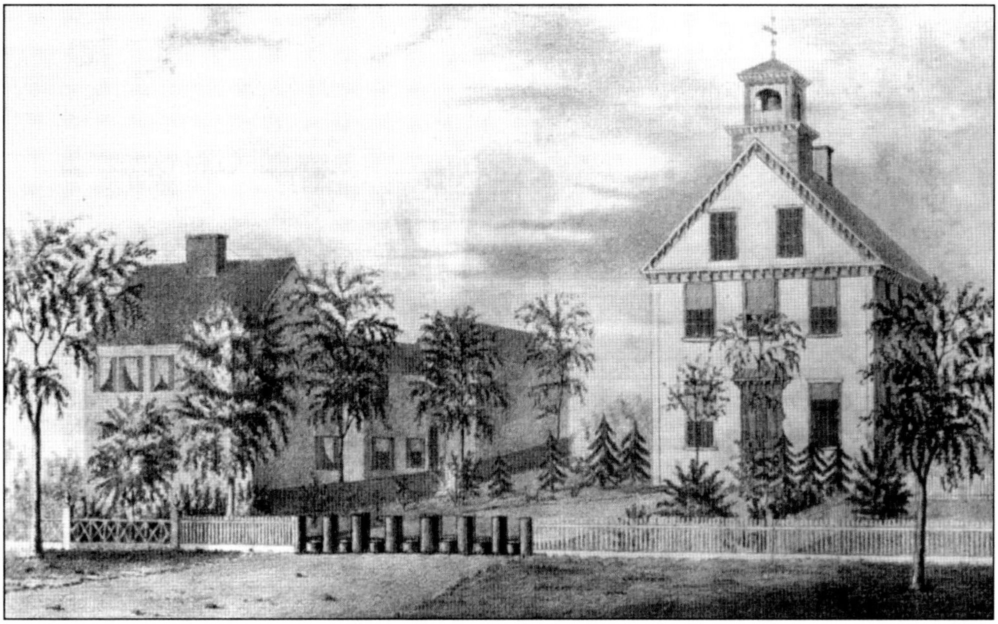

This lithograph from 1851 shows the home of George Woods (left) and Yarmouth Institute, which he established in direct competition with the North Yarmouth Academy. A respected teacher who had been the principal of the English department at the academy, Woods sharply disagreed with its trustees over everything from slavery to theology. Because of Woods's popularity and his impressive new school, even some of the academy's trustees transferred their children to Yarmouth Institute. (Collection of Lois Rogers Lippincott.)

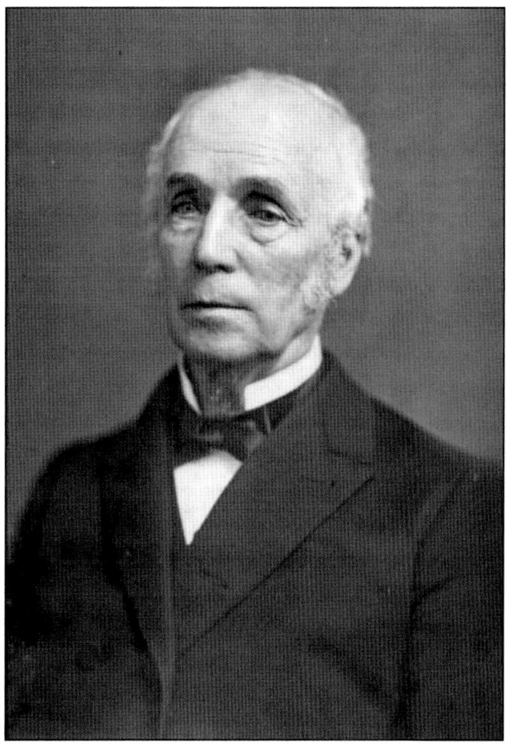

George Woods's independent streak may have come from his father, who was a local abolitionist. Although George Woods (shown here) attracted students from as far away as Cuba, his institute lacked an endowment and closed after five years. He moved on to become the chancellor of the University of Pittsburg, but a lawsuit involving his dispute with North Yarmouth Academy precipitated the split in the First Parish Church in 1859. (Collection of Lois Rogers Lippincott.)

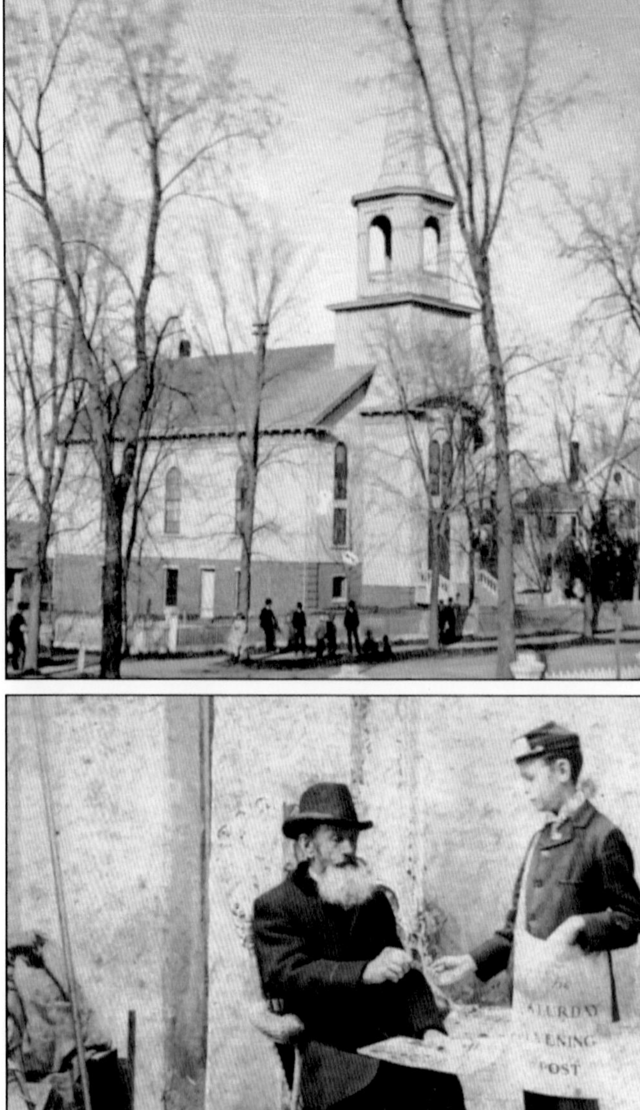

The Central Congregational Society built this church in 1860 after a schism split the First Parish. The shipbuilders and captains who financed the new church felt that the First Parish had become too liberal in its approach to individual morality and too radical in its opposition to slavery and alcohol. It is therefore somewhat ironic that the conservative Central Parish (as it became known) eventually became a reform-minded Unitarian Universalist church in 1886. (Collection of Alan M. Hall.)

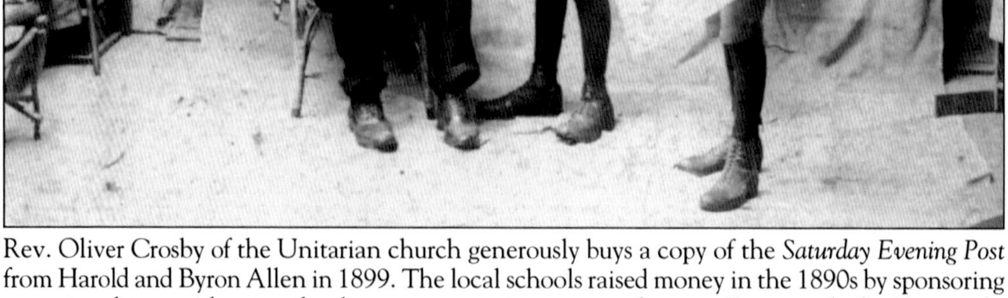

Rev. Oliver Crosby of the Unitarian church generously buys a copy of the *Saturday Evening Post* from Harold and Byron Allen in 1899. The local schools raised money in the 1890s by sponsoring magazine drives with prizes for the most aggressive young salesmen. Fortunately for Yarmouth, Cyrus Curtis, the publisher of the *Saturday Evening Post*, reinvested some of these profits in the town by donating large sums to the academy in 1930. (Collection of Alan M. Hall.)

For approximately 10 years after the Civil War, Yarmouth experienced an economic boom. With its handsome Italianate facade and ornate interior, the current First Parish Church symbolizes that prosperity. Perhaps feeling some competition from the new Central Parish, which had just installed the town's first organ, the members of the First Parish Church spent the extravagant sum of $35,000 to construct their new church in 1868, including a large pipe organ. (Collection of Alan M. Hall.)

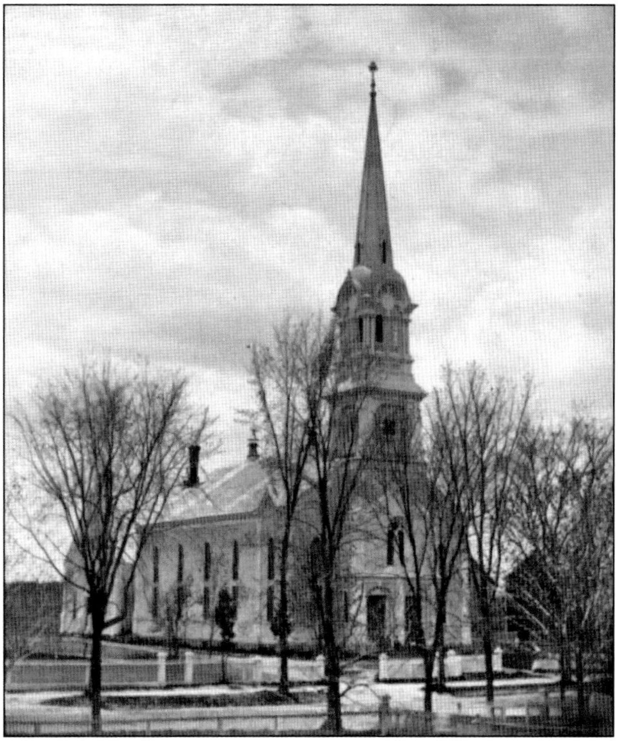

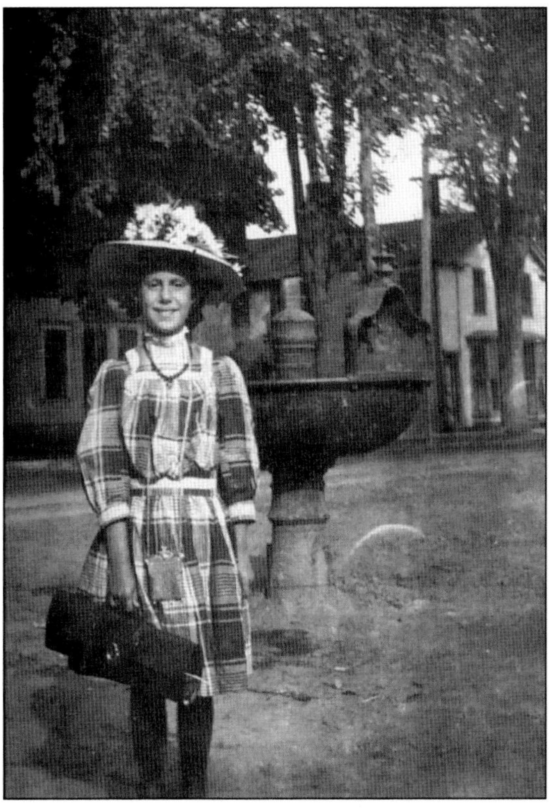

In this 1912 photograph, Elizabeth Drinkwater pauses near the ornate horse trough that once stood at the intersection of Main and Portland Streets. In her hand is the sheet music she needs for her piano lesson, and on her head is a floral creation from Susan Kinghorn's millinery shop, where she worked after school. That store was located behind her on the corner of Portland Street, a location that has more recently been occupied by pizza and sandwich shops. (Collection of Alfreda Drinkwater Thurston.)

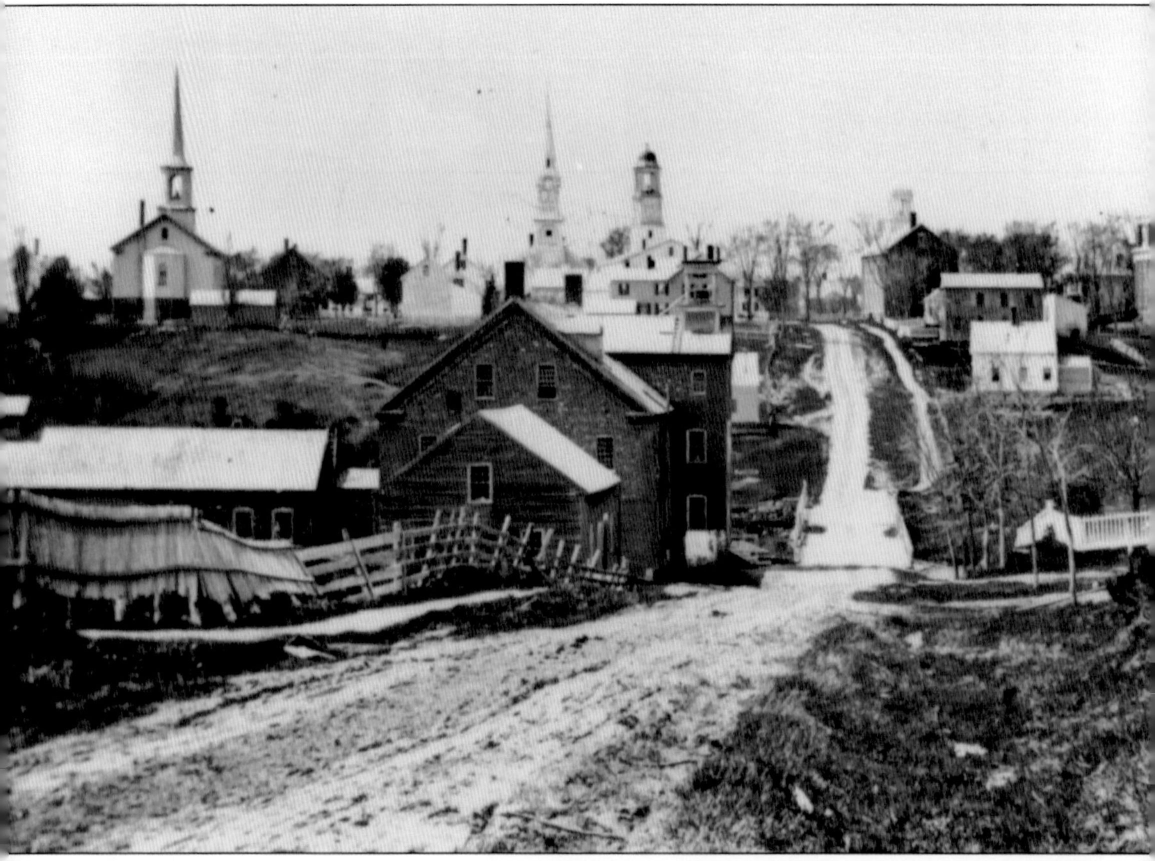

Viewed from Bridge Street in the early 1870s, the skyline of Yarmouth was dominated by the spires and cupolas of churches and schools. Seen here are, from left to right, the Central Parish church (now Unitarian), the First Parish Church, the Old Sloop, Academy Hall, and finally Russell Hall. Capt. Paul Blanchard's mansion can be seen through the trees in front of Russell Hall. The cupola of the Yarmouth Institute is barely visible above Blanchard's roof. The building with a white roof just below Academy Hall was North Yarmouth Academy's original school of 1811. The large brick buildings in the center are Yarmouth's cotton mill. (Collection of the Maine Historic Preservation Commission.)

Two

The Upper Village

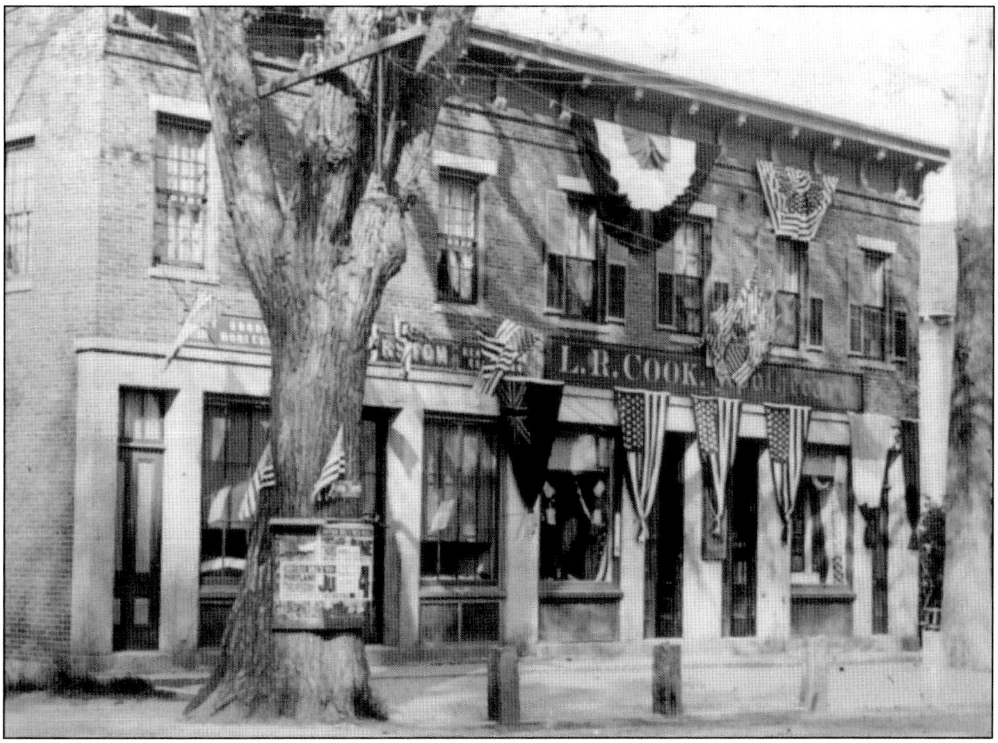

There was a time when people living near the Elm Street corner would not think of shopping at the other end of Main Street. For more than 150 years, much of the retail activity in the Upper Village centered on the area near these old brick stores. Founded in 1859, William Marston's dry goods business was a landmark that lasted until the early 1960s. Next door, L.R. Cook operated a drugstore that sold not only medicines but also items for the home, such as wallpaper and window glass. The elm tree with the bulletin board was used by local residents as early as 1817 for posting public notices, circus posters, and satirical comments about town affairs. Like so many of Yarmouth's majestic elms, it succumbed to Dutch elm disease and was cut down in 1980. (Collection of the Yarmouth Historical Society.)

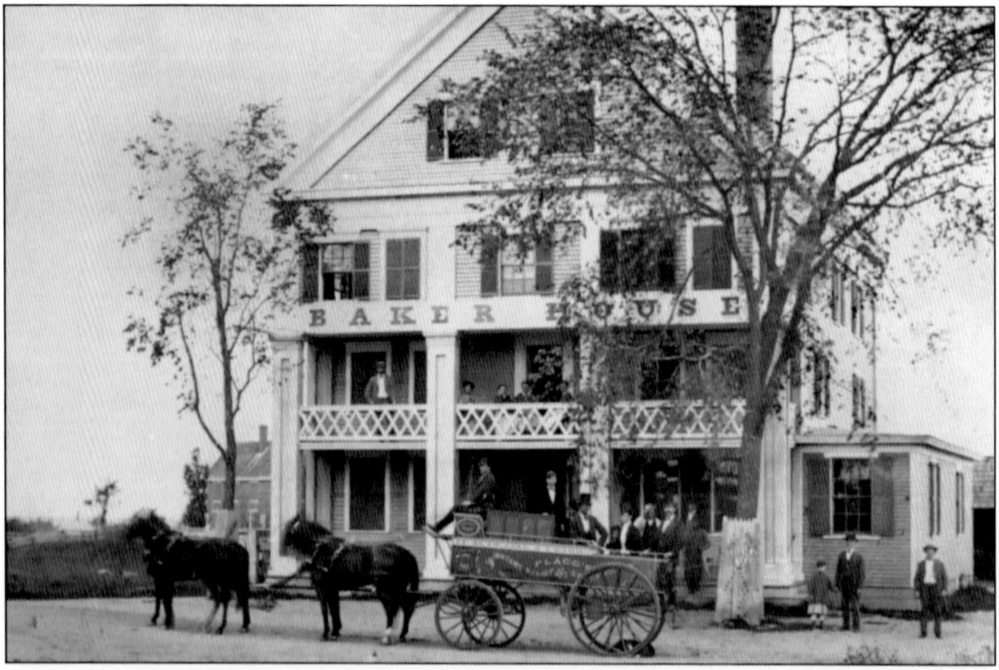

As the rails of the Atlantic and St. Lawrence Railroad (later the Grand Trunk) snaked toward Yarmouth in 1848, local citizens were caught up in a speculative frenzy. They enthusiastically bought railroad bonds and drove up the prices of land near the depot on Main Street. To serve the anticipated crowds that never actually materialized, Jeremiah Baker built a hotel called the St. Lawrence House, which included a bowling alley and ballroom. In this *c.* 1872 view, it had been renamed the Baker House, the first of many name changes before it burned in 1928. The site is now a gas station. (Collection of the Yarmouth Historical Society.)

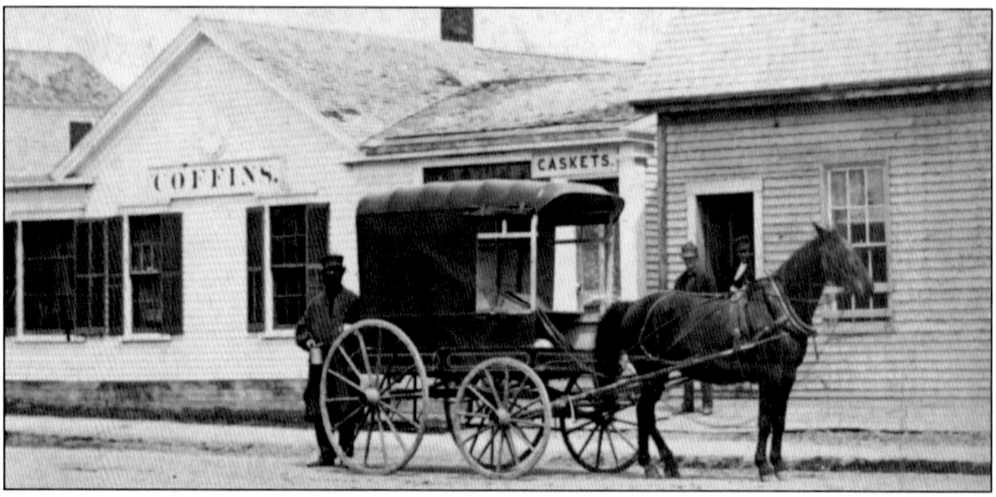

Across from the Grand Trunk depot and just to the east of the Baker House was a low building used by J.O. Durgan in the 1860s as a daguerreotype salon. Later, it became Gad Hitchcock's showroom for caskets and coffins, a curious sideline for the son of a capable local doctor. Gad Hitchcock later sold the coffins out of his paint shop on the waterfront, where he became famous for his ability to put the fine decorative touches on the shipmasters' cabins. (Collection of Lois Rogers Lippincott.)

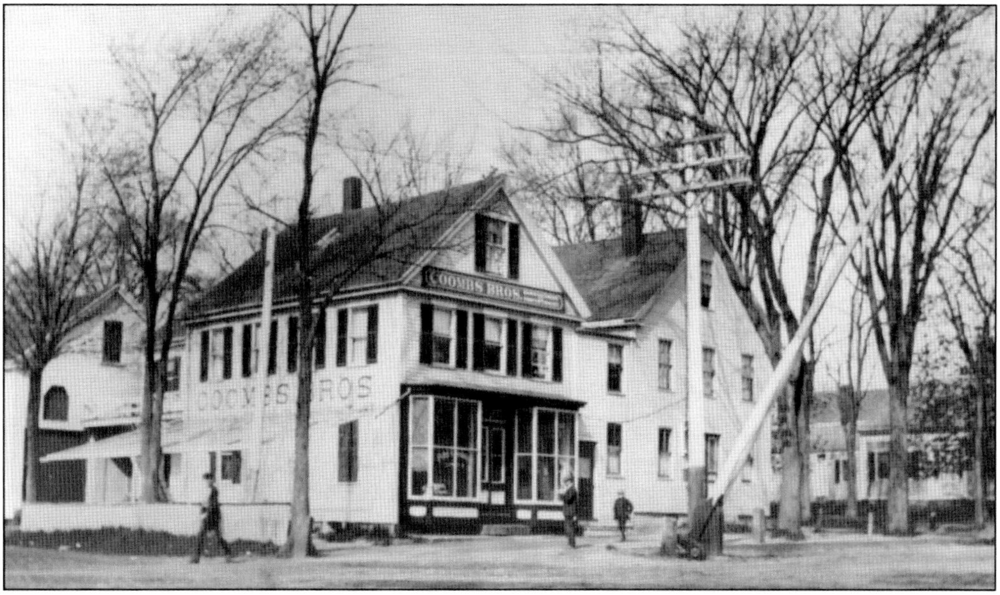

When he was just six years old, Albert Coombs used a little cart to sell lemonade and molasses candy to shipyard workers. He and his brother George later purchased two adjacent buildings on the corner of South Street to manufacture candy and sell groceries. By connecting a horse to an ice-cream freezer, he also manufactured ice cream. Bert set up the town's telephone service in the 1880s and later hired Myrtle McCrae as the first operator. In 1909, he was so impressed with his new Model T that he established a Ford dealership on South Street. (Collection of the Maine Historic Preservation Commission.)

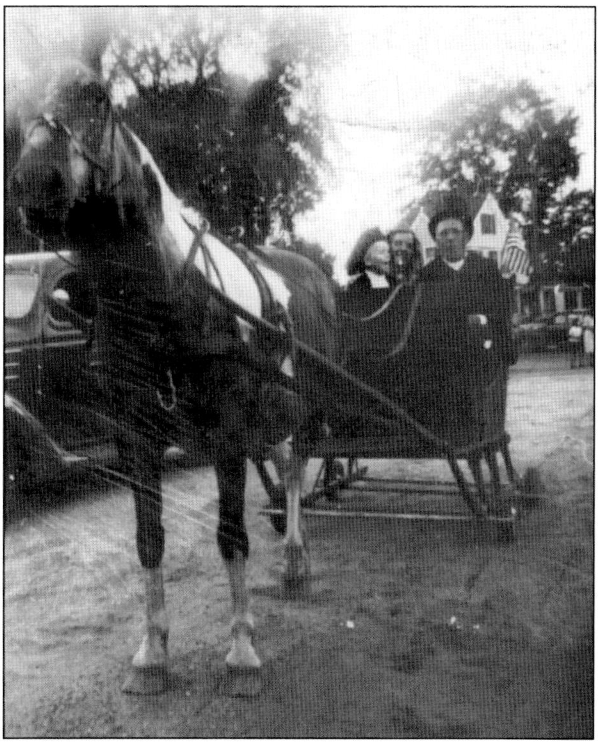

Eventually, the Coombs building was purchased by a colorful local entrepreneur named Elmer Ring. After making significant changes to the roofline and facade of the building, Elmer set up a variety of businesses, including a "washerette," a hardware store, a heating and plumbing service, and a coal yard. During the 1949 centennial parade, Elmer and his family received third prize for riding down Main Street in one of Bert Coombs's old sleighs, which Elmer had rigged with wheels. (Collection of Virginia Turner.)

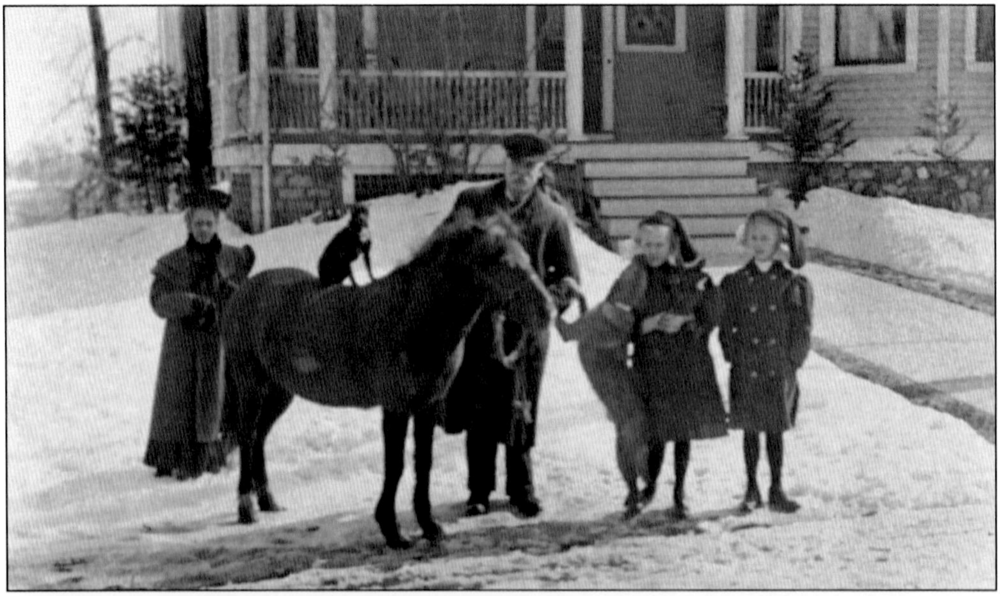

South Street was laid out in 1848 as part of Yarmouth's first modern housing development. House lots were carved out of farm land and sold to merchants and sea captains, such as Ansel Loring and Perez Blanchard. Although the names of the residents seen here are unknown, they were photographed *c.* 1915 with their enthusiastic pets in front of 62 South Street. (Collection of the Yarmouth Historical Society.)

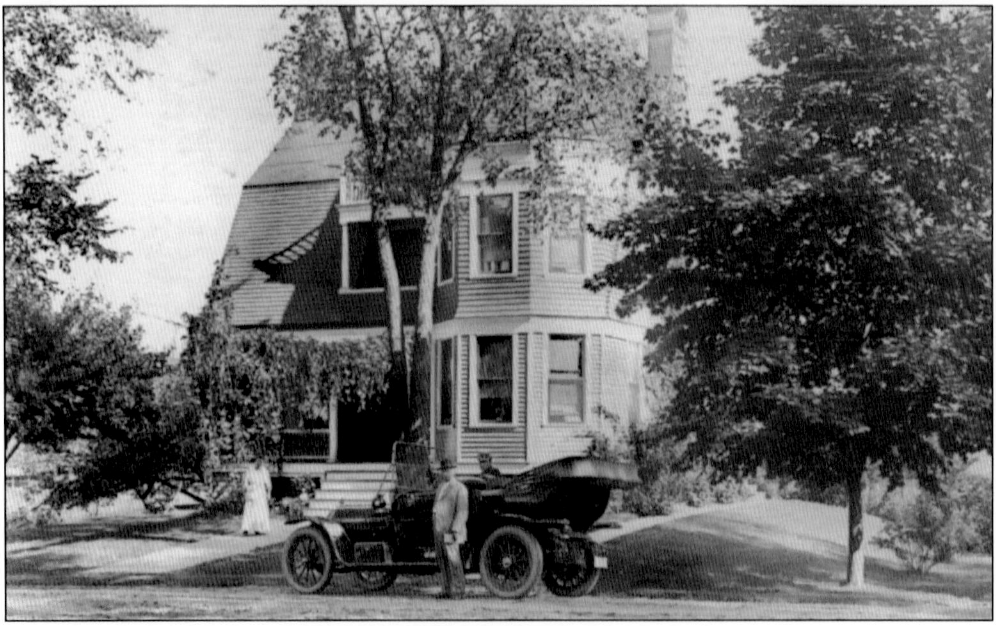

Frederick Gore's home at the corner of Cumberland and South Streets suggests some of the rewards of being the manager of the Forest Paper Company. In this photograph from 1915, a chauffeur-driven Locomobile is parked in front of Gore's neatly landscaped Queen Anne–style house. His wife, Angie, stands on the walkway, while the driver, Joseph Hincks, waits in the car. Mrs. Gore reportedly enjoyed the lifestyle but lamented that they never had any children. (Collection of the Yarmouth Historical Society.)

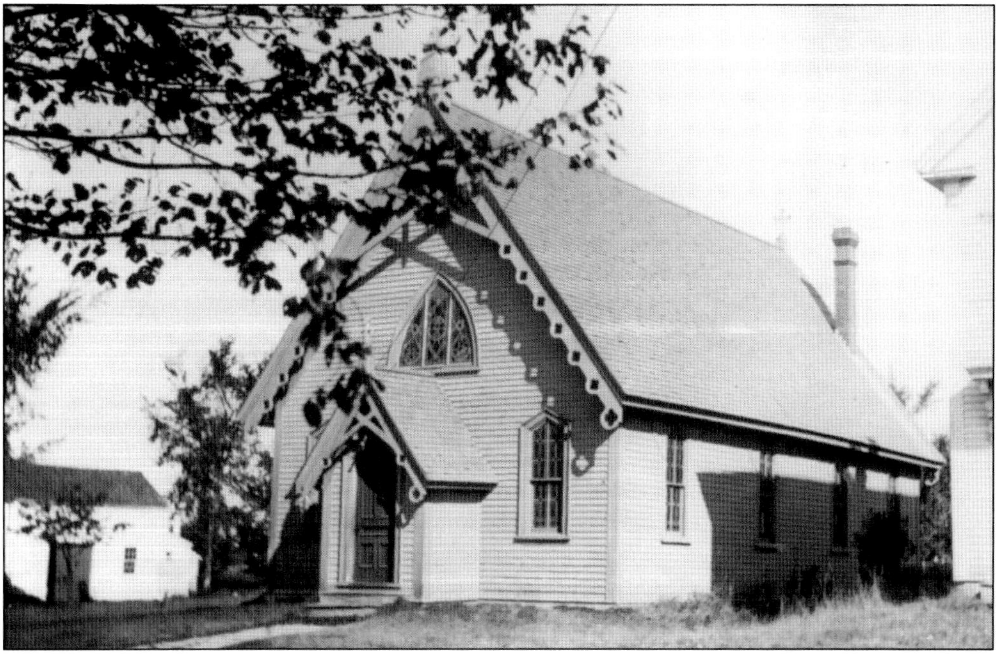

Yarmouth was a rigorously Protestant town when the first Catholic railroad workers and farmers showed up in the 1840s. The Irish and later some French Canadian families from Prince Edward Island settled in the Upper Village, a section of town that had earlier sheltered the town's few Democrats and Unitarians. In 1879, the Catholics finally built their own church, although it was tucked away on Cumberland Street out of concern that it might be vandalized on Main Street. The structure still stands as a private home, but it has been turned sideways to the road. (Collection of the Maine Historic Preservation Commission.)

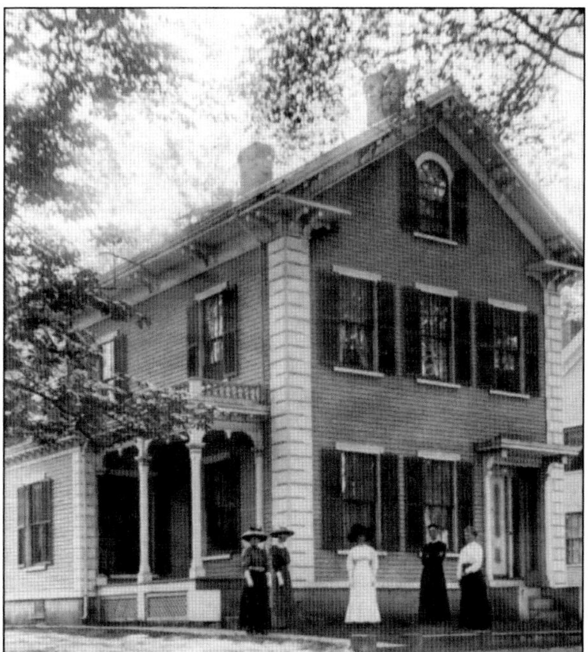

Capt. Eben York's mansion at 326 Main Street became the rectory of the Catholic church in 1910. Fr. Joseph Quinn held services in the barn until it burned in 1913. Here, Father Quinn is standing beside his sister and some of the ladies of the church in front of the rectory. In 1920, the present Sacred Heart Church was constructed next door out of granite quarried in North Yarmouth. (Collection of the Yarmouth Historical Society.)

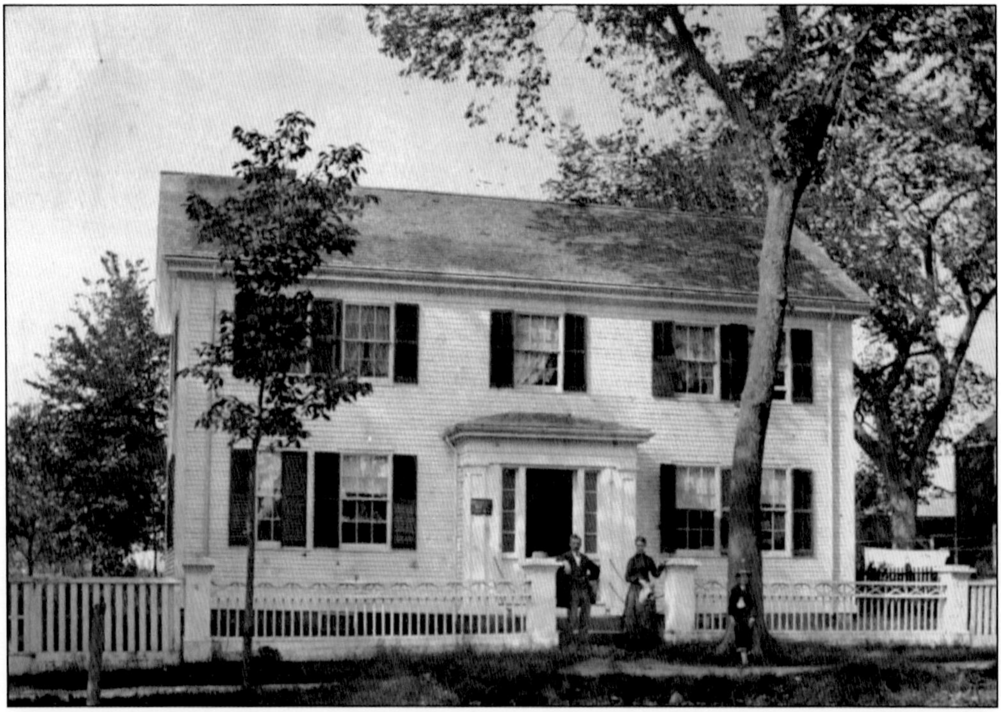

Some of the oldest buildings on Main Street are the Federal-style homes clustered between the Catholic and Baptist churches. The Daniel Wallis house, located at 330 Main Street, was built *c.* 1810. In the middle of the 19th century, it was owned by Capt. Cushing Prince, who was an influential shipowner, a representative to the legislature, and a somewhat cantankerous deacon in the Central Parish. (Collection of the Yarmouth Historical Society.)

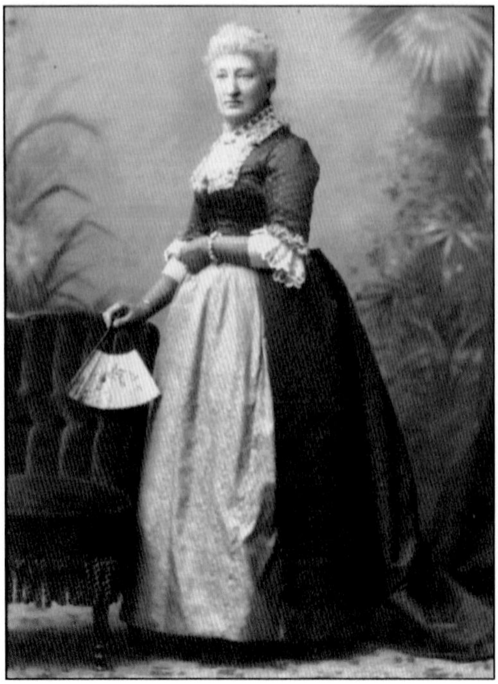

Captain Prince and his wife raised their two daughters, Isabelle (shown here) and Mary, to be independent and adventuresome. After lengthy teaching careers throughout the United States, the sisters were invited to Japan to assist the Japanese as they tried to open their culture to the ideas and industry of the west. Despite the exotic fan that she holds in this Japanese portrait, Isabelle still looks like a no-nonsense Yankee schoolmarm. (Collection of the Yarmouth Historical Society.)

Across Center Street from the Baptist church was a tiny barbershop operated by Harold "Snap" Moxcey. As early as 1924, Snap advertised, "Children's hair-cutting given special attention." It is therefore fitting that Snap was photographed cutting the hair of his great-grandson, Jeffrey Adams, not long before he retired in 1966. (Collection of the Yarmouth Historical Society.)

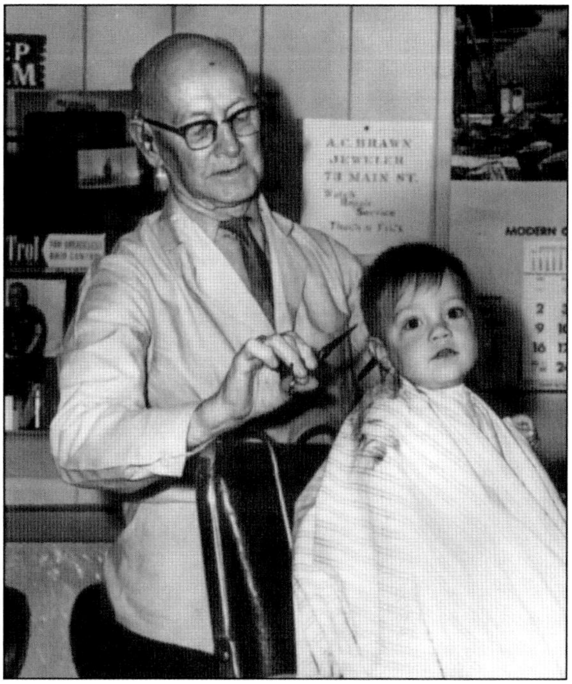

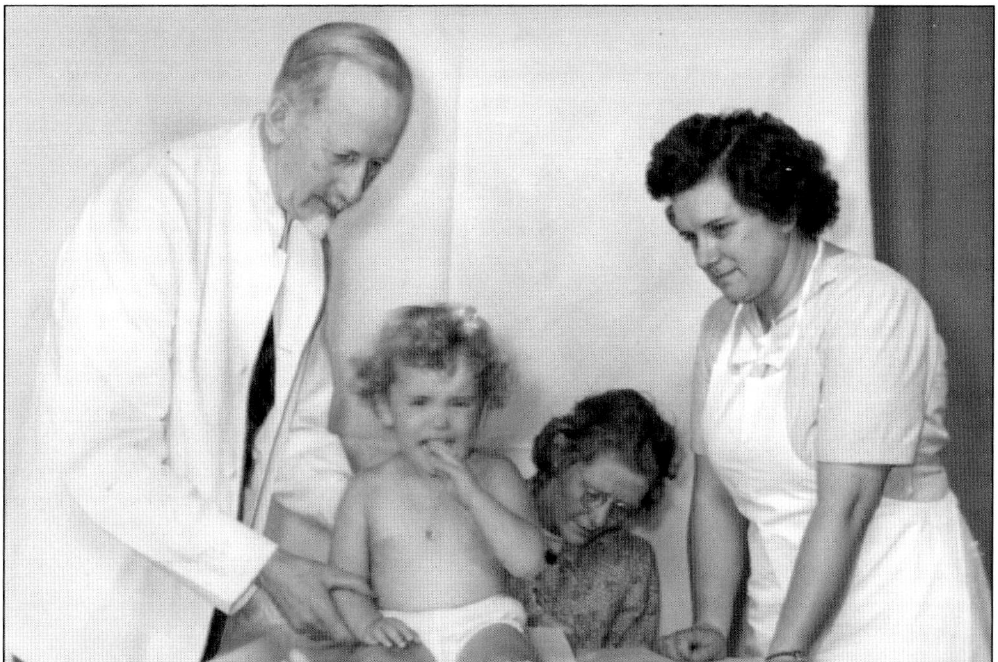

For many years, Dr. Nat Barker and his wife, Catherine, lived on the corner of South Street in the house now owned by the Roys. This photograph from the summer of 1947 shows Dr. Barker working with the town's public health nurse, Theresa McNeil. The Yarmouth Health Council arranged physical exams and immunizations for preschool children who lacked regular health care. (Collection of the Yarmouth Historical Society.)

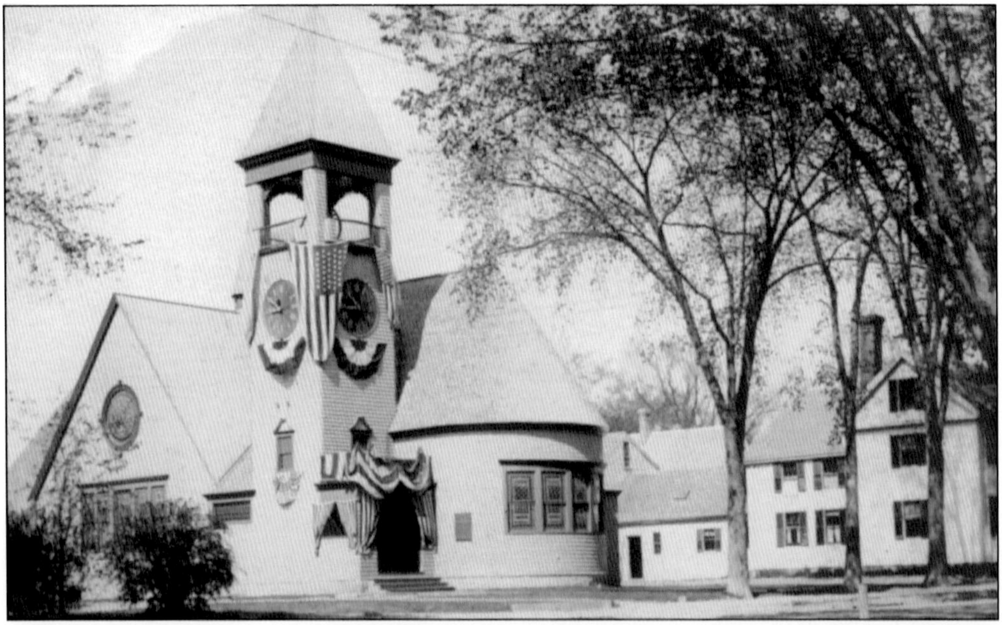

After a religious revival swept Yarmouth in 1877, the town's Baptists began to look for room to expand onto Main Street. In 1889, they finally abandoned their old church on Meetinghouse Hill and relocated into a stylish new building on the corner of Center Street. Designed by noted Portland architect John Calvin Stevens, the soft curves and sweeping roof reflect his well-known Shingle style. Except for the clock that was donated later, the cost for the whole project was $9,000. (Collection of the Yarmouth Historical Society.)

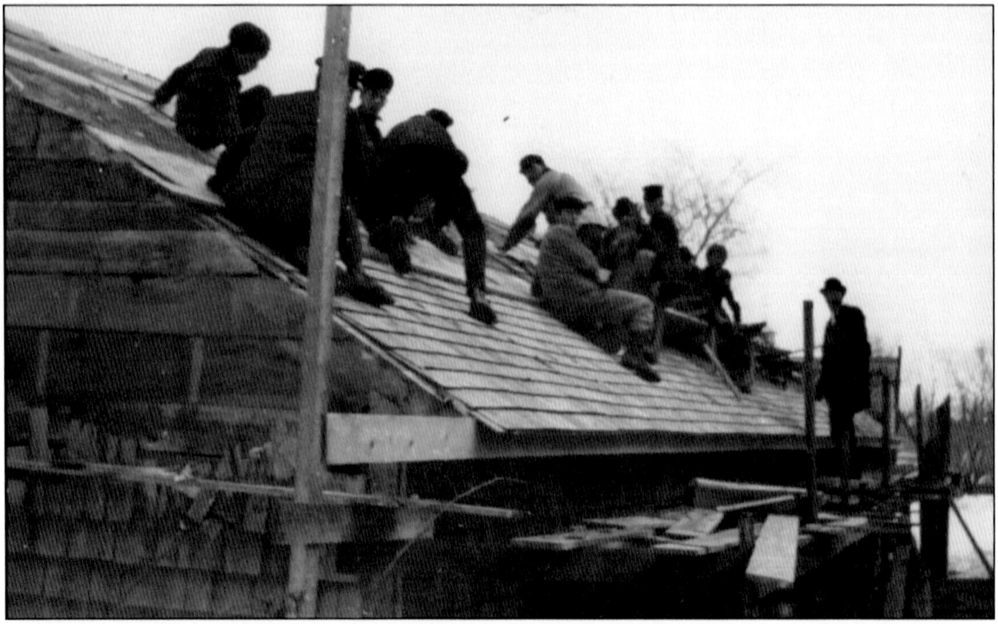

When the new Baptist church opened in 1889, its congregation arrived either on foot or in horse-drawn carriages. To protect the animals from harsh weather, a horse shed was constructed nearby on Center Street. This scene from 1907 shows a group of men reshingling the building shortly before automobiles rendered the shed obsolete. (Collection of the Yarmouth Historical Society.)

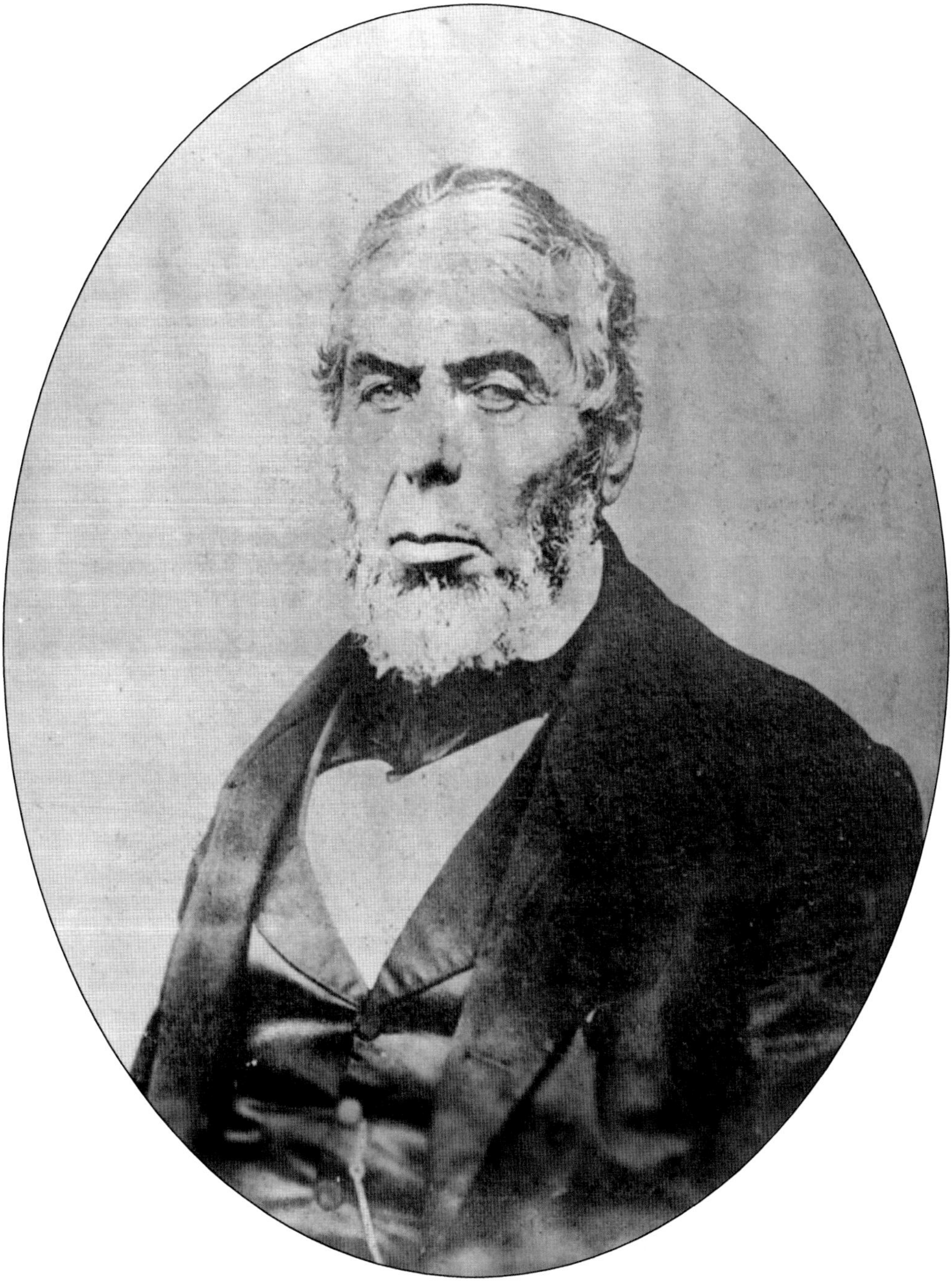

One look at Zadoc Humphrey's portrait reveals the firmness of his convictions. He was a Baptist deacon who led social reformers in Yarmouth into battle against slavery and alcohol. Although he was the great-grandson of Rev. Tristram Gilman (who tried to keep Baptists out of town), Humphrey was a firm believer who named several of his sons for Baptist preachers. After many years of being a shopkeeper, he served as the station agent at the Grand Trunk Railroad depot until his death in 1862. (Collection of Lois Rogers Lippincott.)

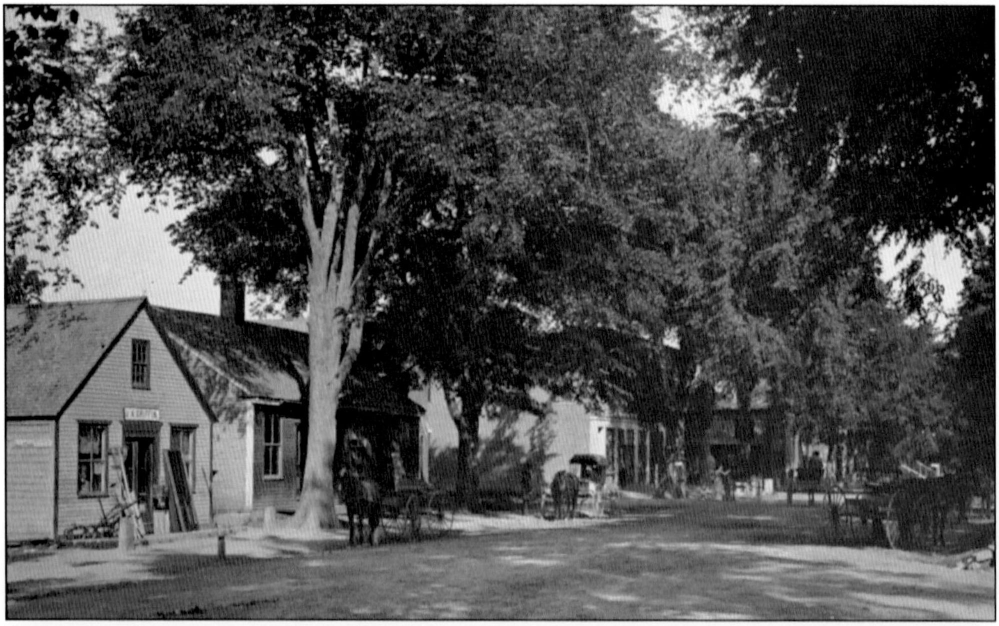

Yarmouthville was sometimes called "the Corner" because of the major intersection at Elm Street. Draped with the towering elms, this c. 1892 view looks east toward L.R. Cook's brick store. In the little shop on the left, John A. Griffin sells hardware and Clarion stoves, and the adjacent store advertises, "Groceries at Portland prices." (Collection of Alan M. Hall.)

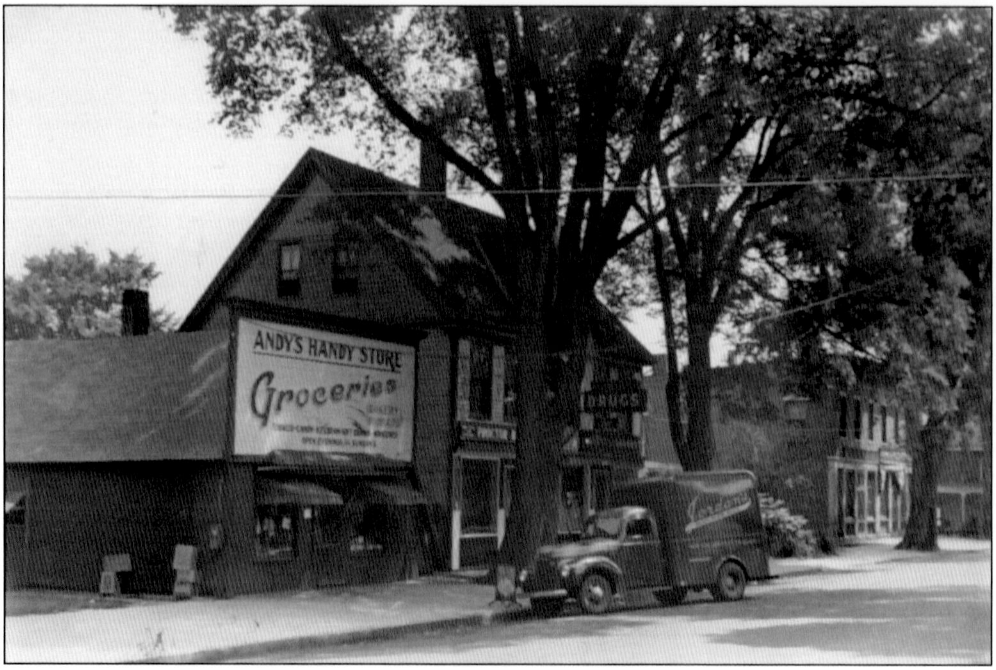

In 1935, Leland "Andy" Anderson combined the two wooden buildings shown in the previous photograph to create Andy's Handy Store. Although the business has changed hands several times since then, it remains a popular landmark that has outlasted a variety of chain stores along Main Street. (Collection of the Yarmouth Historical Society.)

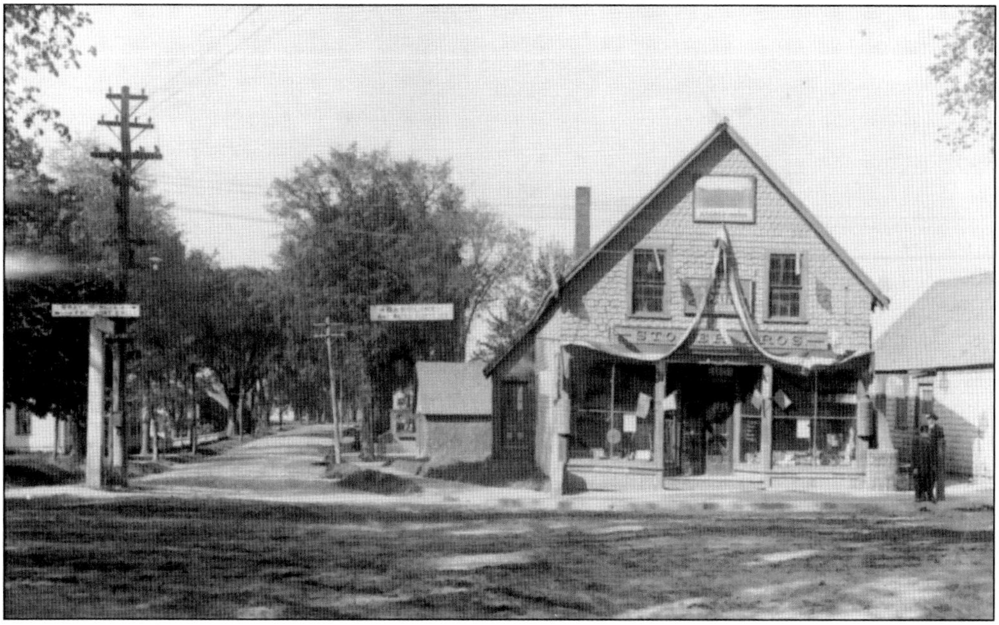

Since 1807, when a nail mill occupied the site, more than 30 different businesses or owners have set up shop on the corner of East Elm Street. In 1891, Foster's Pottery was torn down and a new building was constructed. Eventually, the building became Storer Brothers hardware, which operated from 1906 until 1935, when it became Andy's Handy Store. (Collection of the Maine Historic Preservation Commission.)

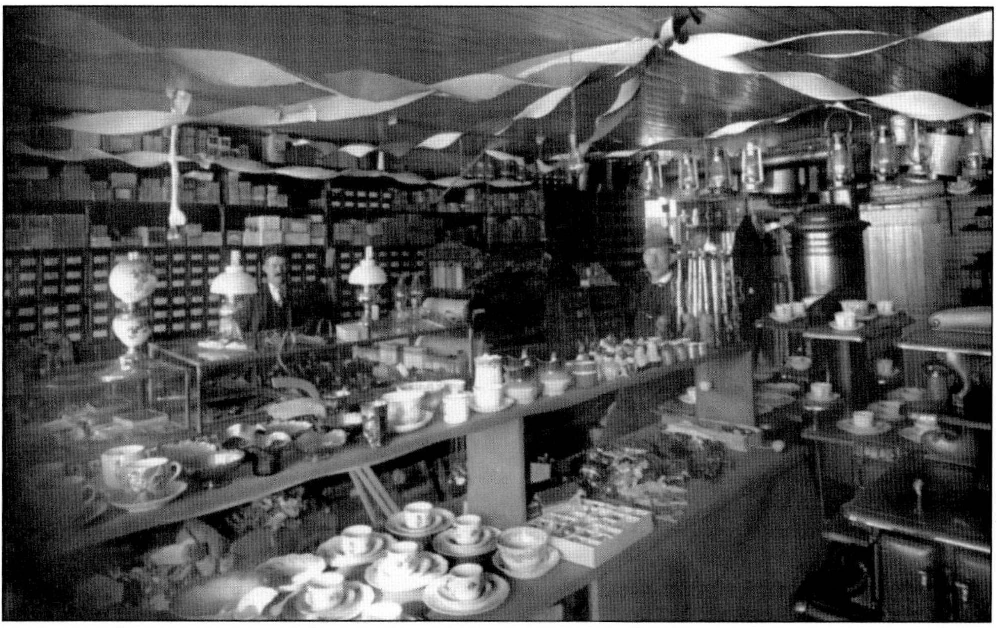

Arthur and Harry Storer sold everything from stoves and plumbing supplies to hockey sticks. Frank Knight, a longtime Yarmouth resident, recently recalled that he purchased fireworks in this store *c.* 1918. Harry Storer, who is also pictured with a big-wheeled bicycle on page 93, used the store as the base for his own plumbing and heating business. (Collection of the Yarmouth Historical Society.)

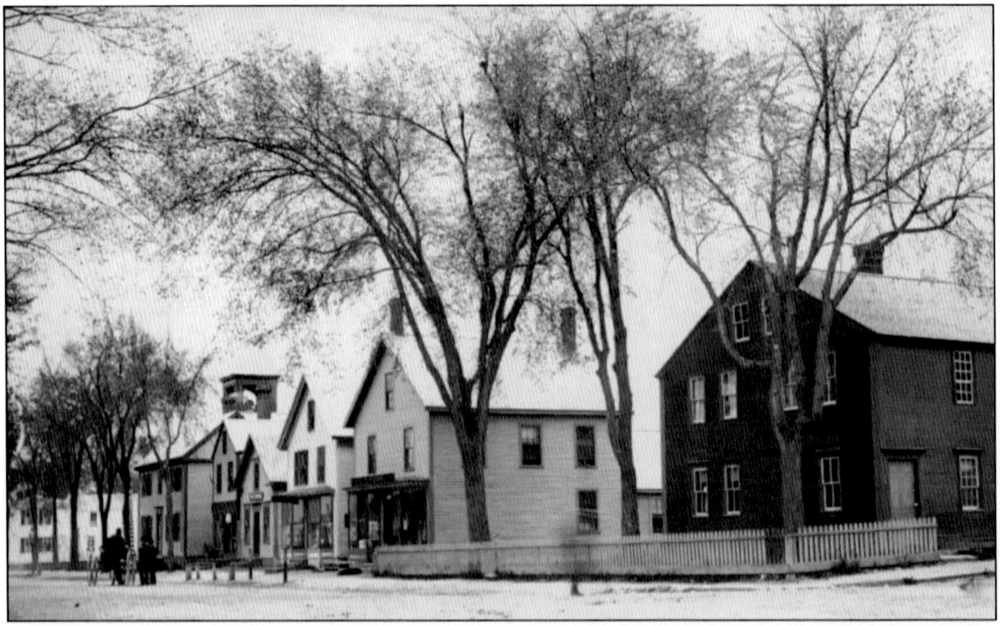

In 1788, Dr. William Parsons built this brown colonial home, which was torn down in 1950 for a supermarket. In this *c.* 1893 photograph, Sam York's grocery is located to the left of the old house. Beyond that is a millinery shop, the post office, and George Jeffords's harness shop. A former slave named Isaac Johnson operated a barbershop over the Jeffords business, and his striped pole can be seen by the wagon. This section of town officially became Yarmouthville in 1882 when Mrs. W.L. Haskell, the widow of a Civil War hero, was appointed postmaster. (Collection of Alan M. Hall.)

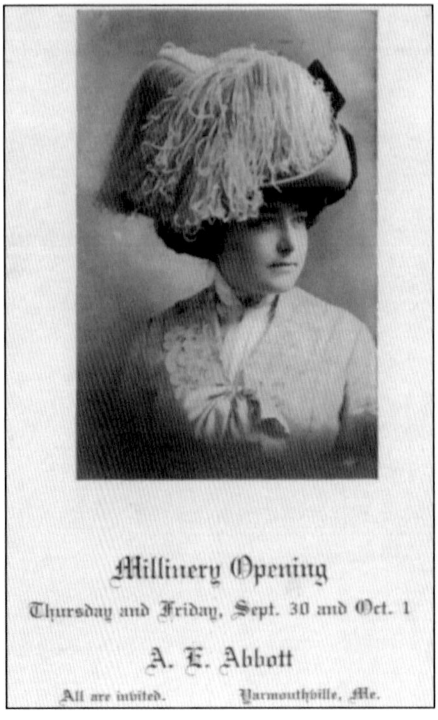

The career opportunities for most women in the late 19th century were limited to working in the cotton mill, teaching school, or opening a millinery shop. In 1909, Adelaide Abbott sent this postcard to entice customers into her shop at 60 Main Street. Due to competition and probably insufficient capital, the life expectancy of most of the hat shops was only about four or five years. (Collection of the Yarmouth Historical Society.)

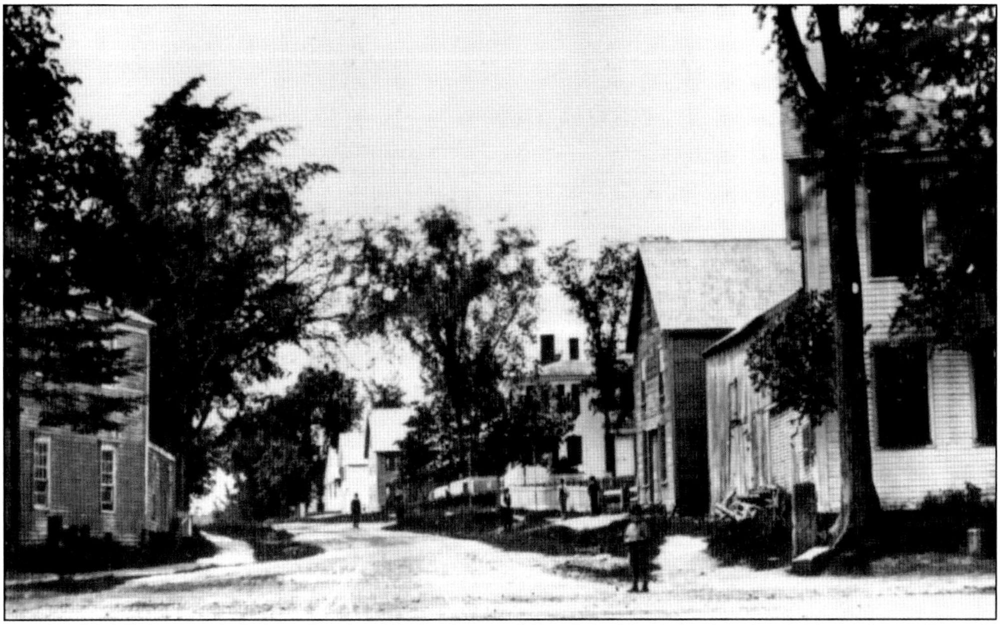

Latchstring Park now occupies the site of Jeremiah Mitchell's tavern, which is on the right side of this 1874 photograph. Before the Presumpcott River was bridged at Martin's Point, this road was a direct route to Portland and therefore a key stagecoach stop. The large barn visible behind the tavern was built to house the horses. Beyond the barn is the house of Richmond Cutter, which still stands on the corner of Church Street. Despite an ordinance banning baseball in the streets, this was a favorite location for ball games as far back as the 1850s. (Collection of the Maine Historic Preservation Commission.)

William Rowe points out that the story of Methodism in Yarmouth has two chapters. After the first phase died out after the Civil War, this chapel on West Elm Street was constructed in 1898 to mark a revival of Methodism. Unfortunately, its supporters soon died or moved away so that it was necessary to disband the church in 1928. Until recently, the building was used by a fraternal group known as the Red Men. (Collection of the Maine Historic Preservation Commission.)

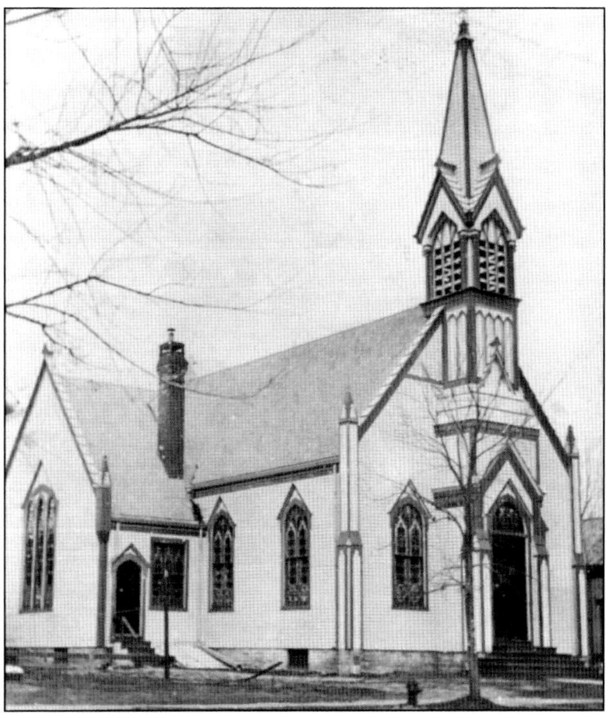

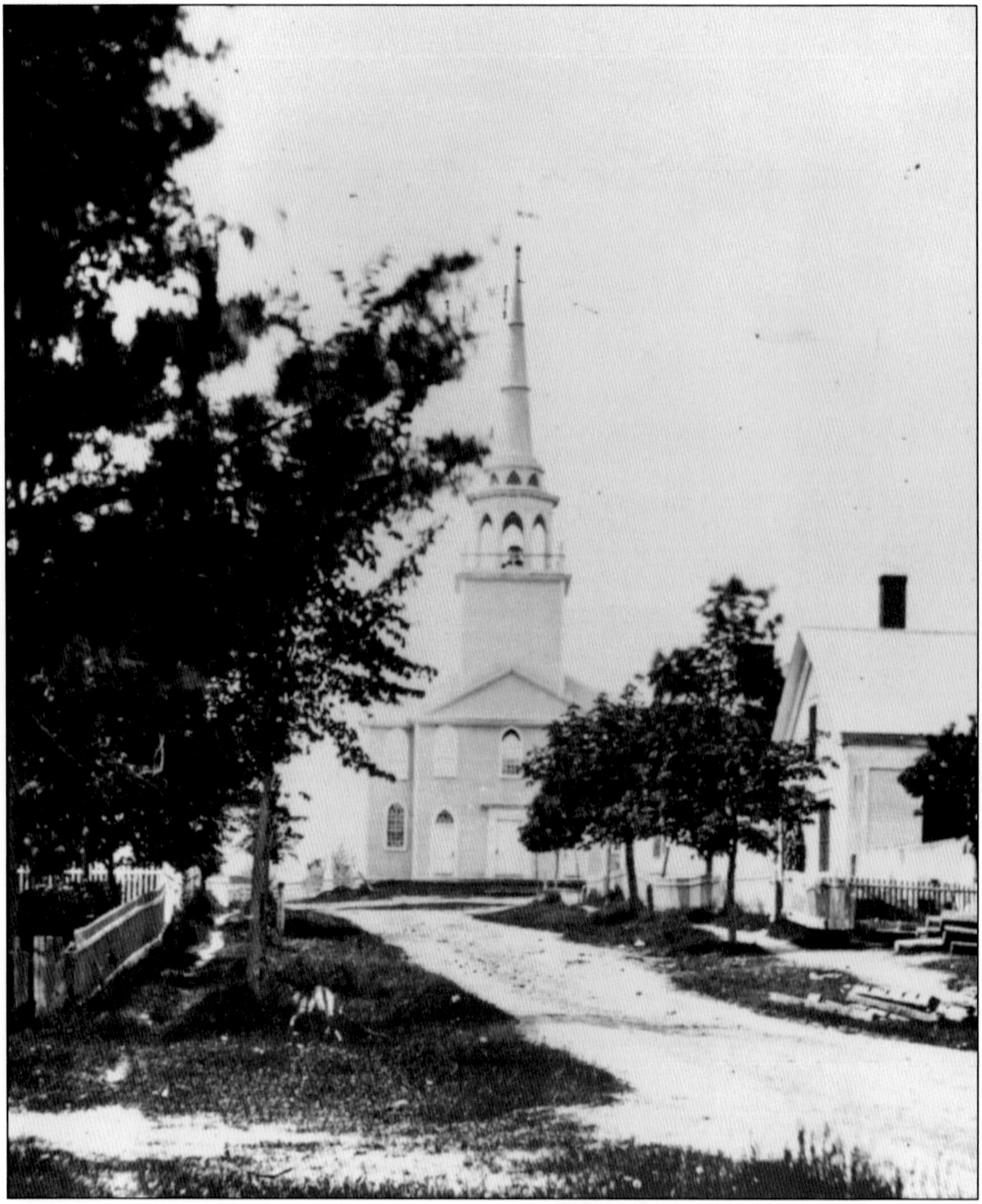

Viewed from Church Street, the old Baptist meetinghouse perches with solemn dignity on the brow of Brimstone Hill. When it was first built in 1796, the building was rather square and somewhat smaller. In 1837, it was it was enlarged and updated with Gothic touches. The result is an architectural gem with a graceful combination of classical and Gothic elements. Fortunately, it was saved for the people of Yarmouth through the efforts of George Hammond when the Baptists relocated to Main Street. (Collection of the Maine Historic Preservation Commission.)

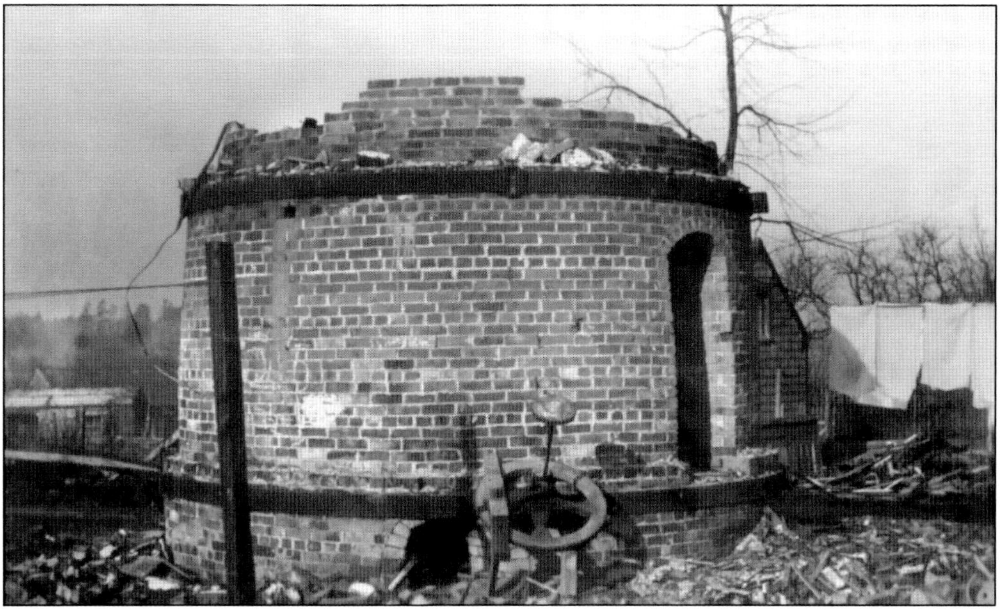

The pottery industry was one of the oldest and most successful industries to thrive in the Upper Village. On East Elm (once called Gooches' Lane), there were several potteries in the 19th century, including Joel Brooks's operation, which lasted from 1851 until 1888. The ruins of his kiln and many broken shards of pottery can be seen in this *c.* 1911 photograph. Yarmouth's extensive beds of marine clay provided plenty of raw material for making bricks as well as redware. (Collection of the Yarmouth Historical Society.)

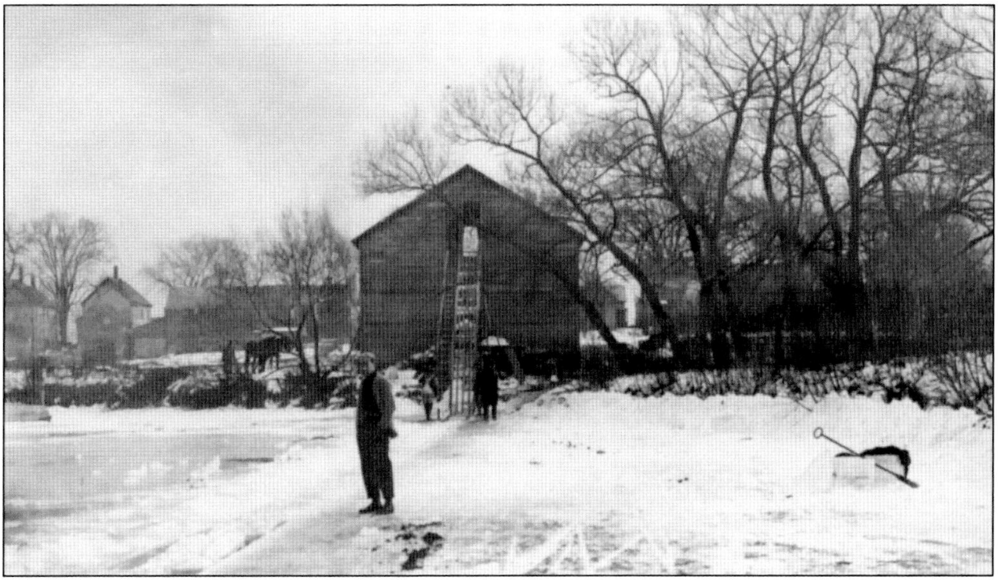

Although some Yarmouth ice was shipped to distant markets like Brooklyn, New York, most of it was cut for home use. Local dealers built icehouses in the 1880s, especially near the fourth falls on Elm Street. When properly packed in sawdust, the ice would last all summer. In 1916, the board of health warned residents not to use local ice in their drinks because of possible contamination from the huge stockyards on Sligo Road. (Collection of the Maine Historic Preservation Commission.)

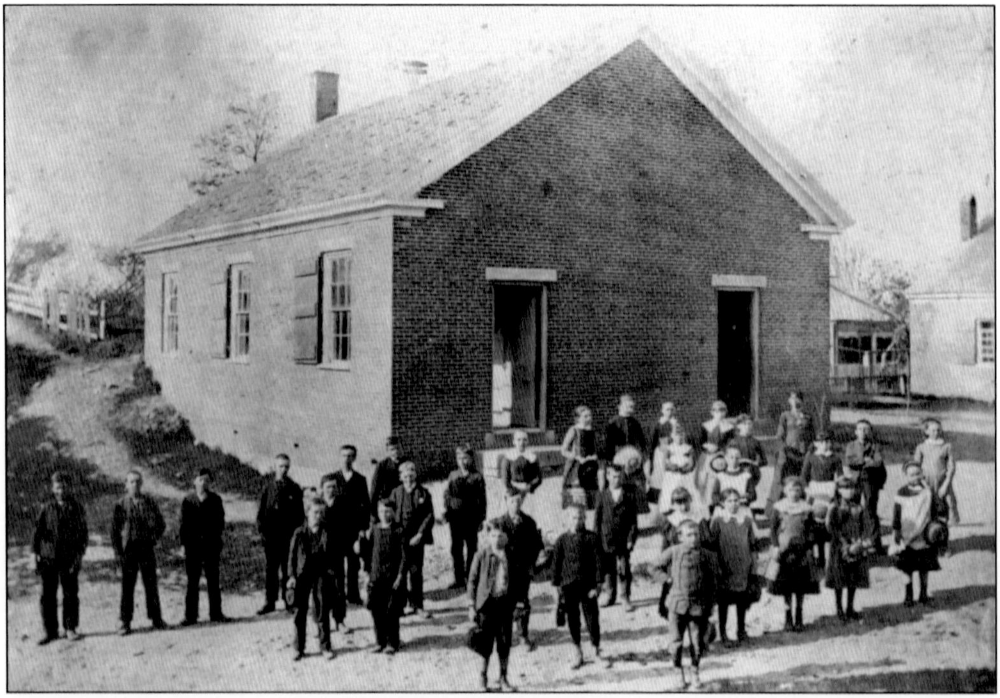

The brick schools near Sligo Road bring back memories for many Yarmouth residents because they were used through the 1980s. Indoor plumbing did not arrive until World War I, and electricity was not added until 1937. In 1847, a teacher named William Osgood had 74 students jammed into the school on the right, explaining why this building was soon added. When this photograph was taken c. 1900, there was an active garbage dump only a few yards to the left. Fortunately, the Village Improvement Society cleaned up the mess in 1915. (Collection of the Yarmouth Historical Society.)

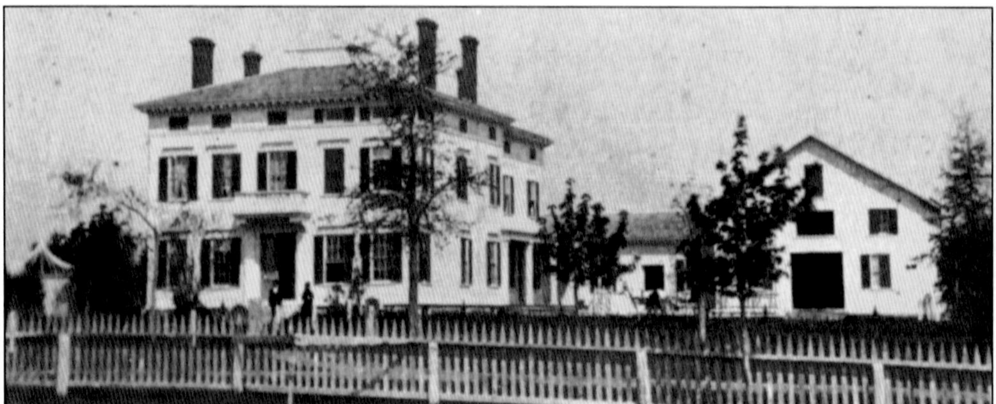

Hidden behind a cedar hedge on West Main Street is an imposing Italianate mansion that was built for Capt. Reuben Merrill. In 1874, Captain Merrill was in Boston, Massachusetts, preparing the *Champlain* for its maiden voyage when he asked legendary clipper ship builder Donald McKay what he thought of the ship. McKay replied, "She will run away with you, Captain." Indeed she did. Captain Merrill was killed by a piece of falling rigging when the *Champlain* went aground near San Francisco, California. (Collection of the Maine Historic Preservation Commission.)

Three

Brickyard Hollow

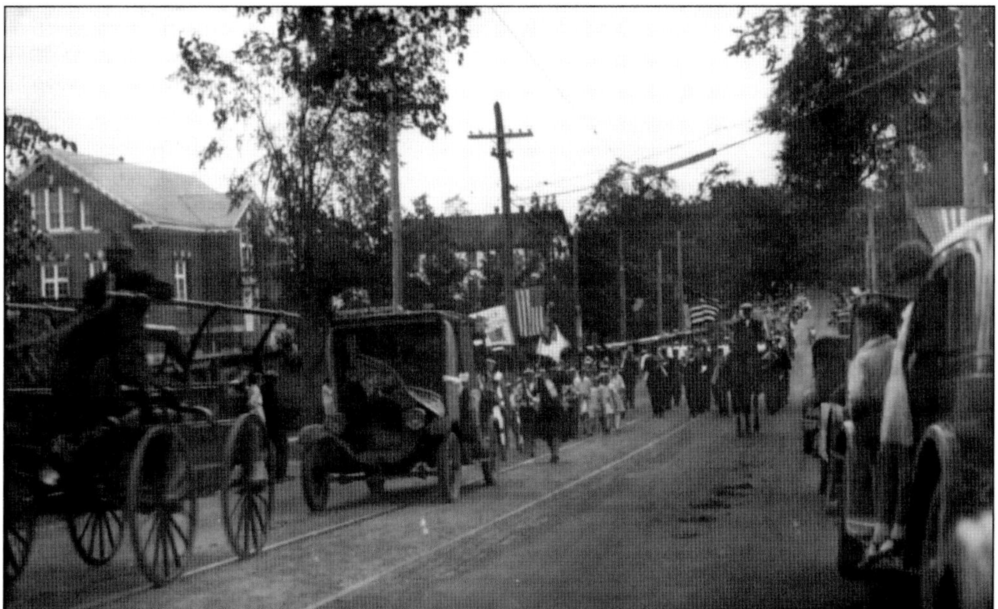

Until the beginning of the 20th century, a muddy valley known as Brickyard Hollow effectively divided the two halves of Yarmouth. Gradually, between 1890 and 1928, the town recognized that this wasteland was strategically located and worth reclaiming as a civic center. After constructing two new schools, the Merrill Memorial Library, and a war memorial, town officials also decided to rename the area Centervale in order to improve its muddy image. In the end, the new name was no more successful than the town's early efforts to prevent Brickyard Hollow from flooding. The vehicle on the left is *Pumgustuk*, preserved today as the town's oldest piece of fire equipment. (Collection of Stan Milton.)

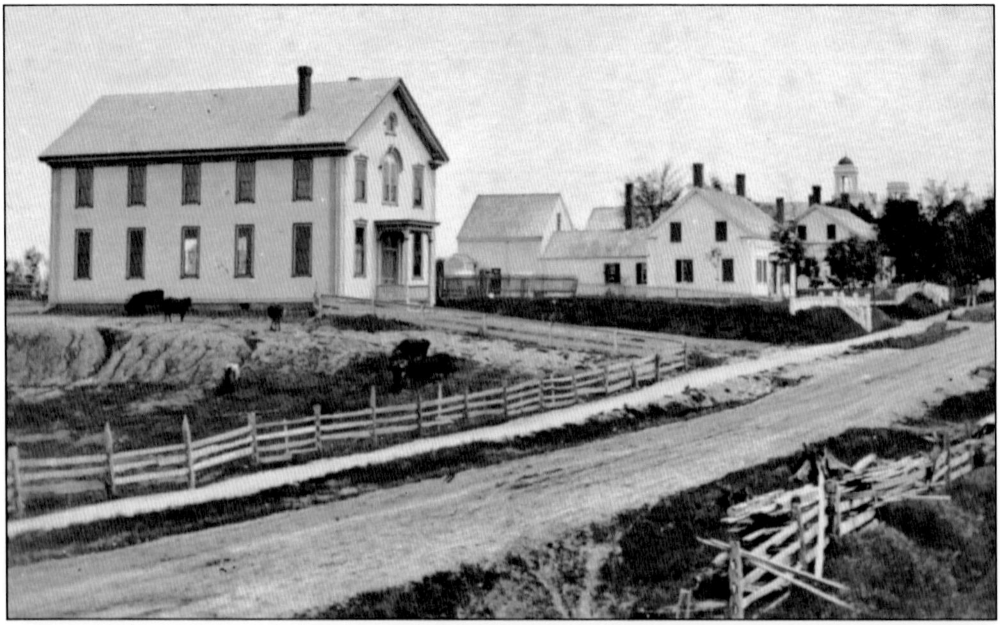

Seeing all these cows gathered around the Masonic Hall in 1874 explains why fences were necessary even in the heart of town. John Collins, who owned the brickyard across the street, donated this site for the new Casco Lodge. The plank sidewalk in the foreground was built in 1831 as an early effort to improve ties between the two villages. Although all these buildings are still standing, this view is now obscured by the U.S. Route 1 overpass. (Collection of Alan M. Hall.)

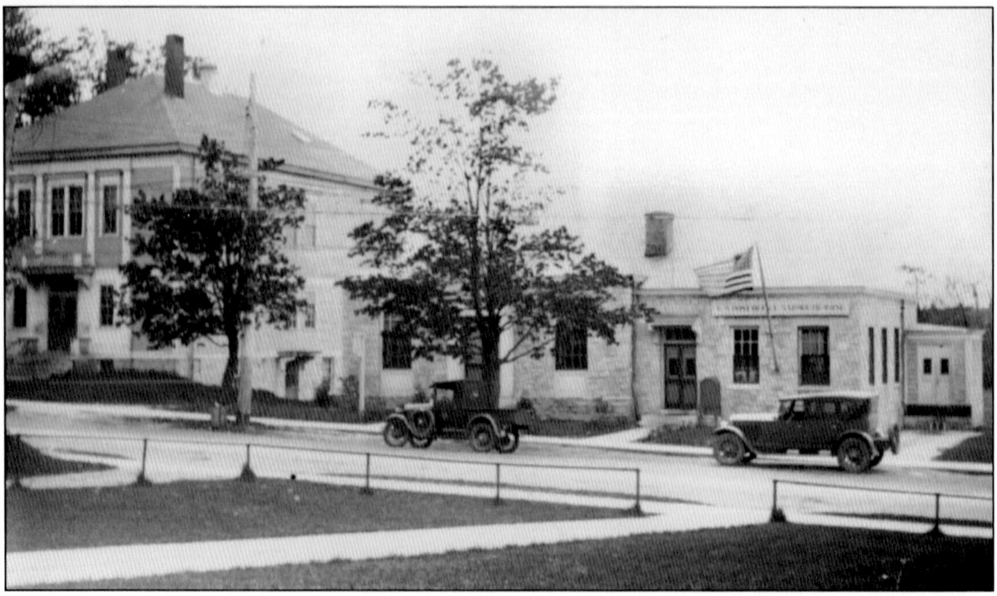

A new centralized post office was built across from the Masonic Hall in 1929. On the left side of the new building (behind the Ford pickup truck) was the Fidelity Trust Company. Unfortunately, the bank failed early in the Great Depression. The large building on the left was the Knights of Pythias Hall. In 1931, the land to the right of the post office was sold by the town to the American Legion for a dollar. A Presque Isle company donated the materials, and the World War I veterans soon completed their log cabin Legion Hall. (Collection of Virginia Turner.)

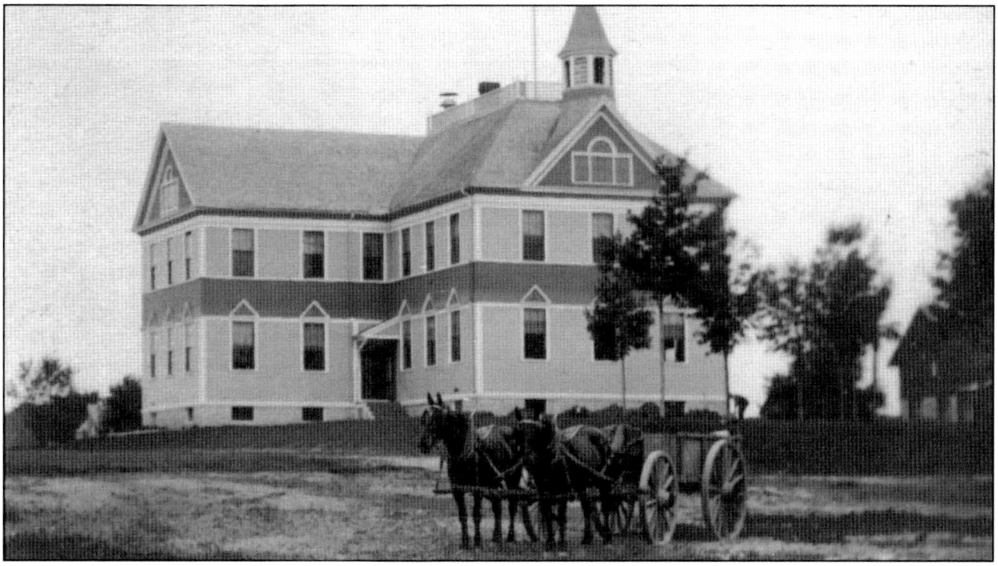

In 1890, Yarmouth constructed a large new school building on the site of the present town hall. Grades five to eight were on the first floor, and the high school occupied the second floor. Although the rooms were spacious and well lit, the building lacked indoor plumbing for 14 years. The wagon in the foreground belonged to Joseph Porter, who was hired by the town in 1905 to put loam over the two-foot layer of black ash that the paper company had used to level Brickyard Hollow. (Collection of Lois Rogers Lippincott.)

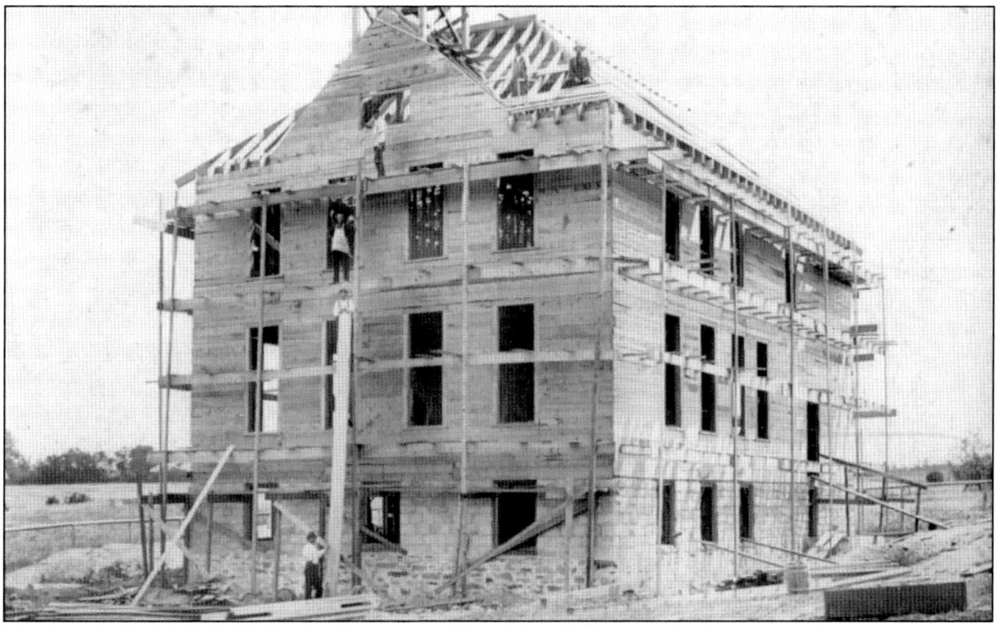

The rapid expansion of the paper mill increased the town's population by 12 percent between 1890 and 1910, making it necessary to construct a separate high school in 1900. With central heating, indoor plumbing, and desks bolted in rows, the building was very modern. When all of the high-school students were sent to North Yarmouth Academy in 1930, the building became another elementary school. In 1974, both of these schools were demolished in order to build the present town hall. (Collection of the Yarmouth Historical Society.)

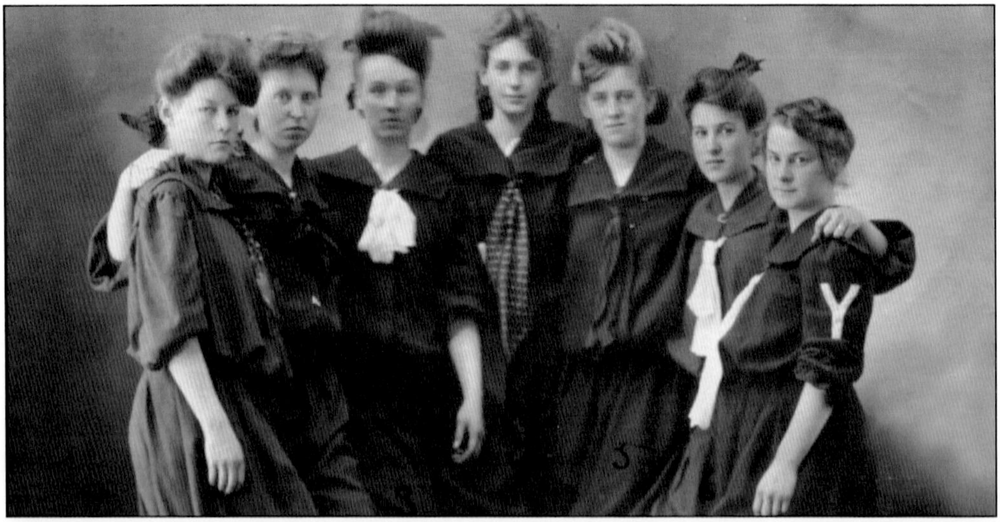

When these girls attended Yarmouth High School in the winter of 1903–1904, there was no gym in the town, and they seem to have practiced in the attic of the high school. After the town voted down a new gym, the Sigma sorority at the high school held an annual minstrel show throughout the 1920s to raise money to build one. Despite these efforts, the students were not able to use proper athletic facilities until they were sent to North Yarmouth Academy during the Great Depression. (Collection of the Yarmouth Historical Society.)

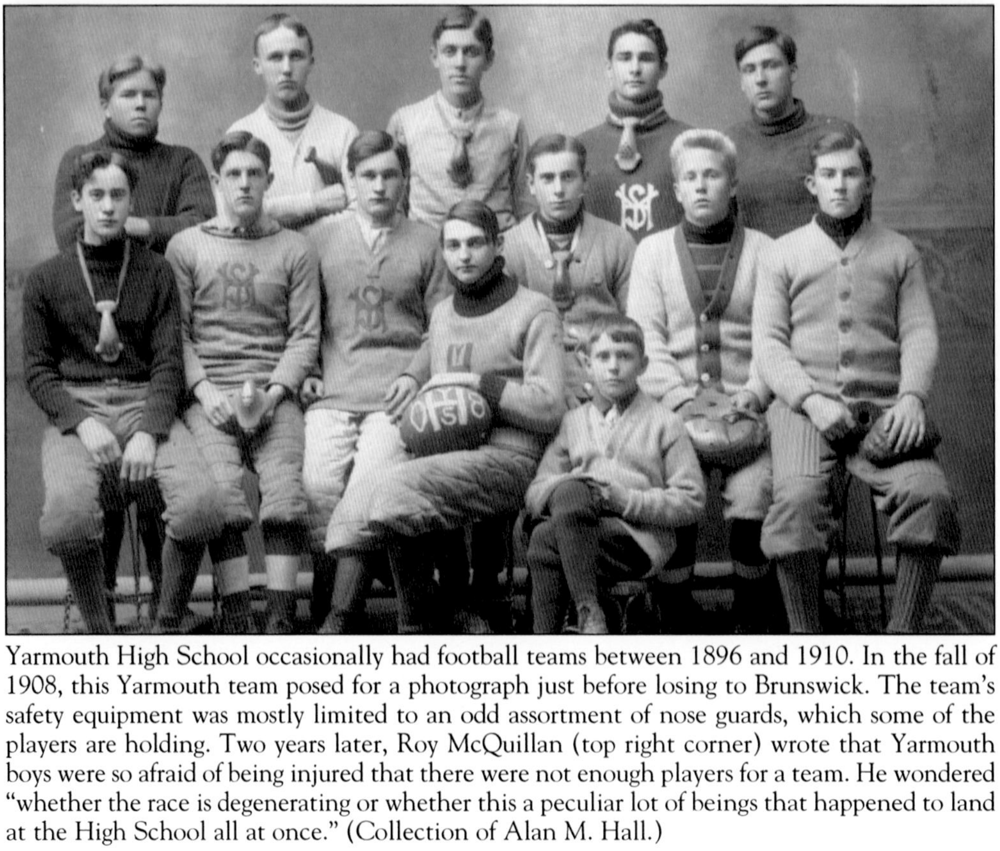

Yarmouth High School occasionally had football teams between 1896 and 1910. In the fall of 1908, this Yarmouth team posed for a photograph just before losing to Brunswick. The team's safety equipment was mostly limited to an odd assortment of nose guards, which some of the players are holding. Two years later, Roy McQuillan (top right corner) wrote that Yarmouth boys were so afraid of being injured that there were not enough players for a team. He wondered "whether the race is degenerating or whether this a peculiar lot of beings that happened to land at the High School all at once." (Collection of Alan M. Hall.)

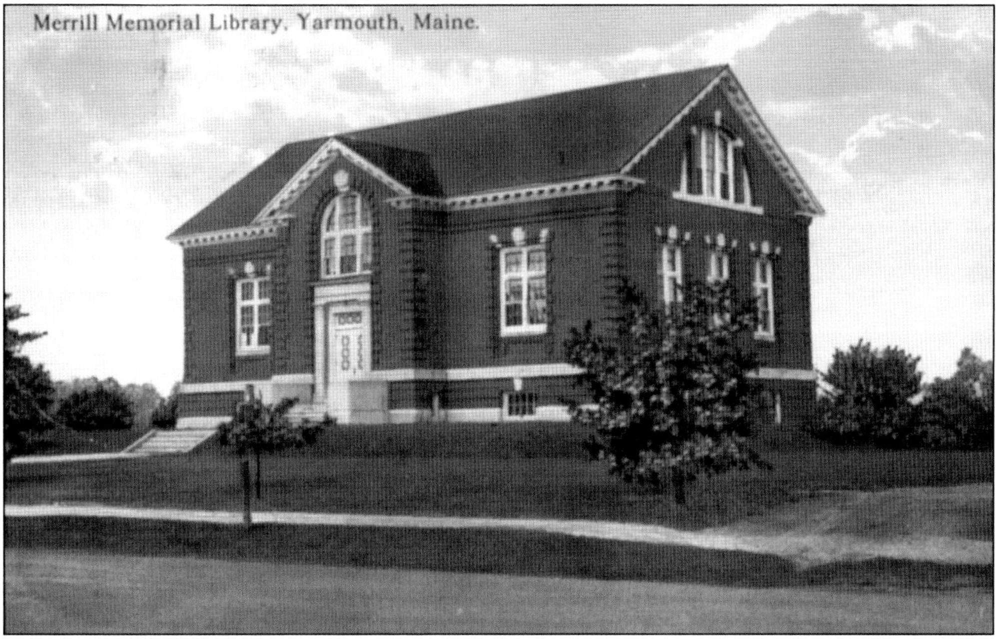

In 1894, a proposal to build a combination town hall, library, and selectmen's office was rejected at the town meeting. Finally, Joseph Merrill offered to donate the funds for a new library in 1903, and the town agreed to support the project. The architect was Alexander Longfellow, a nephew of the poet Henry Wadsworth Longfellow. Despite periodic flooding, town offices were eventually established in the basement. (Collection of Brenda Roy.)

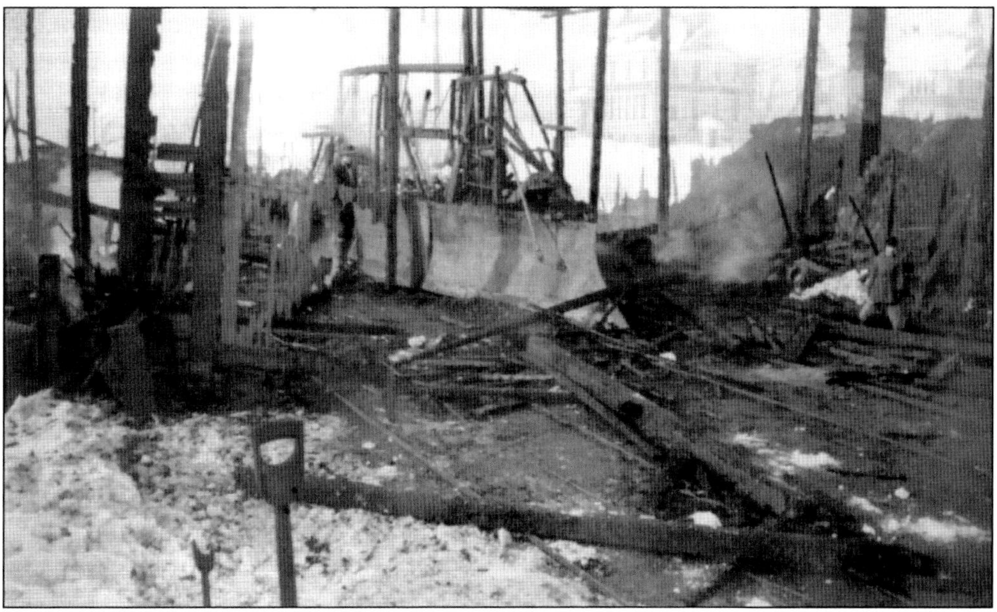

After the Merrill Memorial Library and the schools were built, Brickyard Hollow became a bit more civilized. Tons of black ash were piped from the paper mill to level the area, but the landscaping efforts were hindered by frequent floods and odd buildings, such as the carbarn for the trolleys. In 1921, a fire destroyed the freight shed and carbarn, leaving this smoldering skeleton of a snowplow trolley. (Collection of the Yarmouth Historical Society.)

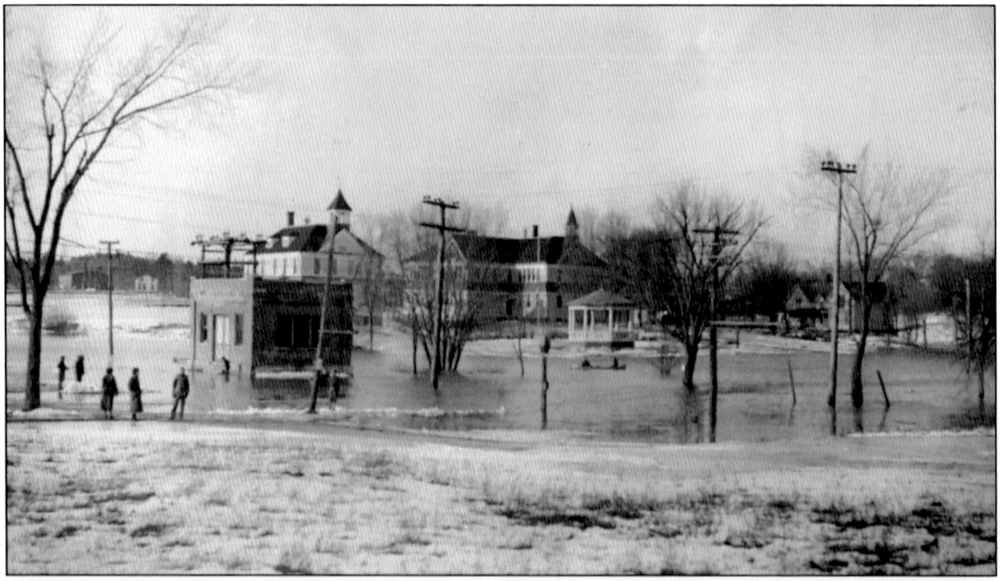

Contributing to the periodic floods, Cleaves Brook—which drained the whole center of town—was blocked up when Brickyard Hollow was filled. As recently as the 1980s, residents turned out to rescue flooded library books and to watch canoeists paddle about on Main Street. The brick structure in this 1930 photograph was the generating plant for the trolley cars, a site now covered by the U.S. Route 1 overpass. (Collection of Virginia Turner.)

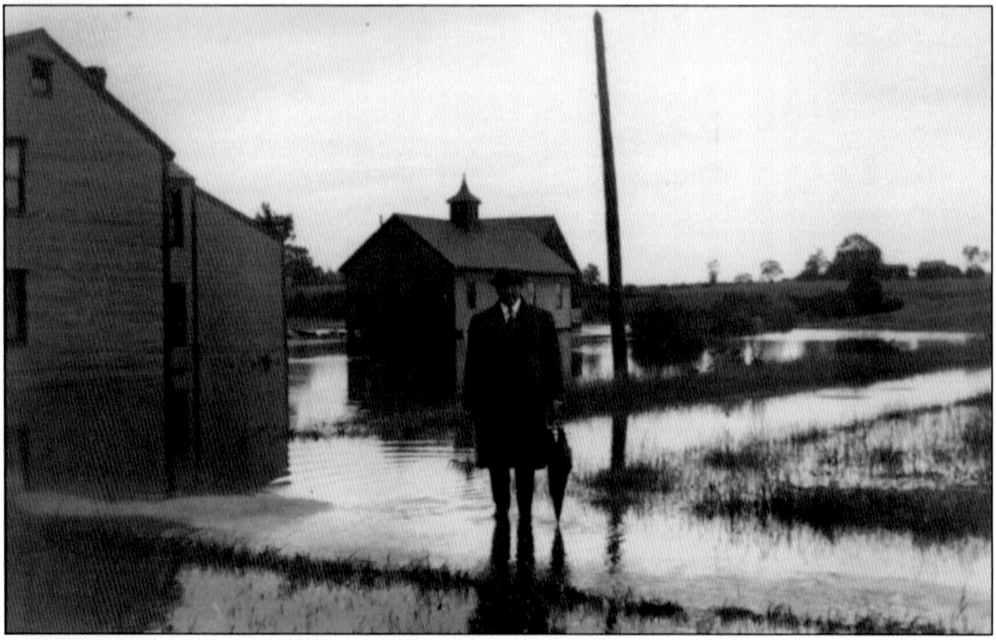

As a politician and an insurance agent, Howard Gooding must have grasped that this flood in Brickyard Hollow was a fine photo opportunity. In his role as chairman of the selectmen, Gooding was undoubtedly instrumental in the town's decision to acquire the Dumphy property in the flood zone, directly across from the Merrill Memorial Library. The house and barn were auctioned off in 1921, creating more public space in Centervale. (Collection of the Yarmouth Historical Society.)

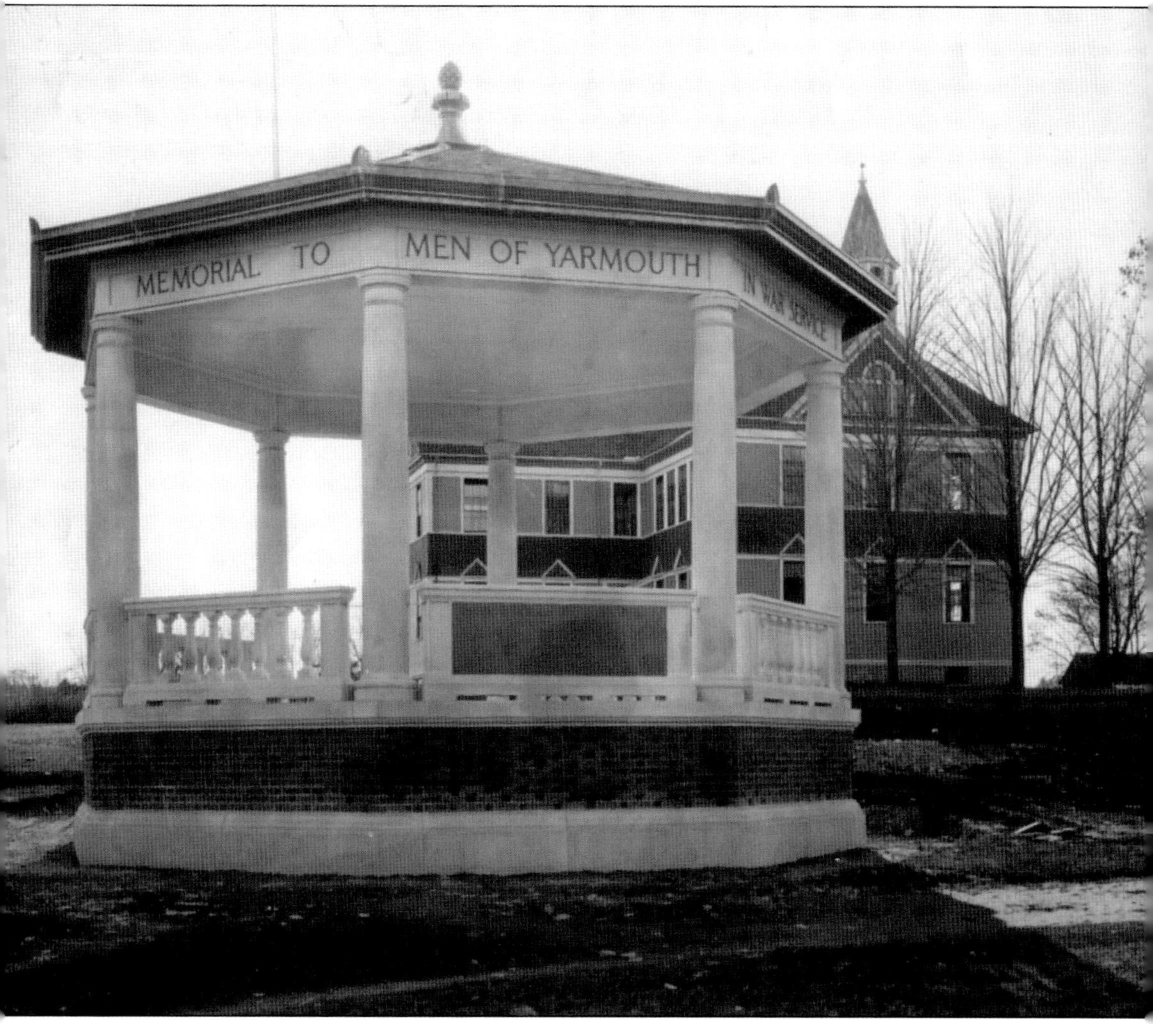

In 1904, the town's Civil War veterans asked permission to place a soldiers monument in front of the new schools in Brick Yard Hollow. Lacking the necessary funds, the project was put off until after World War I, when it was combined with a board of trade plan to erect a bandstand. The result was a beautifully proportioned bandstand with Doric columns and a memorial plaque that honored all Yarmouth veterans. Unfortunately, the structure was inadequately maintained and had to be removed when rotting boards caused injuries. The plaque is now in the basement of the nearby American Legion hall. (Collection of the Yarmouth Historical Society.)

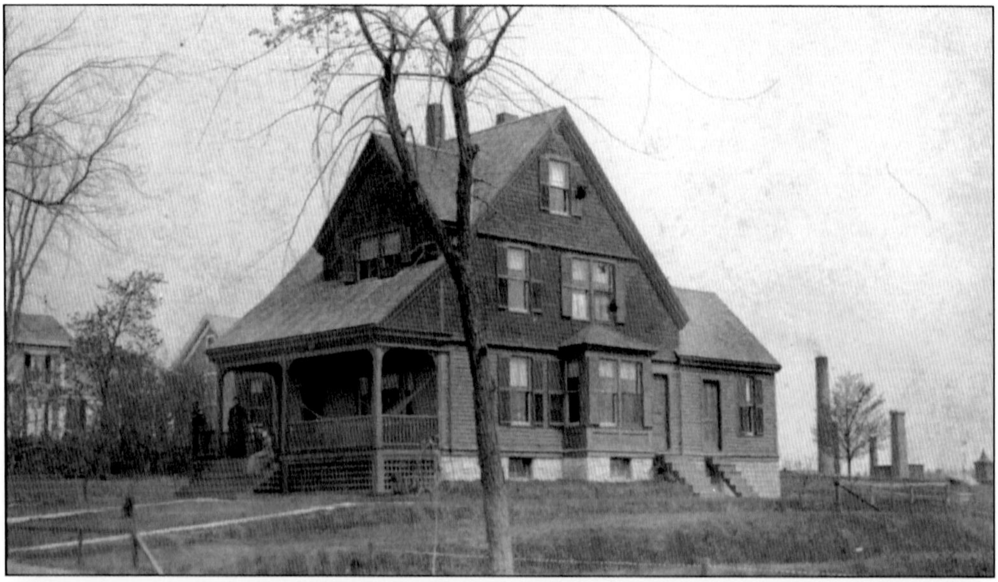

Although most of the land reclaimed in Brick Yard Hollow was used for public buildings, one new home was constructed. In 1889, Dr. Herbert Merrill set up his dental practice in the back of this house, which has since been moved closer to the Rowe School. As a member of the Yarmouth Rifles, the Masons, the board of trade, and local theater groups, Merrill was fully engaged in the life of the town. It is likely that he even rode the big-wheeled bicycle that is leaning against the porch. (Collection of the Yarmouth Historical Society.)

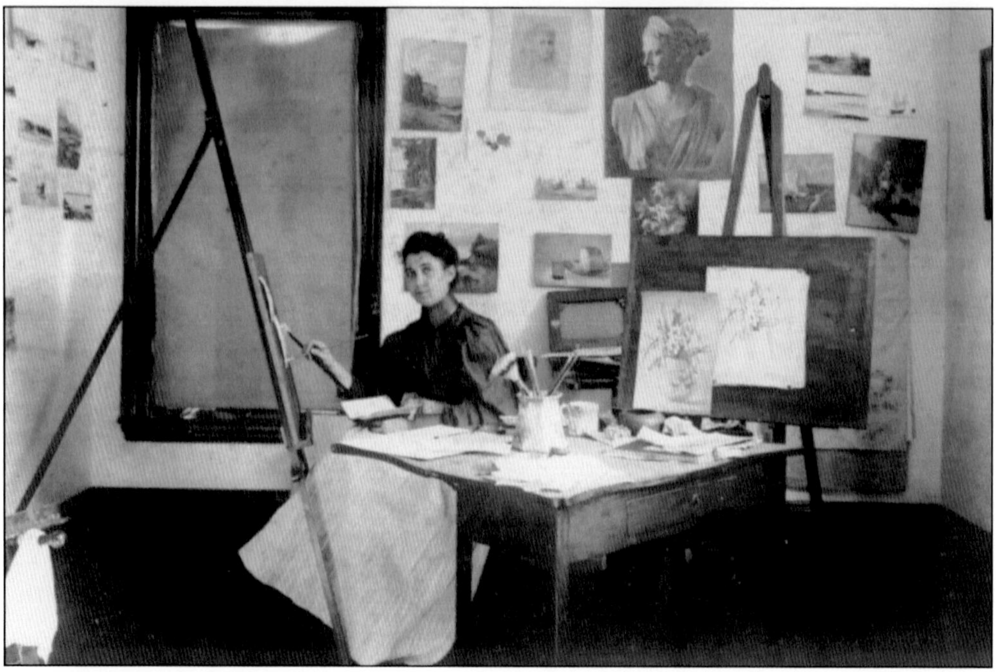

Merrill's wife, Leila, was talented in both music and art. After one of her crayon drawings was put on display in Portland in 1878, a newspaper praised her "remarkable talent in this line of art." She was working in her studio in 1896 when this photograph was taken. (Collection of the Yarmouth Historical Society.)

Four

The Shipyards

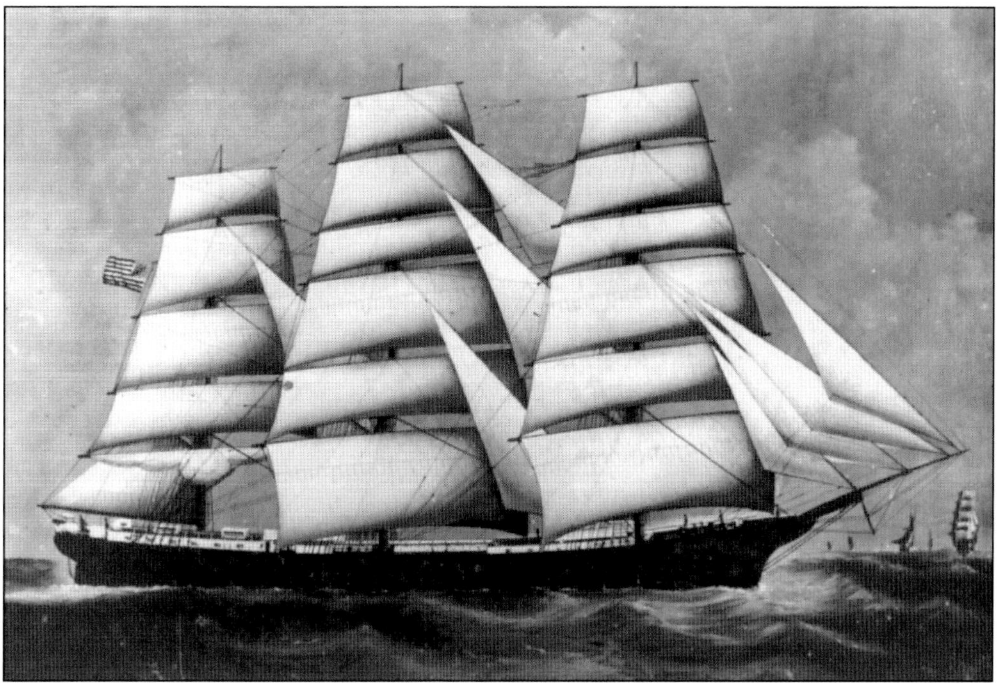

With its full suit of sails and a streaming wake, the largest ship ever launched in Yarmouth is a fitting symbol for the town's maritime heritage. The glorious but brief career of the *Admiral* was like the story of Yarmouth's shipyards, which brought fame and prosperity to the town in the mid-19th century. Scores of sea captains were living in the little town when shipbuilding peaked in the 1870s. Some of Yarmouth's master builders, such as Giles Loring, specialized in small brigs for the West Indian sugar trade. Others, such as the Blanchard Brothers, concentrated on barks and full-rigged ships for distant voyages to Asia and Europe. Still other craftsmen produced the small schooners, stone sloops, and sailing yachts that plied the coast well into the 1930s. (Collection of the Maine Historic Preservation Commission.)

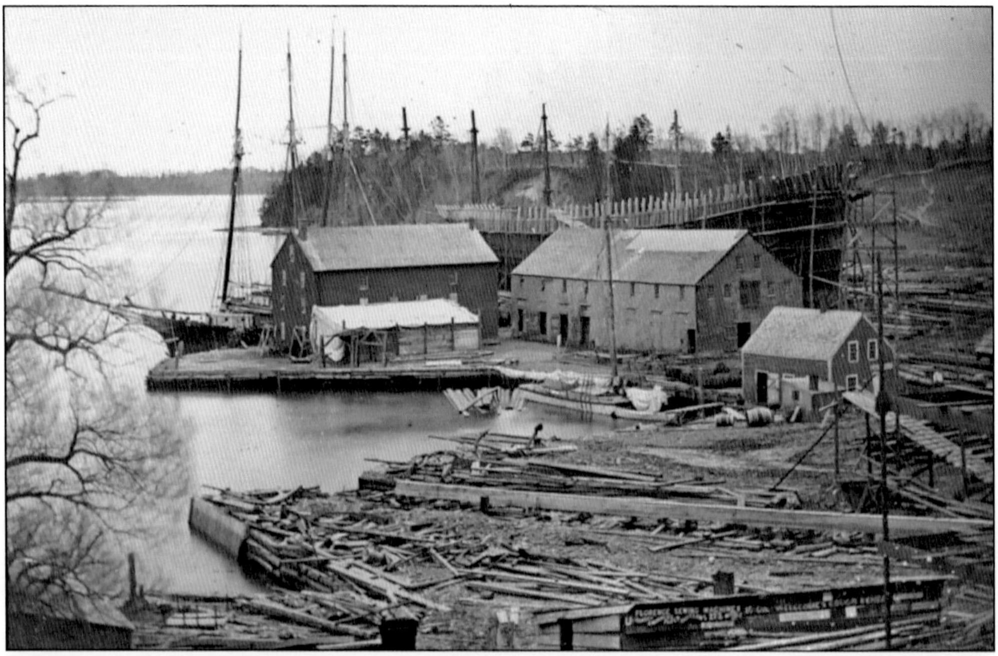

When the country's merchant marine needed to be rebuilt after the Civil War, the shipyards in Yarmouth immediately responded. Twelve ships were launched in 1874, including two from the Hutchins & Stubbs yard in the foreground. The perils of ocean trade are illustrated by the Blanchard's C.F. *Sargent*, under construction behind the long warehouse. Loaded with guano off the coast of Chile, the ship was spun around in circles and nearly destroyed by a huge tidal wave. (Collection of Alan M. Hall.)

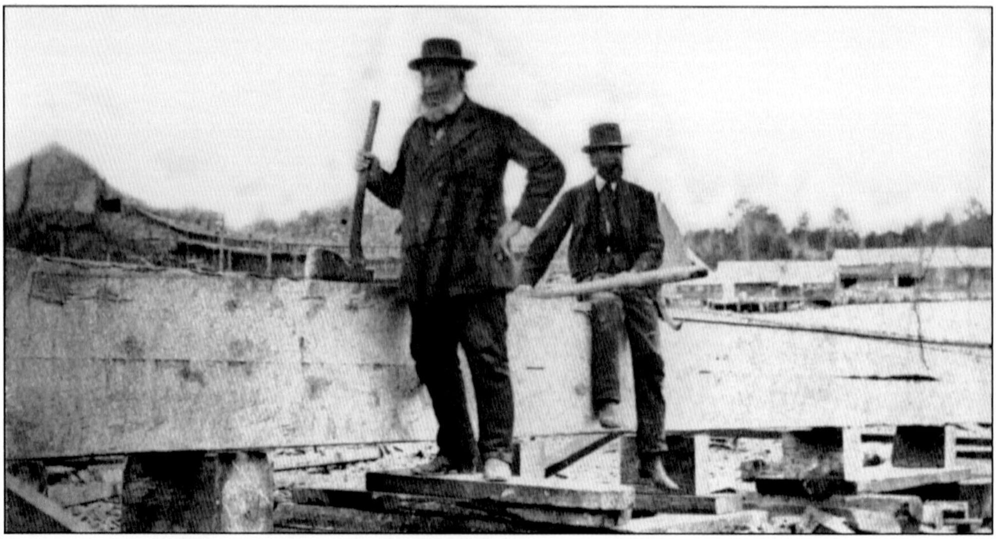

Henry Hutchins (left) and Edward J. Stubbs look a bit overdressed as they pose in their shipyard with a broadax and peavey. This 1874 picture was probably taken on the same day as the previous photograph. That would mean that the keel in the foreground belonged to the bark *Tewksbury L. Sweat*. In 1889, a typhoon hurled the *Tewksbury L. Sweat* onto a Pacific reef, where the crew was captured by hostile natives. After an odyssey of nine months, the captain startled the town of Yarmouth by showing up alive. (Collection of Richard Thoits.)

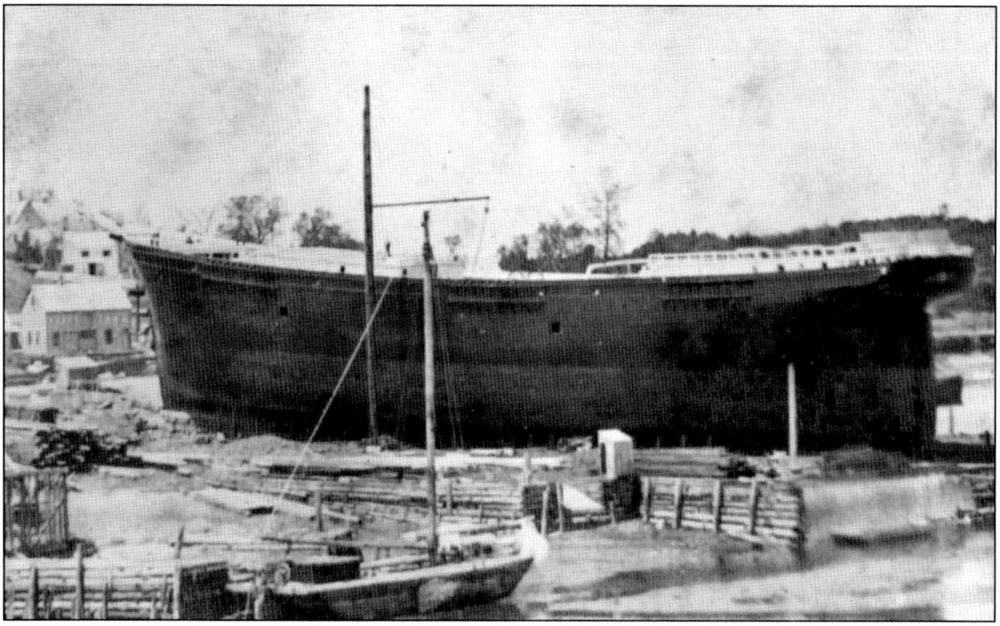

The immensity of the 260-foot ship *Admiral* is illustrated by this 1875 photograph, which provides a contrast with a humble scow sloop. The *Admiral* had iron masts, a steam engine for hauling, and cabins finished with hardwoods and Brussels carpets. The fullness of the lower hull reveals that the ship was built to make a profit hauling cargo, not to be a clipper ship. It should be noted that no clipper ships were built in Yarmouth. The loss of the *Admiral* on its second voyage cost the Blanchard family and its insurers almost four million in today's dollars. (Collection of the Maine Historic Preservation Commission.)

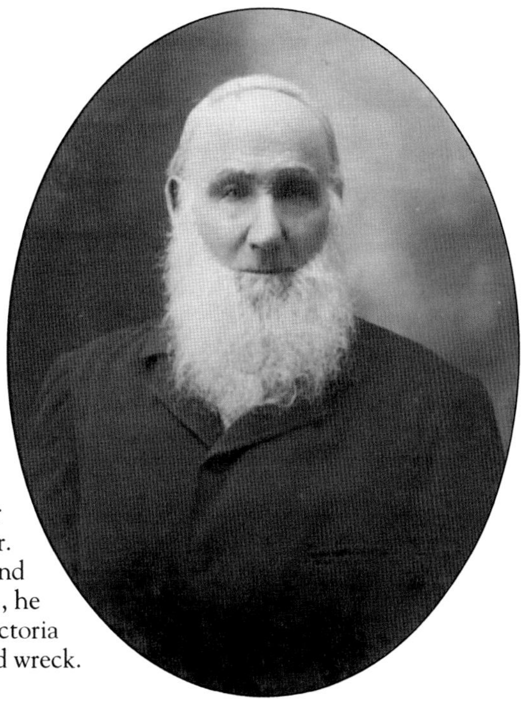

Sea captains often made enough money to retire early and buy beautiful homes or farms, but they earned every penny. Poor judgment in securing cargoes, navigating, or disciplining the crew could lead to disaster. Levi Marston first went to sea at age 14 and eventually commanded his own brig. In 1851, he was awarded a medal for heroism by Queen Victoria for saving 325 immigrants from a storm-tossed wreck. (Collection of Lois Rogers Lippincott.)

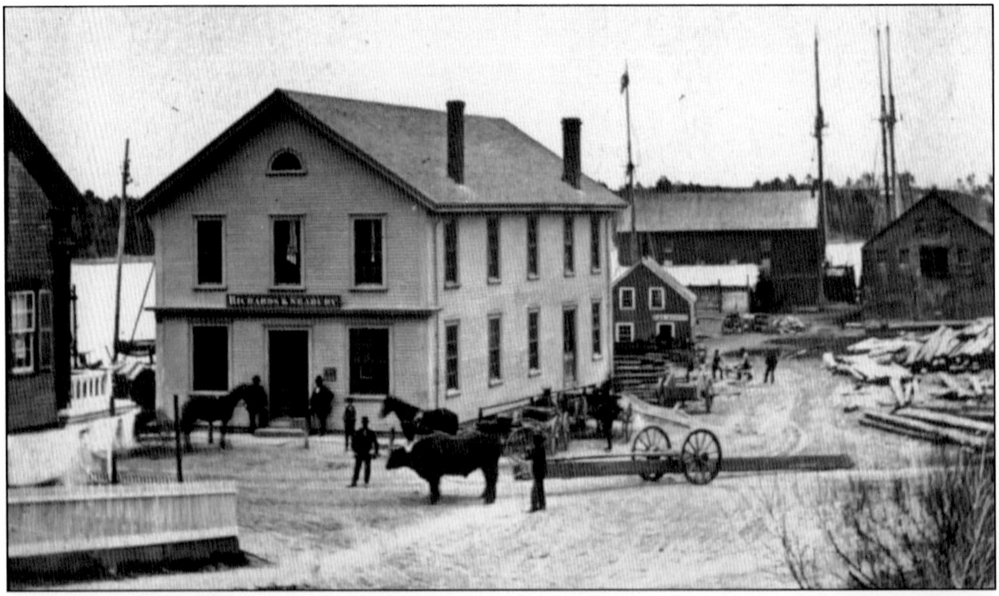

The bustle and vitality of Yarmouth's waterfront are evident in this 1874 view of Union Wharf. Ammi Mitchell and his ox team are hauling a timber in the direction of Craig's sawmill. Men lounge in front of the Richards & Seabury general store and the little fish market behind it. A relic from the old West India trade, the warehouse on the end of the wharf once had sailmakers in its loft and later stored cargoes of screwed (baled) hay. This site is now covered by the southern end of the interstate bridge. (Collection of Bruce Ingraham.)

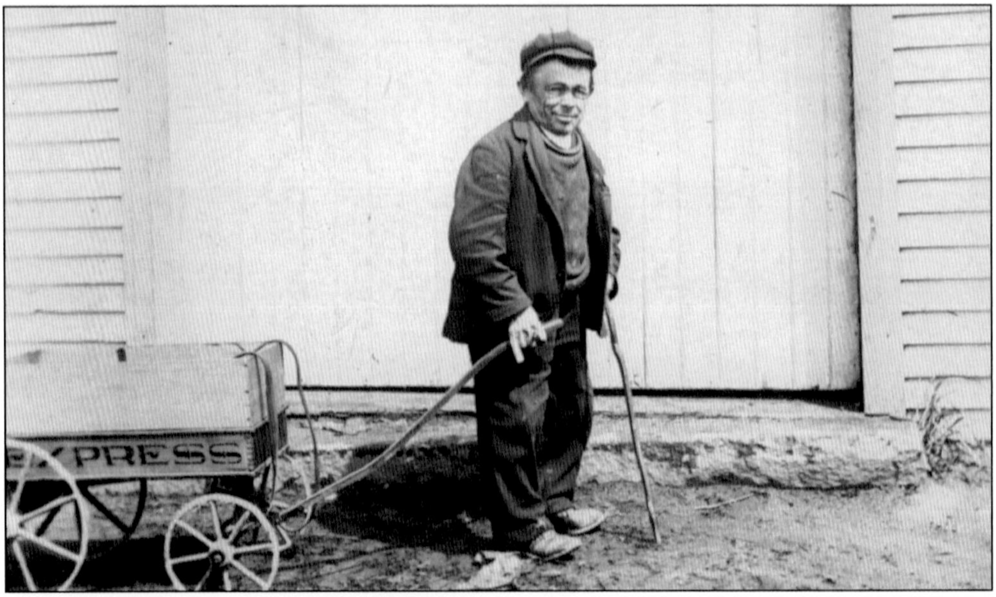

With his growth stunted by a childhood accident, "Billy" Lawrence was a memorable figure around Yarmouth's waterfront in the late 19th century. Pulling a wagon loaded with candy and popcorn, he made his living by selling refreshments at ship launchings and at the railroad station. The Lawrence family built the big Richards store, seen in the previous picture, but they went bankrupt around the time of the Civil War. In this photograph, Lawrence is standing in front of J.B. Dennison's blacksmith shop. (Collection of Richard Thoits.)

In 1854, when he was 30 years old, Giles Loring, or "Master Giles," began his illustrious career as a shipbuilder by launching two schooners. By combining several small yards on the eastern side of the harbor, he was able to construct as many as four vessels at the same time. When Loring finally retired in 1890, he had launched 34 vessels. Unfortunately, he went bankrupt two years later when his investment in a North Yarmouth mineral spring failed. (Collection of Lois Rogers Lippincott.)

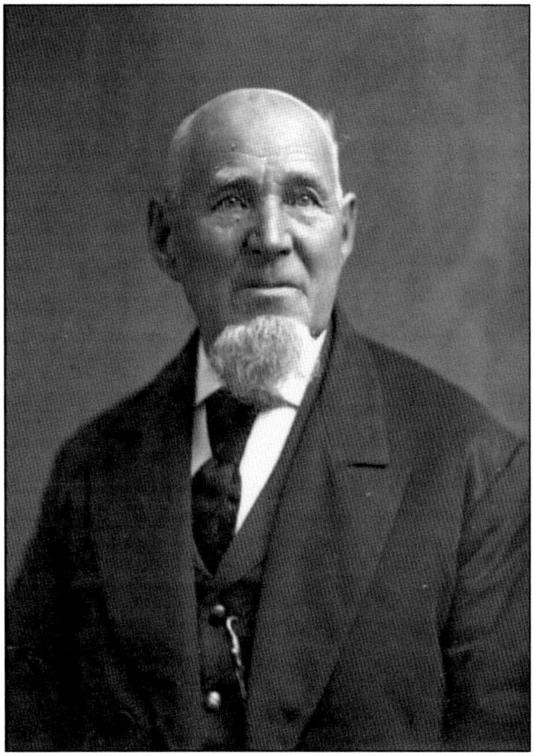

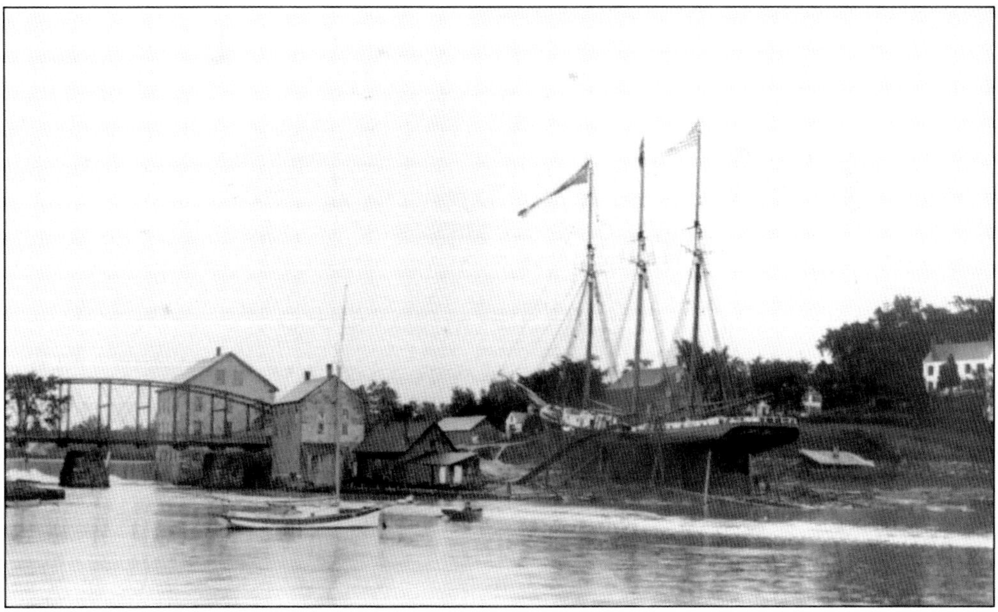

With its flags snapping in an easterly September breeze, the *Damietta and Joanna* is ready to be launched. Giles Loring came out of retirement in the summer of 1890 to build this 350-ton schooner for Horace Sargent of Portland. At 1:00 p.m. on September 3, 1890, Yarmouth's last big wooden ship slid into the water and was immediately towed down the river by a little white tugboat. For a few more years, local craftsmen built small steam yachts and sloops similar to the gaff-rigged *Maud*, which is in the foreground. (Collection of the Maine Historic Preservation Commission.)

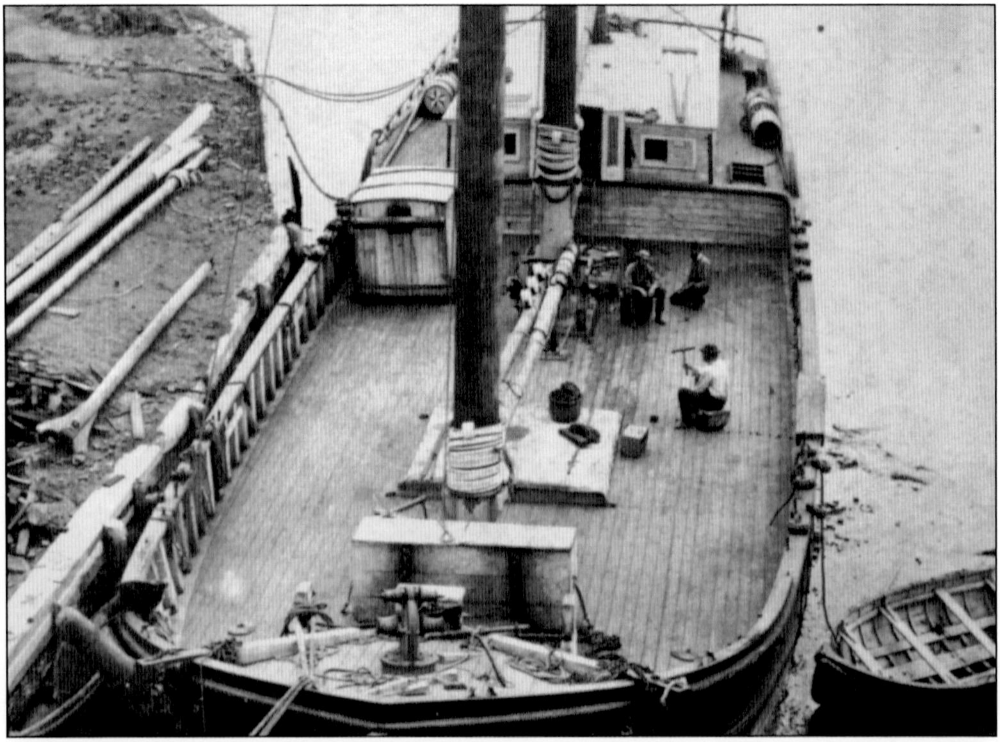

This little schooner, the *Casco Lodge*, was built by Joseph Albert Seabury in 1867. Having learned his trade in a shipyard where Alan Dugas now has his marina, Seabury usually teamed with his father on Union Wharf to build big ships for the Blanchards. In the 1870s, many schooners like this one operated out of Yarmouth, often hauling local hay and bricks and returning with coal or wood. This unusual view shows caulkers at work on the schooner's deck. (Collection of the Maine Historic Preservation Commission.)

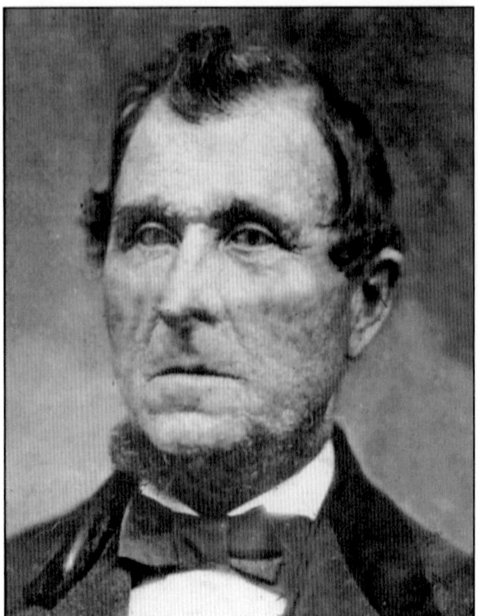

David Pierce, the captain of the *Casco Lodge*, was a grizzled old salt who was still sailing the schooner in his 60s. Captain Pierce had a deep voice, and he never yelled louder than the time he misjudged the speed of his schooner as it approached Union Wharf. His jib boom struck one of the shipyard outhouses and sent its startled occupant fleeing—to the delight of the other shipyard workers. (Collection of Lois Rogers Lippincott.)

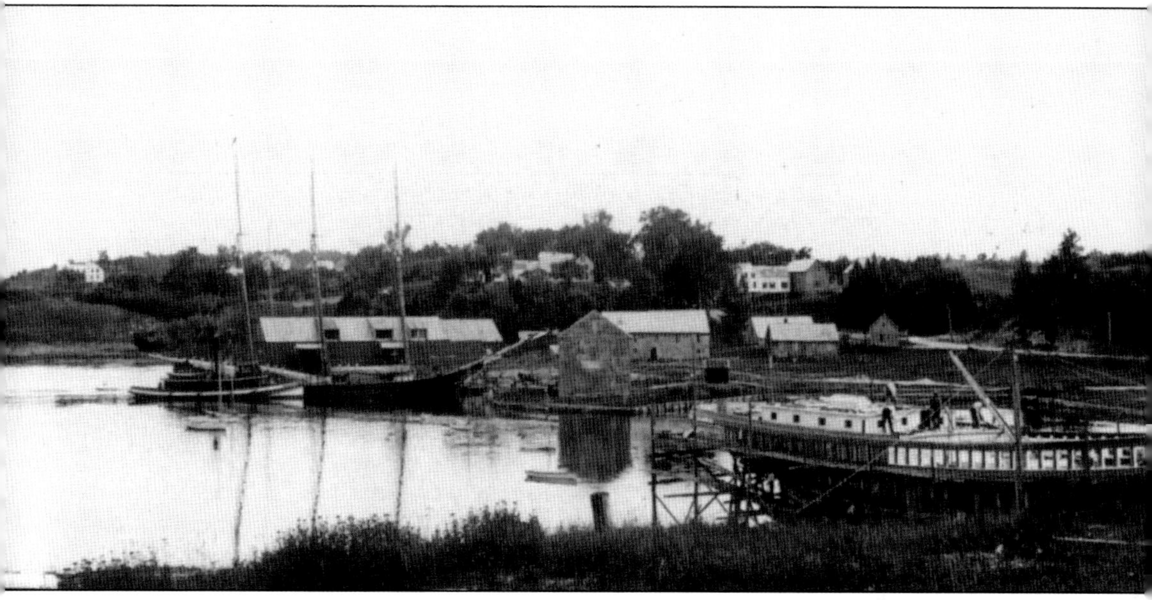

This view from Giles Loring's shipyard in 1884 shows his crew at work on the schooner *Ethel M. Davis*. In the background, another schooner, probably loaded with coal, has just been docked at Union Wharf. It will very likely be moved around to Lyman F. Walker's coal shed, which is visible behind the schooner's masts. The Yarmouth Boat Yard now occupies the site of that coal shed. The *Ethel M. Davis* was eventually abandoned at sea during a storm off Cape Hatteras and floated twice across the Atlantic as a ghost ship before making an eerie final return to the North Carolina shore. A year before this picture was taken, Yarmouth's last square-rigged ship, the *Onaway*, sat in the same spot in Loring's yard and was reluctant to go into the water. Not until the shipwrights filled its stern with large rocks did the vessel slide down the ways. (Collection of the Yarmouth Historical Society.)

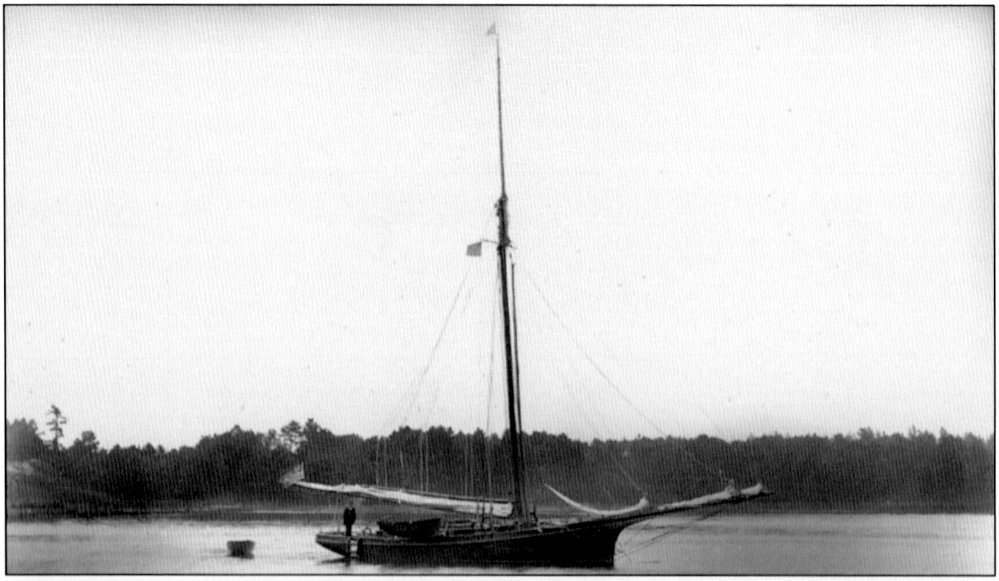

As the era of wooden shipbuilding began to ebb, John Walker was one of the craftsmen who kept it alive by producing yachts and first-class steamers. In 1880, he launched the handsome sailing yacht *E.W. Hill*, which promptly won the Casco Bay regatta. The boat caught the eye of a wealthy Chicago man who asked Walker to lengthen it into a cruising yacht. The vessel seems to have been relaunched in 1885 with the name *Vixen*. The owner, J.H. Richardson, used the boat for summer cruises to Bar Harbor. (Collection of Lois Rogers Lippincott.)

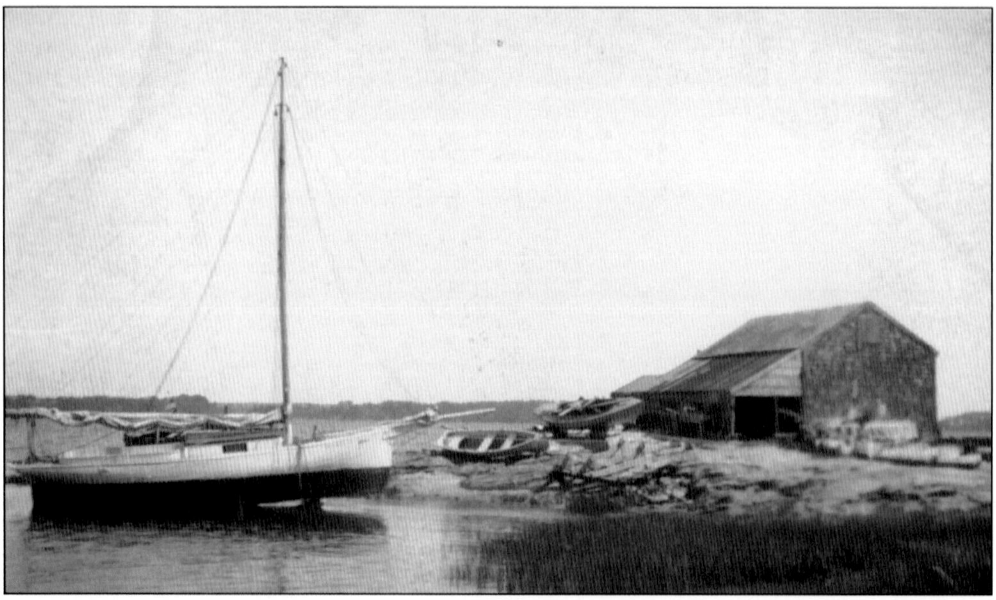

Other Yarmouth men, such as Henry Hitchcock, John Drinkwater, and Alfred Drinkwater, provided boats and sailing parties to Yarmouth's growing tide of summer visitors. The centerboard sloop *Georgia* was used by Woodbury Hamilton for fishing and charter groups. It is shown here in 1921 at the old town landing on Princes Point. Woodbury's boathouse (right) was very likely the fish oil factory that occupied the site *c.* 1870. (Collection of Alfreda Drinkwater Thurston.)

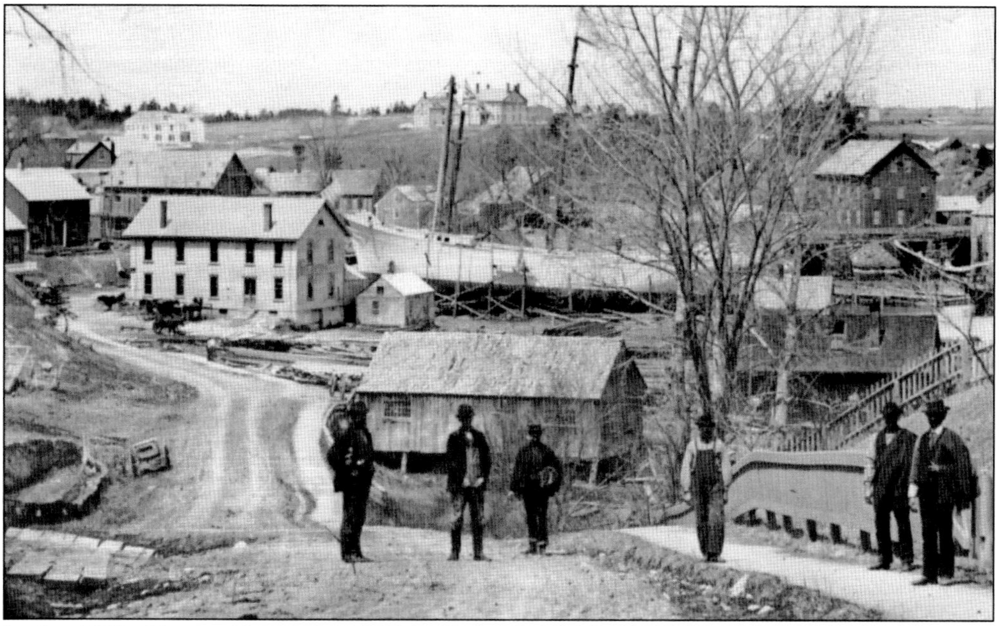

In the 1870s, Pleasant Street was the home of many shipyard workers. Although the road today still twists down the hill toward a boatyard, very few buildings are left from this 1874 landscape. Behind the men in the road is Edward Seabury's boat shop. In the Hutchins & Stubbs yard, the white barkentine *Hattie S. Jackson* is nearly ready to launch. The large building to the left of that ship is the Richards & Seabury store, which was destroyed by fire not long after this picture was taken. (Collection of Alan M. Hall.)

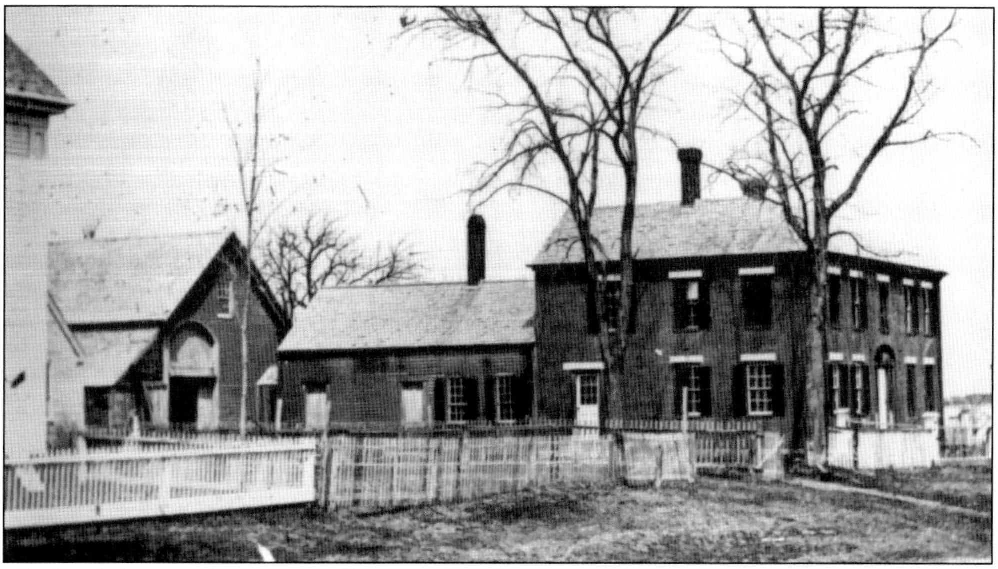

The brick home of Lyman Walker is still a distinctive landmark on Pleasant Street. From 1841 to 1874, his shipyard produced more vessels than any other in town. Although his boast is difficult to believe, Walker once declared that he had more than 100 men working in his shipyard. After he retired from shipbuilding, he and his son built a large storage facility for coal beside Stony Brook, where the Yarmouth Boat Yard is now located. (Collection of the Maine Historic Preservation Commission.)

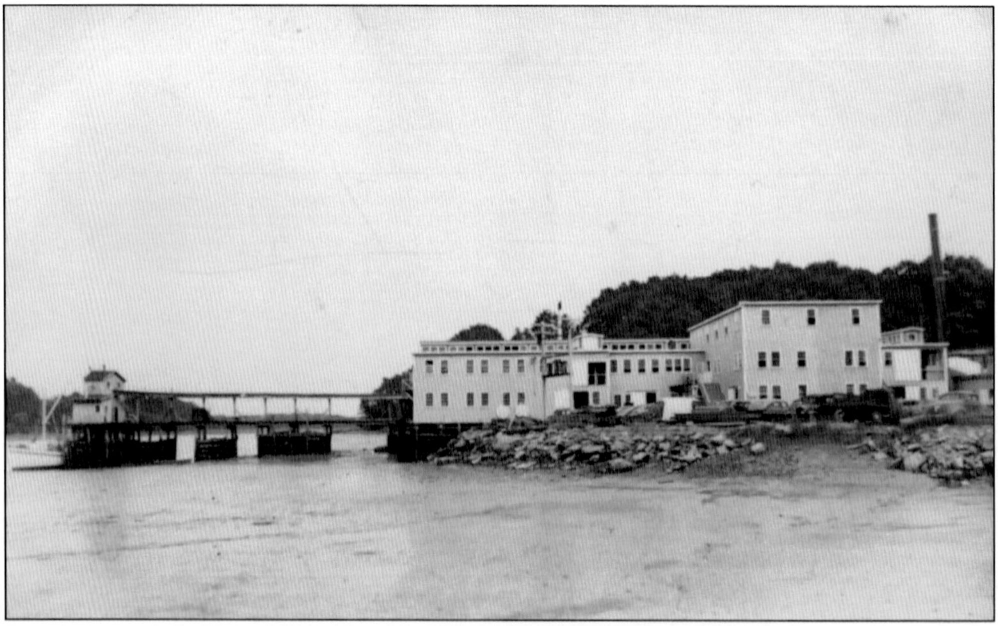

By 1910, grass grew over the wharves of the old shipyards. Except for an occasional schooner that arrived with poplar logs for the paper company, the greatest activity along the waterfront involved the canneries. There were two in Yarmouth in 1916, including Silas Adams' Royall River Packing Company, which was expanding rapidly. Well into the 1970s, packing sardines was a source of seasonal employment for the men and women of the town. (Collection of Stan Milton.)

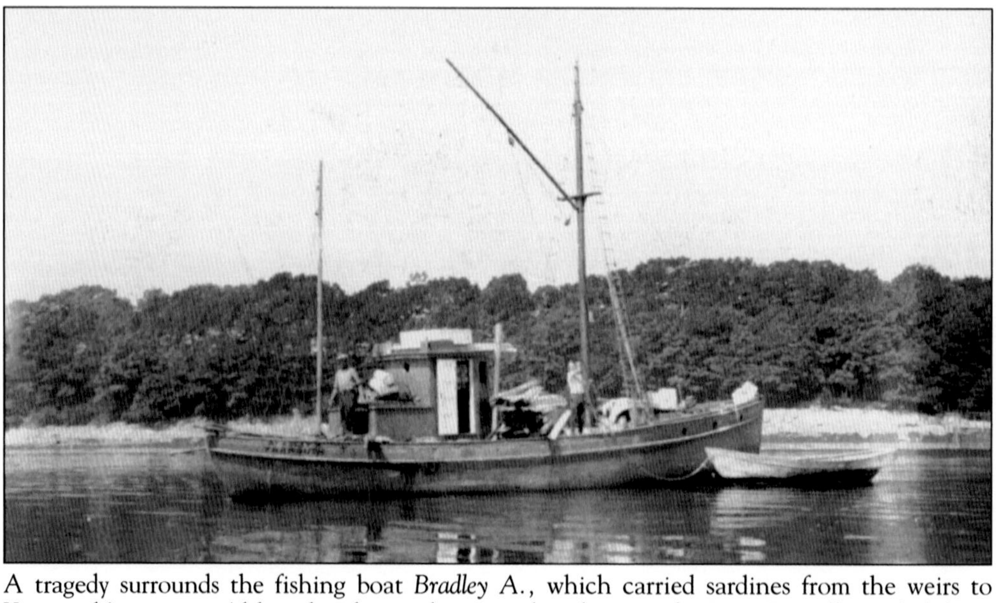

A tragedy surrounds the fishing boat *Bradley A.*, which carried sardines from the weirs to Yarmouth's cannery. Although a dory is shown in this photograph, Capt. Russell Smith did not like to tow them because they slowed his boat. One night in 1925, a sleepy helmsman caused the *Bradley A.* to founder on Bold Dick Rock near Harpswell. Without a lifeboat, three men drowned, including Captain Smith. The only survivor was a young boy who swam to Ragged Island. (Collection of Richard Thoits.)

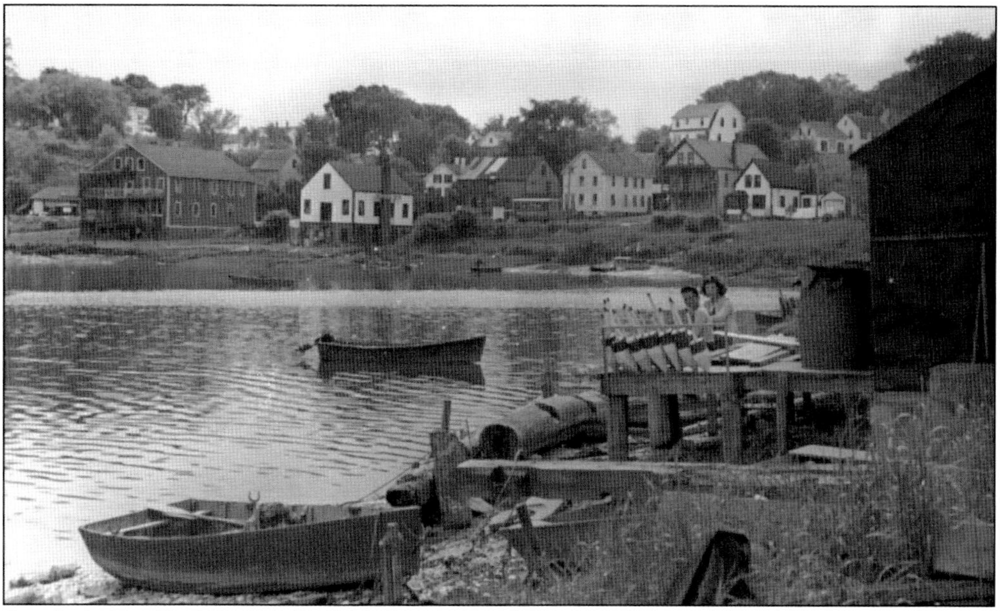

On the east side of Yarmouth's harbor, exactly where the interstate now meets the shore, there was a flat area that had been a cannery and brickyard. From approximately 1910 to 1960, this shore of the harbor became known as Grantville because of the numerous members of the Grant family who settled there. Many of them made their living from the sea, either by fishing or by providing clams to the Howard Johnson restaurants. (Collection of Stan Milton.)

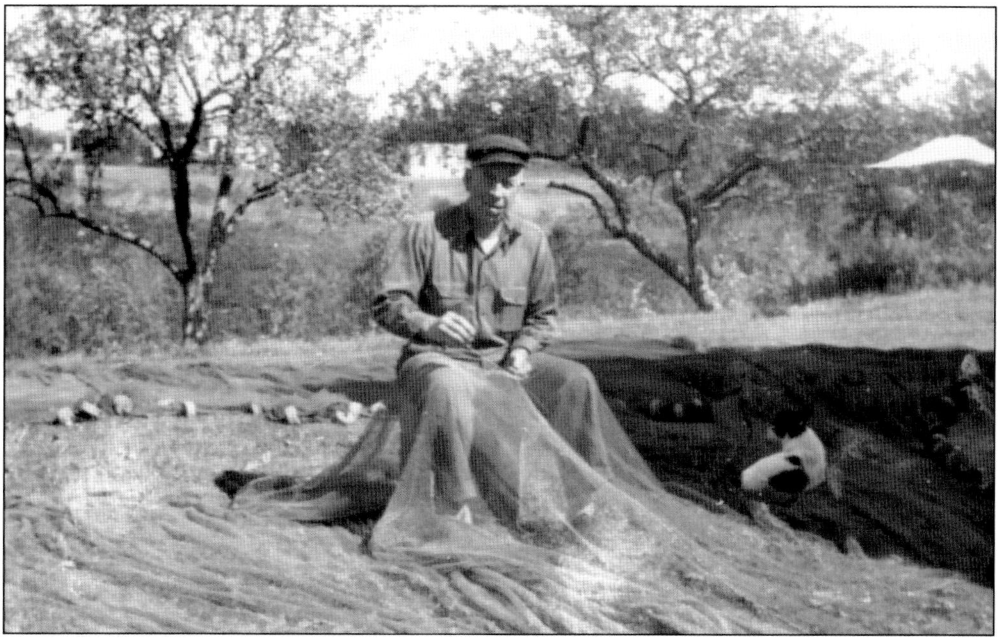

As the grandson of a sea captain and a shipwright, Bob Collins was born to love boats. In fact, the only thing he loved more was a good story about boats, even if he had to make it up. Collins built boats, fished for lobsters and sardines, dug clams, and painted houses. Near the end of his life, he collected his favorite tales into a colorful and important book, *Wescustogo & Aucocisco*. In this c. 1949 photograph, he is mending a fishnet in his backyard. (Collection of Richard Thoits.)

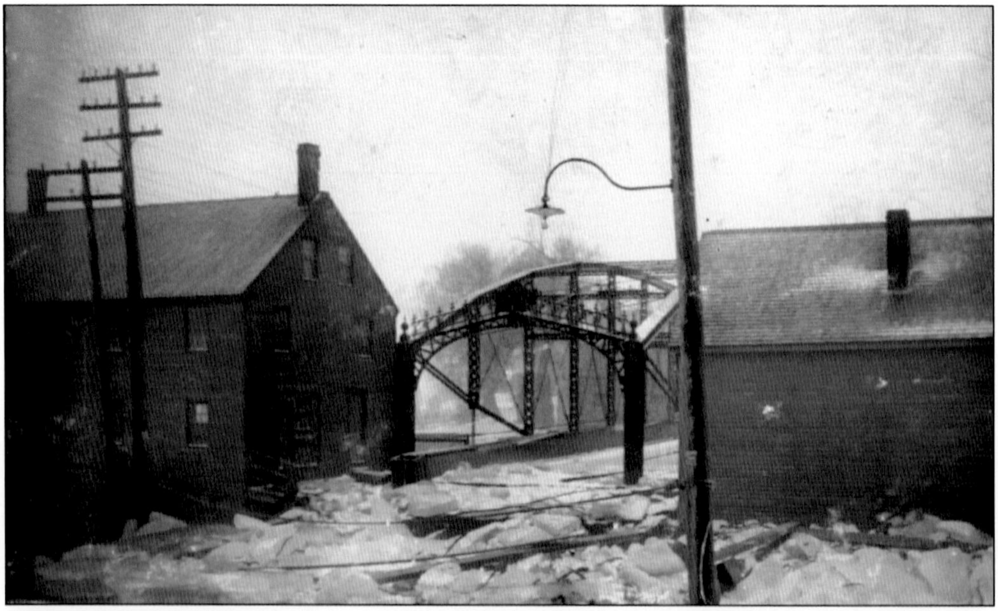

With four dams holding back the watershed of the Royal River, Yarmouth periodically had its bridges swept away by freshets. This 1896 flood forced ice cakes over the new iron bridge that stood on Lafayette Street. The waterpower rights at this location had recently been purchased by a group of local investors who had started to generate the town's electricity. One of their brand-new streetlights is visible in the center of this photograph. (Collection of the Yarmouth Historical Society.)

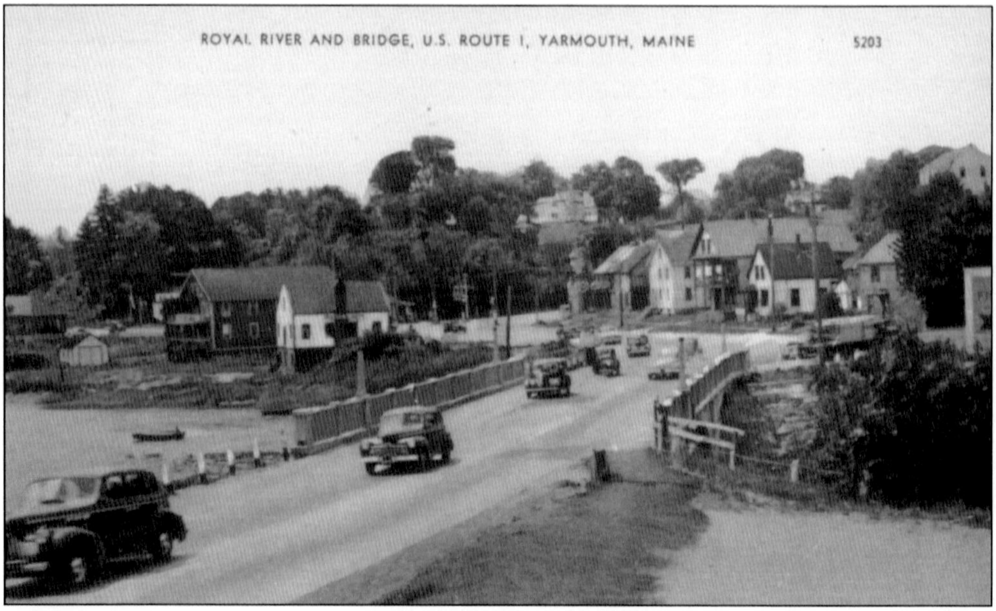

Taken from the same spot 50 years later, this photograph reveals the dramatic changes that occurred when Lafayette Street was widened and paved with concrete as part of the new federal highway. The small boy in the skiff, behind the 1931 Packard, is Tom Dugas. On the right is a sign for the Nichols sporting goods store that occupied the old power plant. (Collection of Frank Witkowski.)

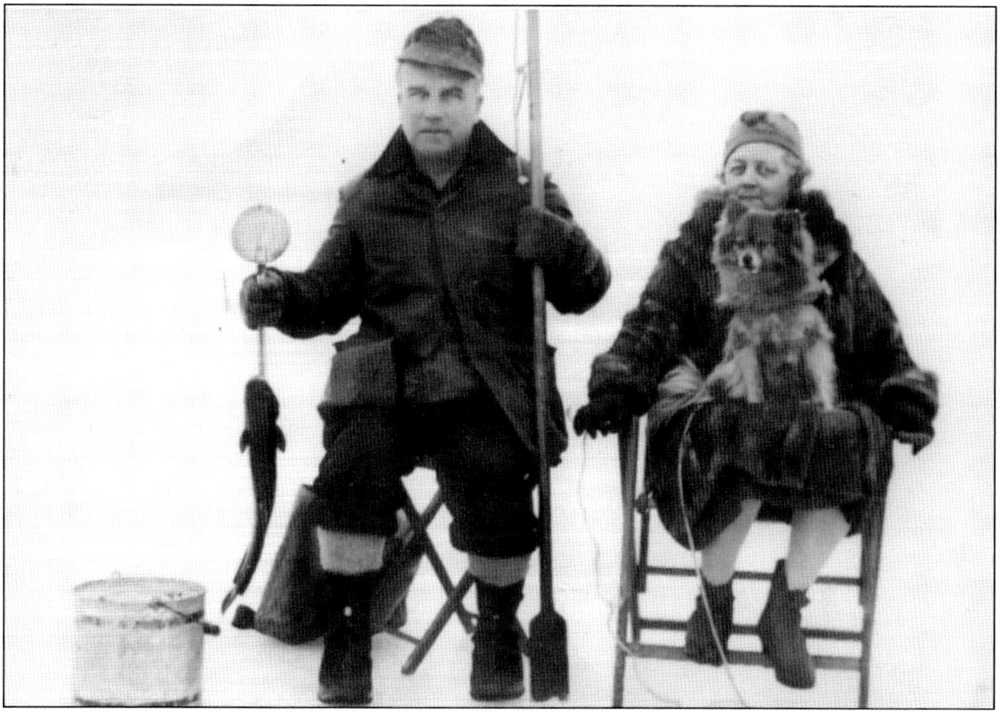

This engaging image shows Herbert Johnson and his wife ice fishing in 1937. Hired to teach a manual training course at Yarmouth High in 1918, he argued that classical studies often force the students to drop out who most need to stay in school to prepare for practical jobs. Then, he immediately asked for a larger classroom and more equipment. A talented but gruff individual, Johnson also led the school orchestra until shortly before he retired in 1950. (Collection of the Yarmouth Historical Society.)

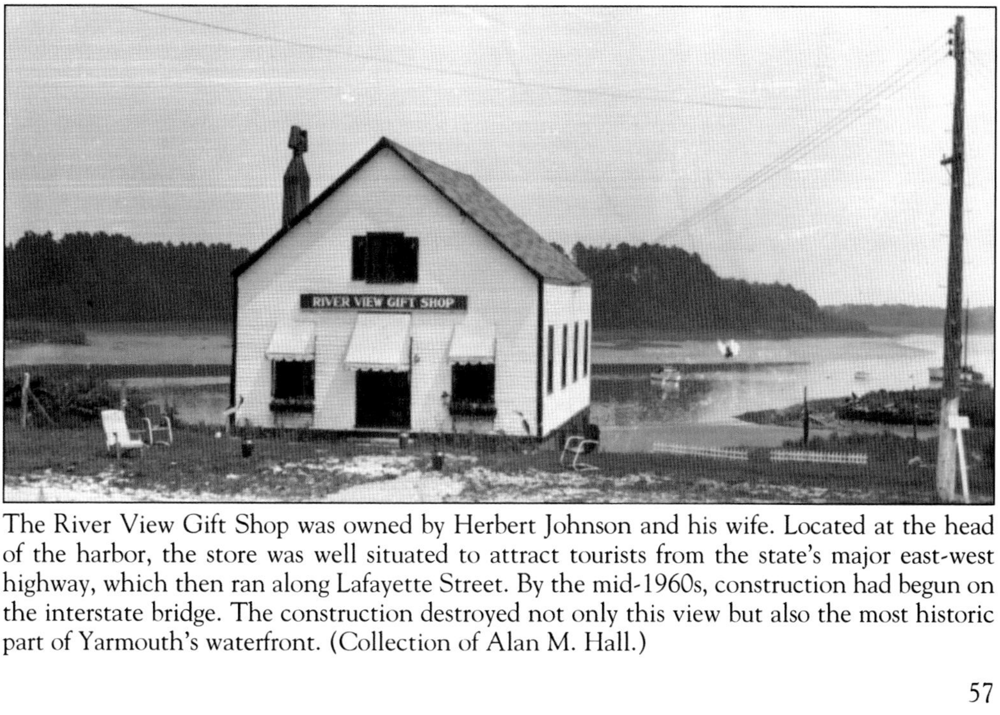

The River View Gift Shop was owned by Herbert Johnson and his wife. Located at the head of the harbor, the store was well situated to attract tourists from the state's major east-west highway, which then ran along Lafayette Street. By the mid-1960s, construction had begun on the interstate bridge. The construction destroyed not only this view but also the most historic part of Yarmouth's waterfront. (Collection of Alan M. Hall.)

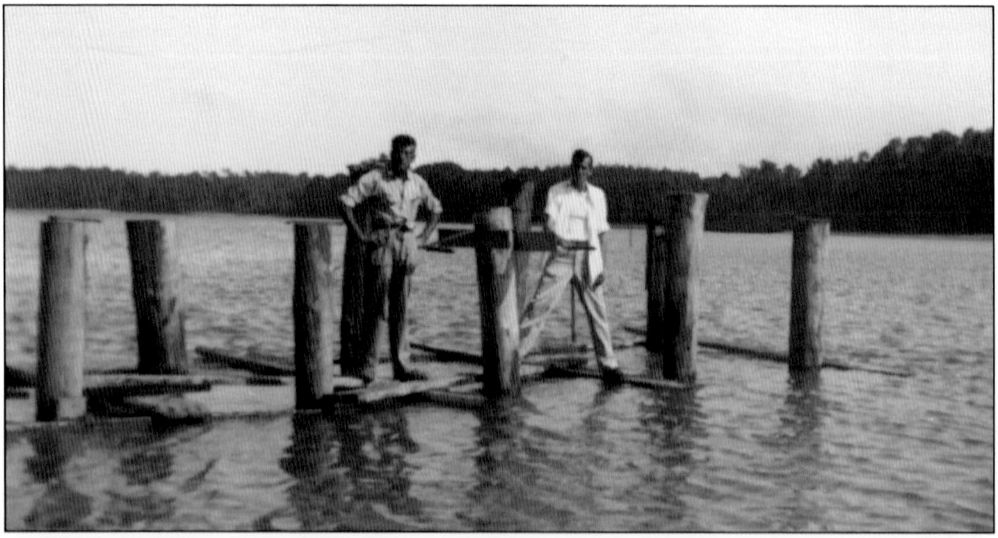

With hydraulic lifts and shrink-wrapped yachts, Yarmouth's boatyards have become sophisticated operations. It is therefore refreshing to see the old-fashioned techniques used by the Dugas family *c.* 1957, when they built the Royal River Boatyard. Adolphus Dugas (left) and his son Joe are using a crosscut saw to level the pilings for their first pier. That pier extends right over the original bed timbers of Albion Seabury's shipyard, which occupied the site from 1831 to 1856. (Collection of Alan Dugas.)

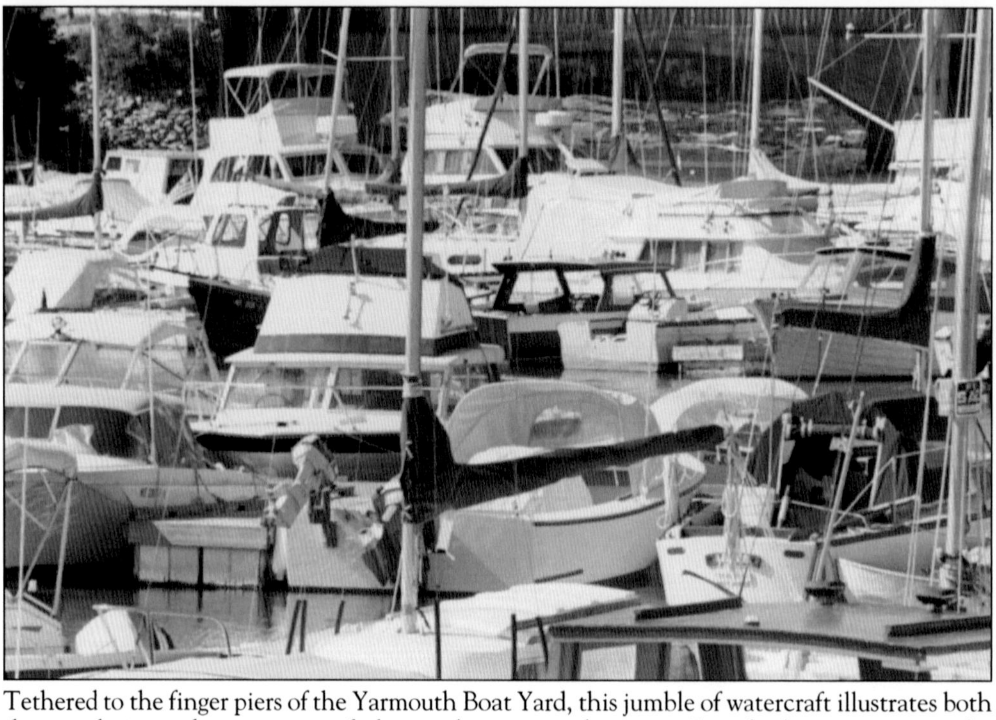

Tethered to the finger piers of the Yarmouth Boat Yard, this jumble of watercraft illustrates both the popularity and importance of pleasure boating in the town. Four facilities now serve the needs of hundreds of yacht owners and commercial fishermen. Although most of these vessels rarely go around Cape Small, let alone Cape Horn, the town is once again being enriched by the bustling activity of its waterfront. (Collection of Virginia Turner.)

Five

Old Number Nine

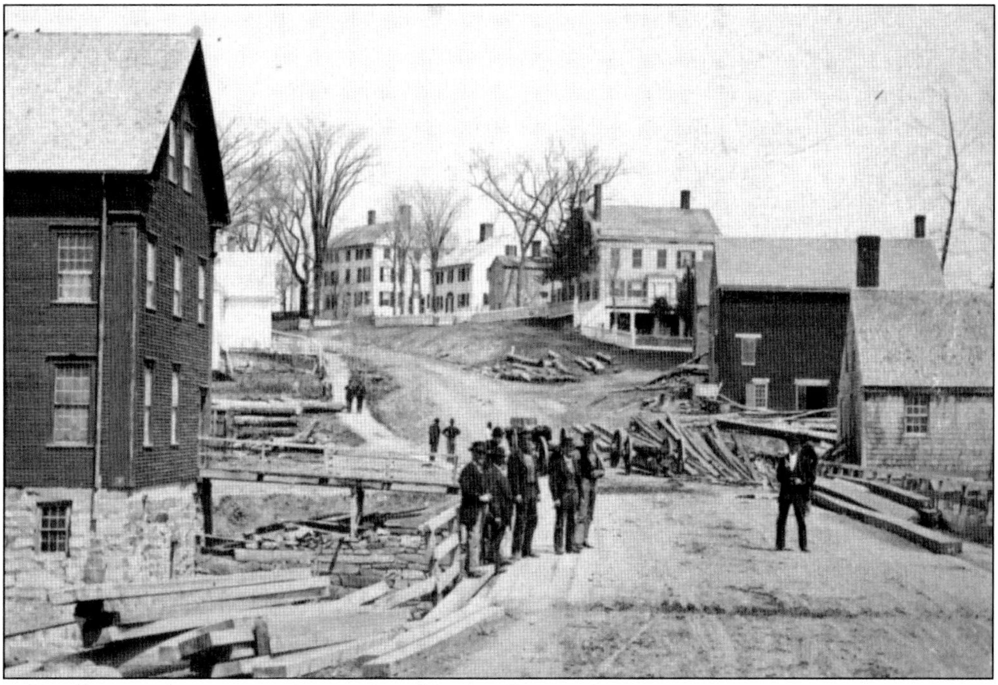

Officially, Number Nine refers to the old schoolhouse that now serves as a community center on East Main Street. It also refers to the eastern corner of town, historically a working-class neighborhood south of Bridge Street and east of the river. Living in this district brought with it a sense of pride that was reinforced by strong social and political ties. In the late 19th century, the Number Nine summer picnics often involved schooner rides and clambakes. At the annual town meetings, Number Nine tended to vote as a bloc and influenced town politics through much of the 20th century. This photograph shows the East Main Street hill *c.* 1874, with Ansel Loring's gristmill on the left. Because General Lafayette once stayed in the three-story house at the top of the hill, this dusty street along Yarmouth's wharves was named for him. (Collection of Alan M. Hall.)

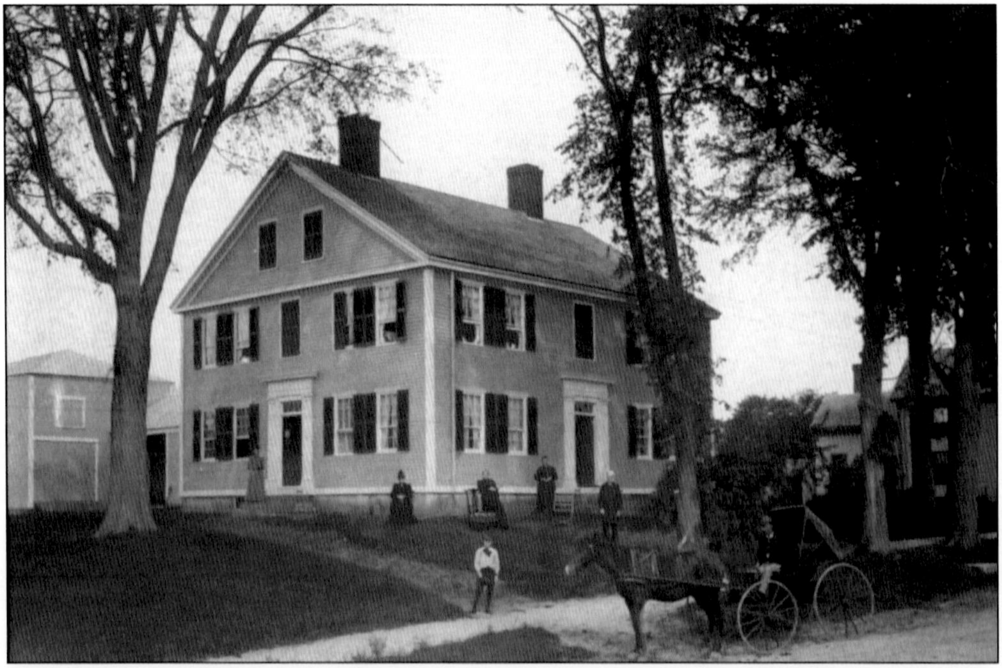

The name of Calvin has always floated piously above Stockbridge Hall. Built in 1785, the building was used by Dea. Calvin Stockbridge both as a home and a store. His son, a Baptist minister named John Calvin Stockbridge, stands in front of the house in this 1885 photograph. His daughter rented the house to Alice and Minerva Dufour *c.* 1900, who used it for a private girls school. (Collection of the Yarmouth Historical Society.)

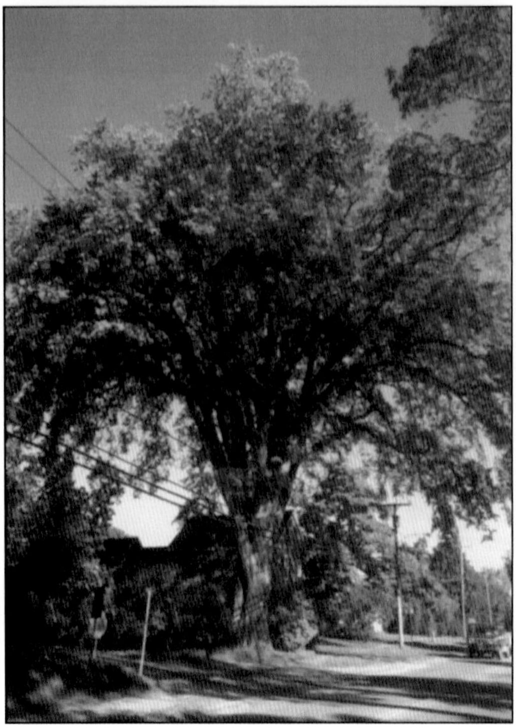

Herbie, the town's monumental elm tree, is located only a few yards east of Stockbridge Hall. Towering 110 feet high, the tree is considered to be the oldest and largest elm in New England, having been planted *c.* 1775. On May 1, 1834, the town gave Herbie some companions by setting out rows of elms along East Elm Street. Despite heroic efforts by Frank Knight (who took this picture), most of them have succumbed to Dutch elm disease. (Collection of the Yarmouth Historical Society.)

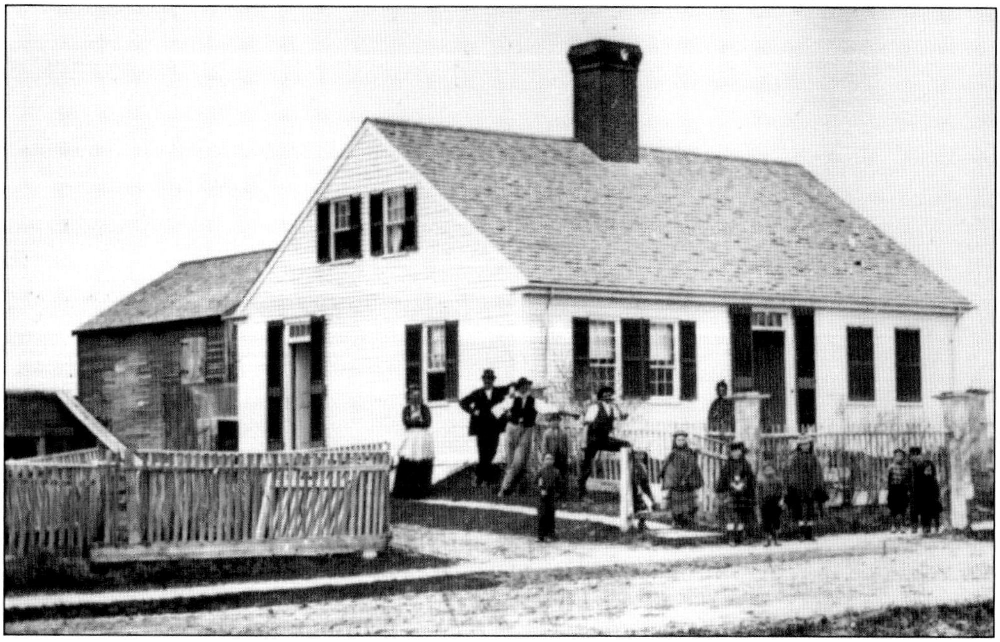

After each coastal voyage, Capt. Steven Harris would sit at the kitchen table in this house near Willow Street and sort coins and bills into piles for the local men who sent him off with their hay, bricks, and pottery. When it was time for the Number Nine summer picnic, Captain Harris scrubbed his old schooner, adorned it with colorful flags, and took the whole neighborhood to Jewell's Island. (Collection of the Maine Historic Preservation Society.)

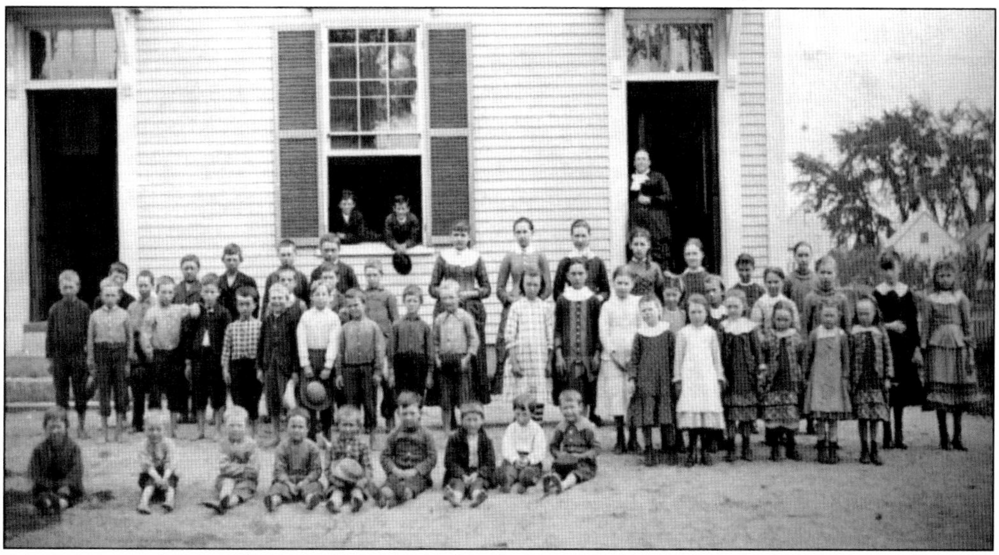

After the Civil War, the Number Nine schoolhouse was known as a difficult place to teach, especially when the older boys would return from sea voyages. Serious problems were handed to Elbridge Wagg, "a man of powerful physique, with an active brain . . . equal to any emergency." With the opening of the central grammar school in 1890, older students no longer attended Number Nine. In this *c.* 1880 photograph, the teacher, Theresa Merrill, has the situation well in hand, even with 50 students, whom she has carefully segregated by gender. (Collection of Lois Rogers Lippincott.)

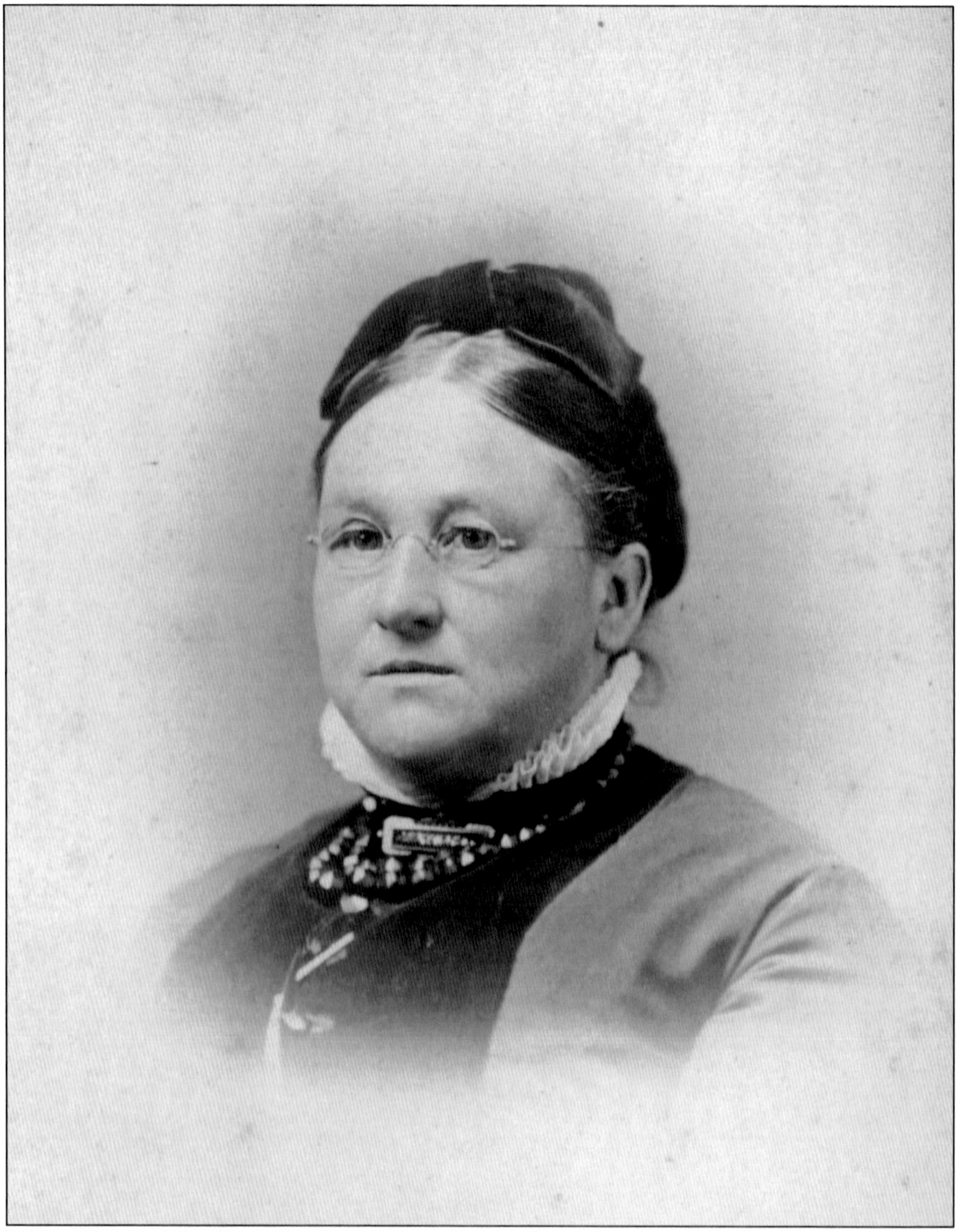

When Theresa Merrill was born *c.* 1840, a Yarmouth teacher was typically a young man who would teach for a year or two before advancing his position by reading the law or clerking in a store. As women like Merrill became teachers after the Civil War, they found low pay and an endless struggle with overcrowded classrooms. In 1905, the starting salary for teachers right out of normal school was usually about $12 per week. Yarmouth's rate was $7.50. Merrill's former students remembered her fondly as a teacher who clearly loved her job and fearlessly maintained discipline by spanking unruly students if necessary. One former student was a sea captain who treasured a pair of red stockings she knit for him when he returned from a shipwreck. She died in 1908 at the age of 69. (Collection of Lois Rogers Lippincott.)

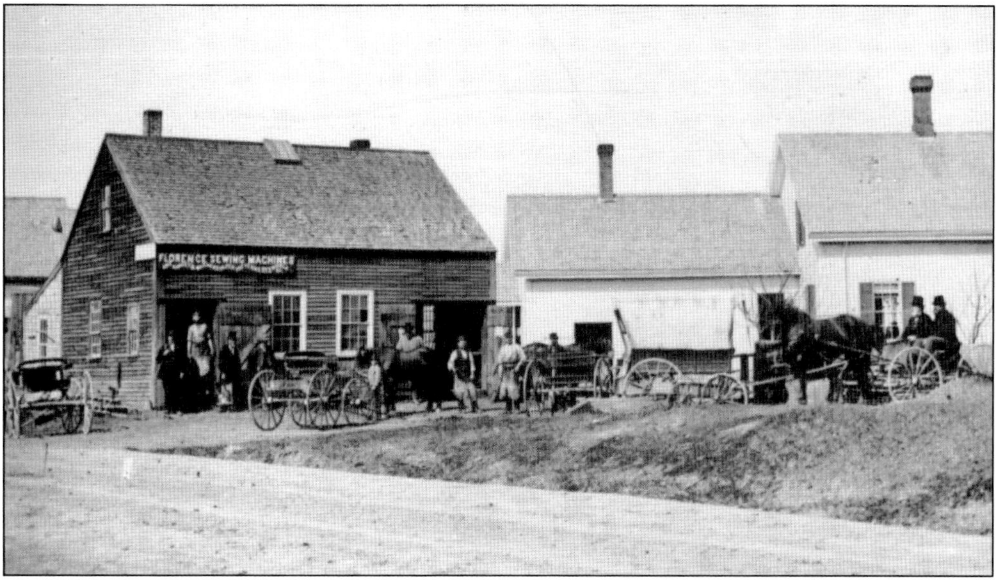

Although Number Nine took its name from the school, its most important meeting place was J.B. Dennison's blacksmith shop, which was located at the fork of Spring Street and East Main Street for 50 years. Horses, carriages, top-hatted gentlemen, and small boys are crowded around the shop in this view from the 1880s. One old sea captain, slightly addled by a belaying pin during a mutiny, brought his horse to the shop almost every day to be shod. (Collection of Alan M. Hall.)

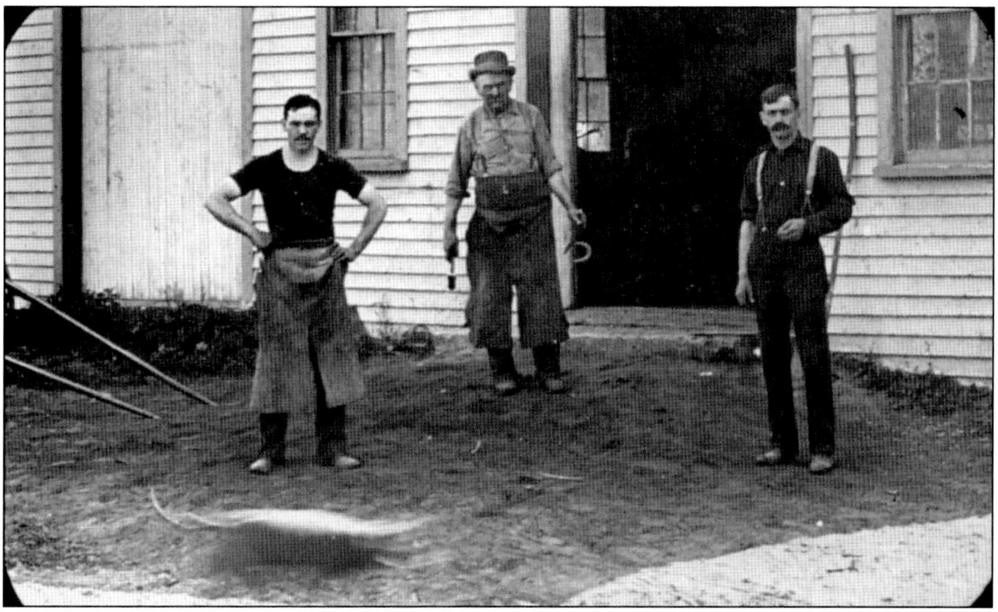

Looking as though they would rather be hammering iron, Jim Dennison (center) and his son William (left) stand in front of the smithy. In a typical week during February 1892, the Dennisons shod 129 horses. Jim Dennison was born in Freeport and set up his shop in Yarmouth in 1863. As a staunch Republican, he loved to stir up lively political debates among his customers and friends. The blur in the foreground is a dog rolling joyously in the dirt. (Collection of the Yarmouth Historical Society.)

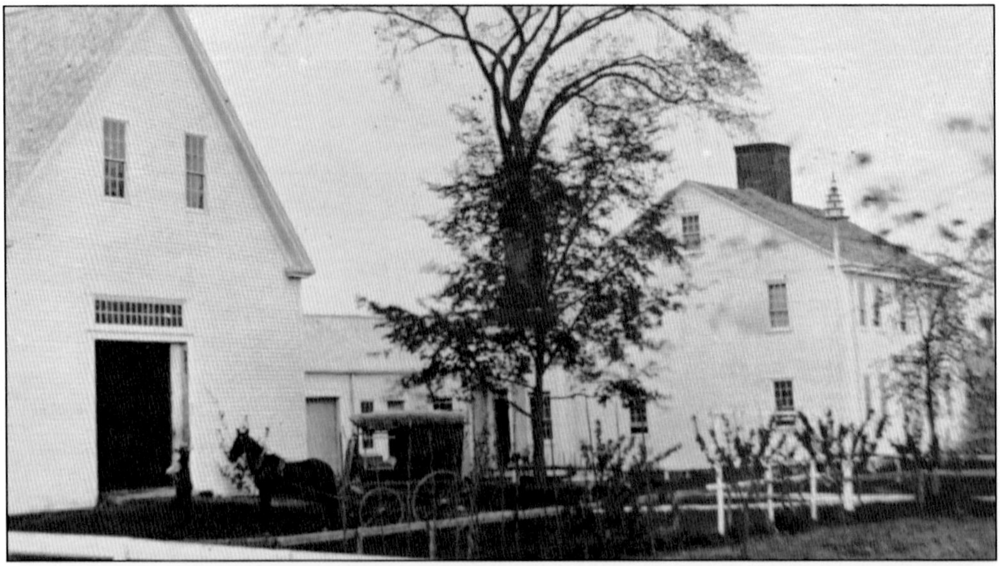

At his farm on East Main Street, Amos Greenleaf stands by the dairy wagon he used for milk deliveries. The town's athletic fields on North Road were once pastures for his dairy cows. Greenleaf was very enterprising, eventually setting up a general store and a laundry in addition to the dairy. In the past century, the house and barn have changed very little, and they are still in the hands of the same family. (Collection of Alan M. Hall.)

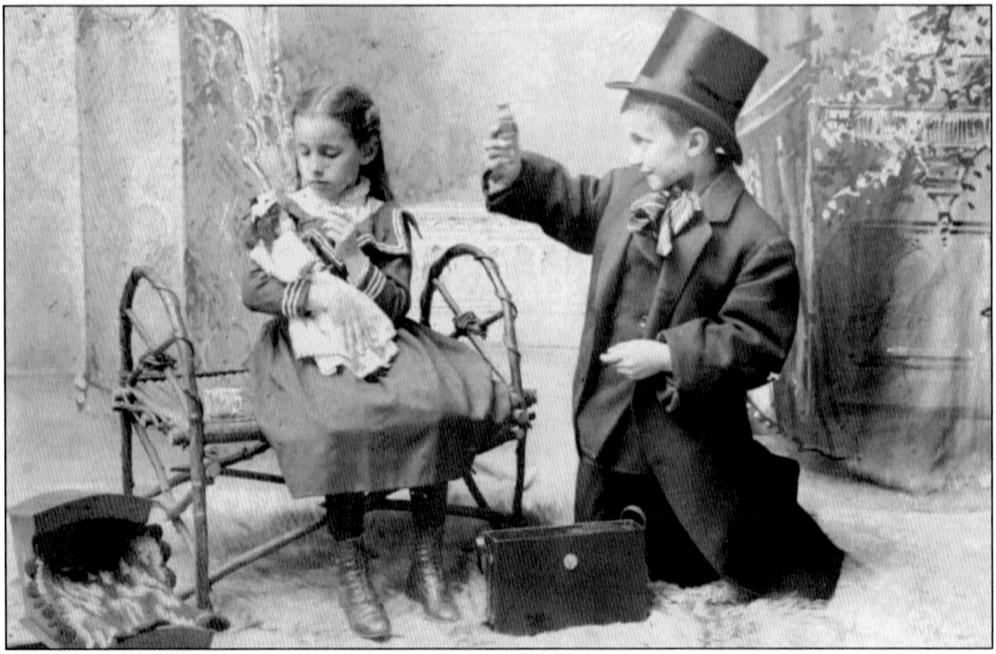

In 1891, James and Mary Rogers inherited the Greenleaf farm from Mary's father, Amos Greenleaf. In this 1901 photograph, two of their children, Annie May and Henry, are attending to the medical needs of Annie's doll. Henry later established a well-known electrical contracting business, Rogers-Wentworth. When Yarmouth sold the town farm and poorhouse, which was adjacent to the Greenleaf farm, Henry purchased it for his own home. (Collection of Lois Rogers Lippincott.)

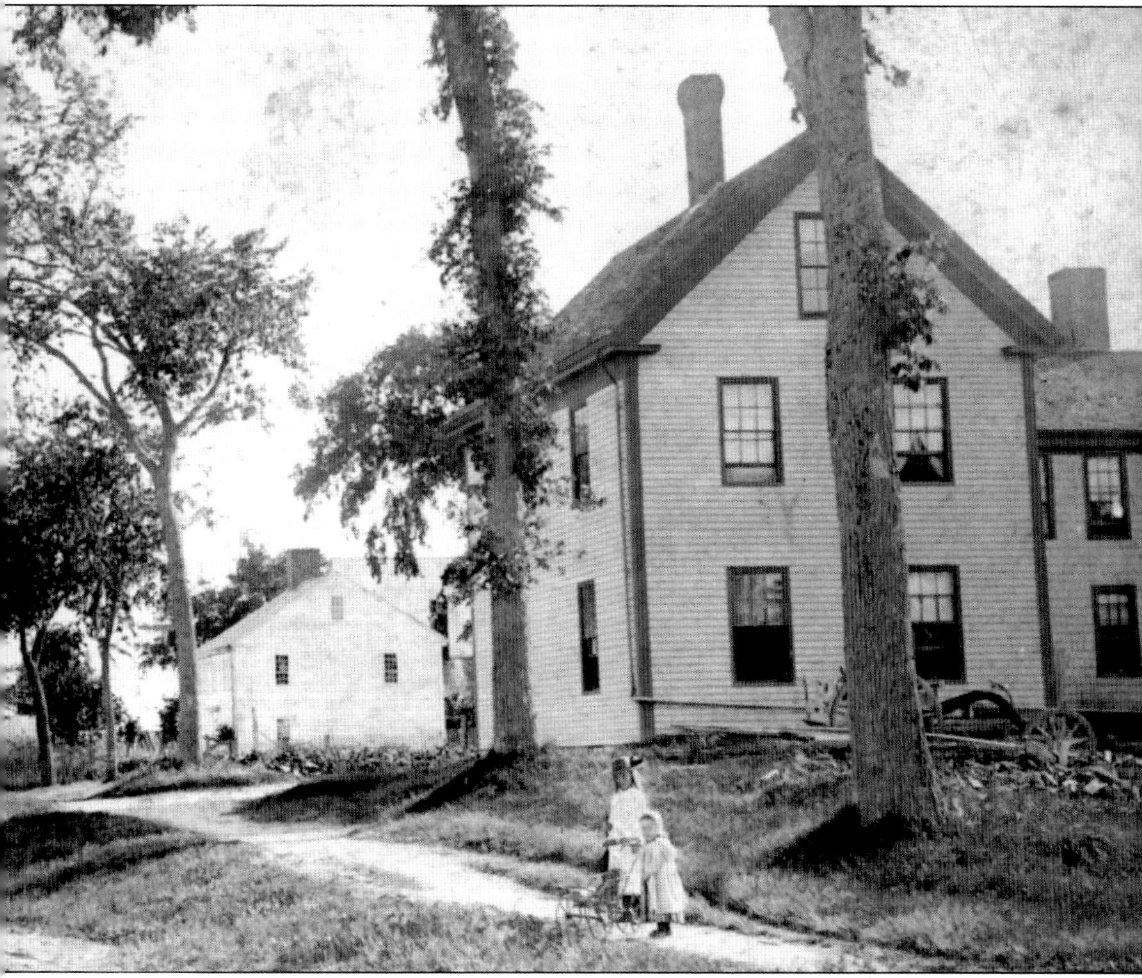

Well into the 20th century, the state of Maine required each town to support its own welfare cases. Yarmouth's town farm and poorhouse eventually ended up on the corner of East Main Street and North Road. Paupers, tramps, and even escapees were all housed in the building on the right, where they were expected to contribute some sort of labor. Notice, for example, that one of Yarmouth's road-grading machines is visible behind the tree on the right. In 1894, during an economic slump, 1,398 tramps were fed and housed at the town farm, sometimes arriving in large gangs of 20 or more at once. Exasperated town officials finally made them saw wood for their meals, declaring that "the professional tramp does not like work and will steer clear of the town in the future." Although many cords of wood were cut, the ambitious scheme did little to stem the tide of tramps. The two little girls with the doll carriage were definitely not residents of the poorhouse. State law prohibited the boarding of children in local facilities of this sort. (Collection of Lois Rogers Lippincott.)

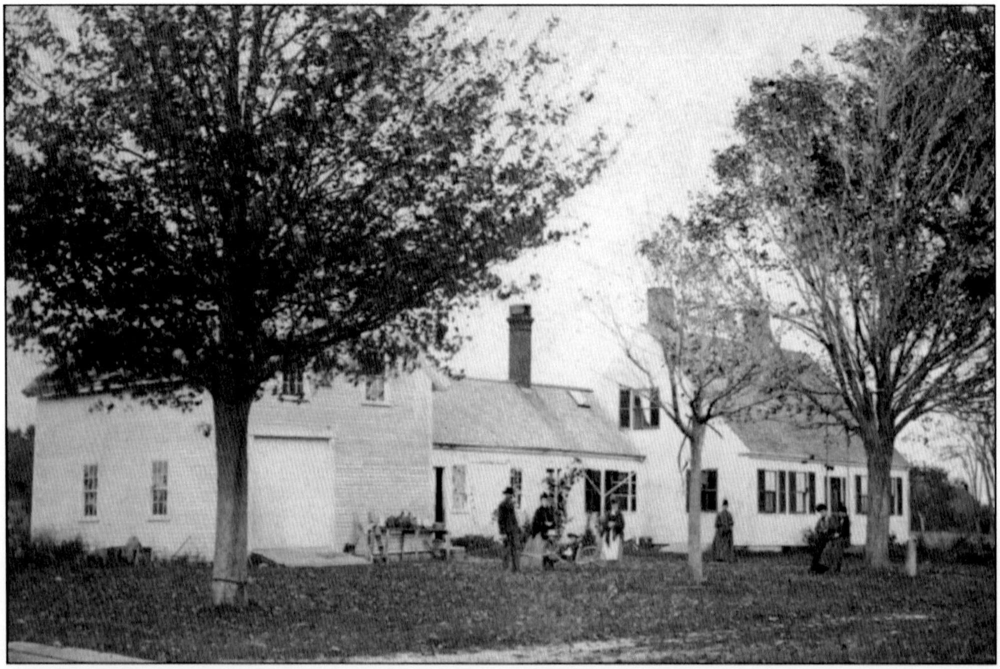

As its name suggests, Bayview Street once provided scenic glimpses of the Royal River and the Cousins River. Saltwater farms dotted the historic peninsula that was the site of William Royal's first settlement in the 1630s. Some of Royal's land on Brown's Point was conveyed to the Browns and held in that family for more than 300 years. At his house on Brown's Point, Capt. John Brown, his wife, and their twins posed for this picture *c.* 1890. (Collection of Lois Rogers Lippincott.)

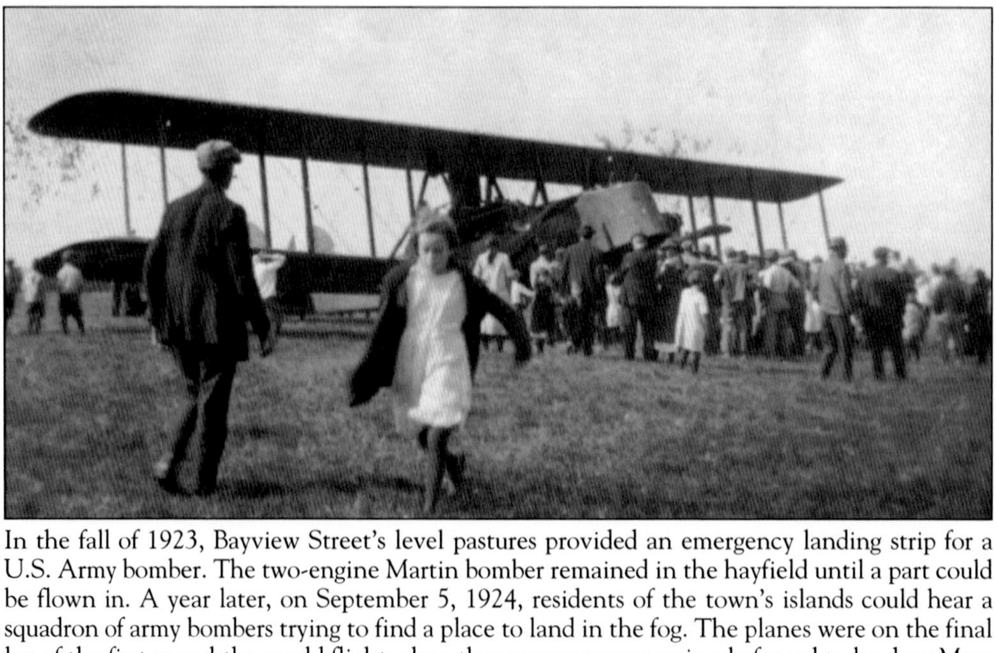

In the fall of 1923, Bayview Street's level pastures provided an emergency landing strip for a U.S. Army bomber. The two-engine Martin bomber remained in the hayfield until a part could be flown in. A year later, on September 5, 1924, residents of the town's islands could hear a squadron of army bombers trying to find a place to land in the fog. The planes were on the final leg of the first round-the-world flight when they were unceremoniously forced to land on Mere Point. (Collection of Alfreda Drinkwater Thurston.)

Six

Civic Spirit

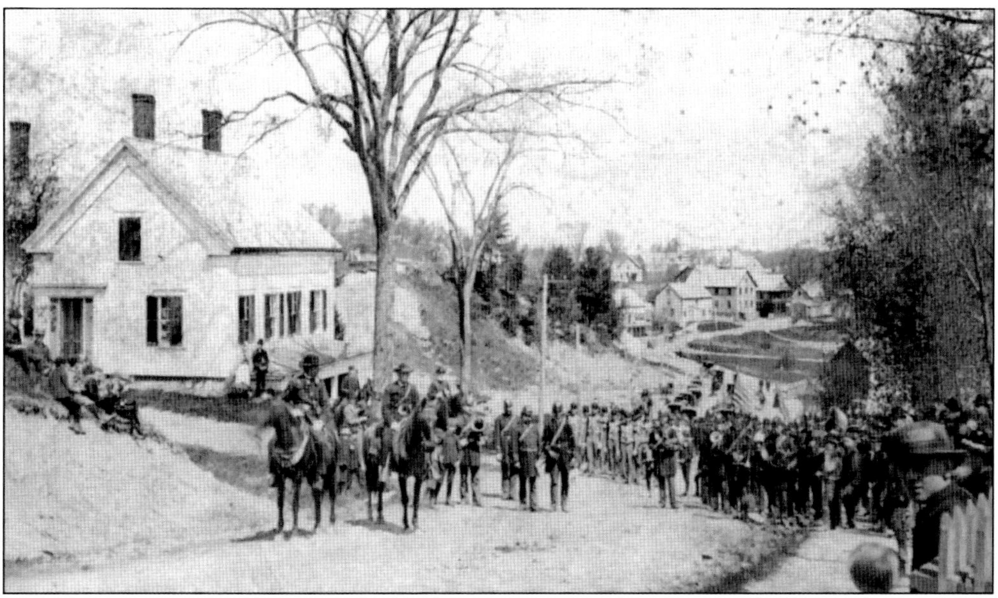

It is very difficult to photograph a parade. Charles Gooding skillfully used the natural curve and slope of Pleasant Street to capture this Memorial Day procession *c.* 1892. While a few Civil War veterans ride horses at the head of the line, many others are certainly in the carriages along the base of the hill. The Yarmouth Band has moved aside to provide a view of the colorful local militia known as the Yarmouth Rifles. From the firemen's musters of the 19th century to the Clam Festival of the present, parades have always been an important part of Yarmouth's civic culture. The colorful mix of brass bands, children in costumes, war veterans, and decorative floats provides not only a delightful spectacle but also a public demonstration of the town's spirit and sense of tradition. (Collection of the Yarmouth Historical Society.)

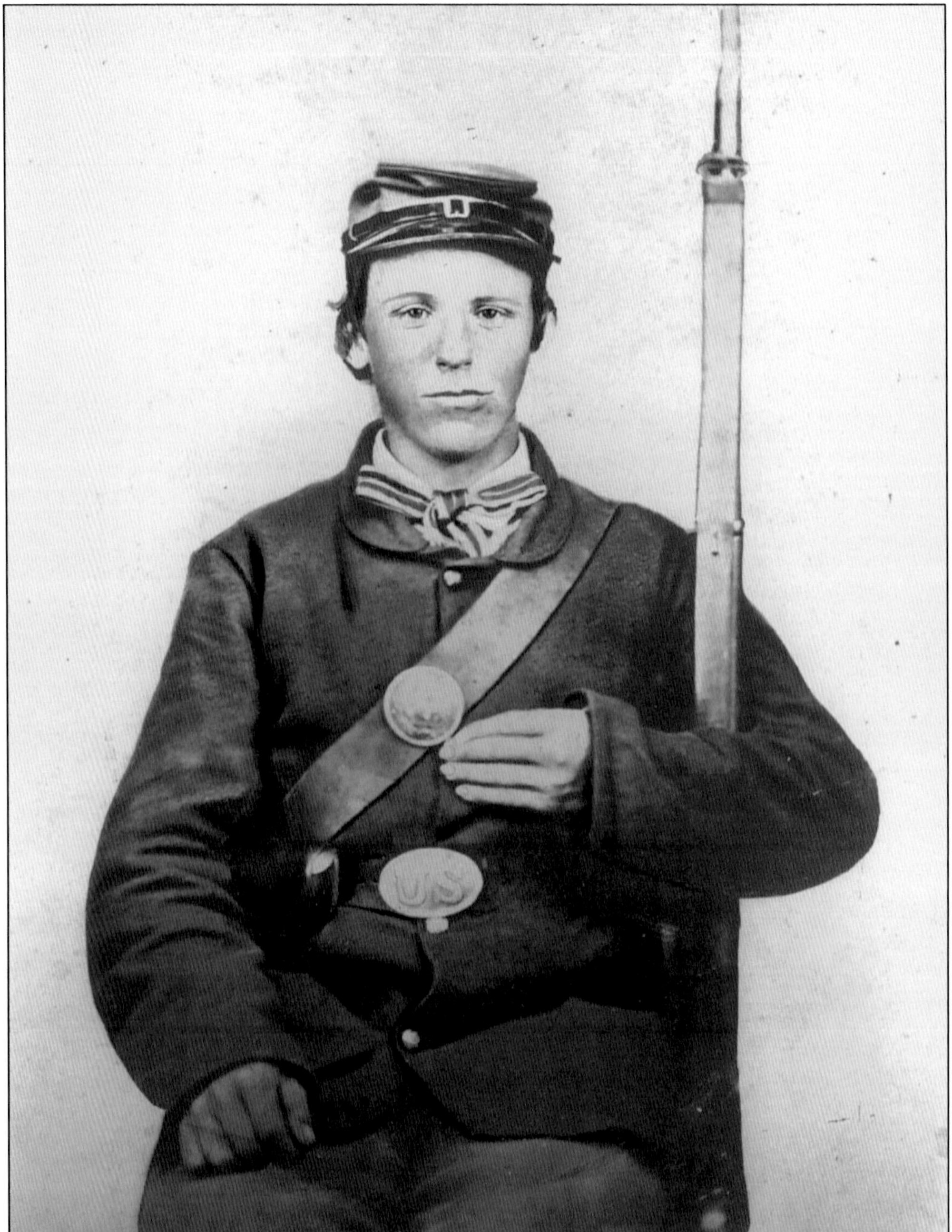

The steady gaze of this young Civil War recruit suggests that he was unfazed either by the prospect of war or the size of his uniform. Although his identity is unknown, he was apparently photographed by James Durgan in Yarmouth. More than 170 men from Yarmouth, one out of every six males in town, served in the Civil War. Some fought with the heroic 20th Maine, some died in Confederate prisons, and one served on the *Kearsarge*, which sank the infamous warship *Alabama*. After the war, the legendary Joshua Chamberlain visited Yarmouth and helped the local veterans raise money for a monument by delivering his famous oration on the Battle of Gettysburg. (Collection of Lois Rogers Lippincott.)

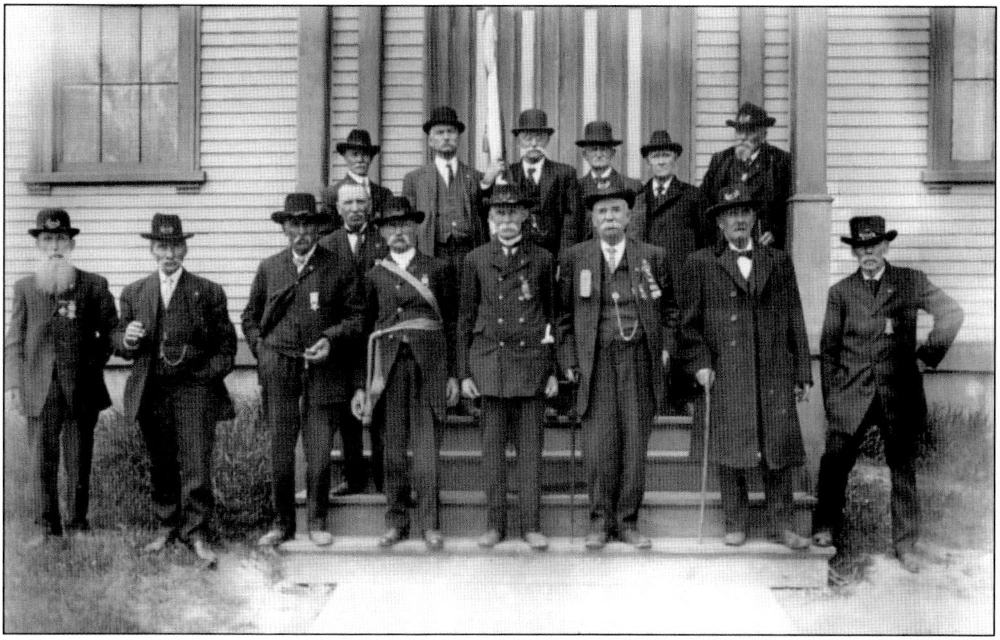

These Civil War veterans, assembled approximately 50 years after the conflict, provide a stark contrast with the last image. They are standing on the steps of their veterans' hall at the old Yarmouth Institute. The man on the far left appears to be Herbert Soule, who fought at Gettysburg and witnessed Lee's surrender at Appomattox, Virginia. The man with the sash is Dr. James Bates, a surgeon in Neal Dow's regiment. (Collection of the Yarmouth Historical Society.)

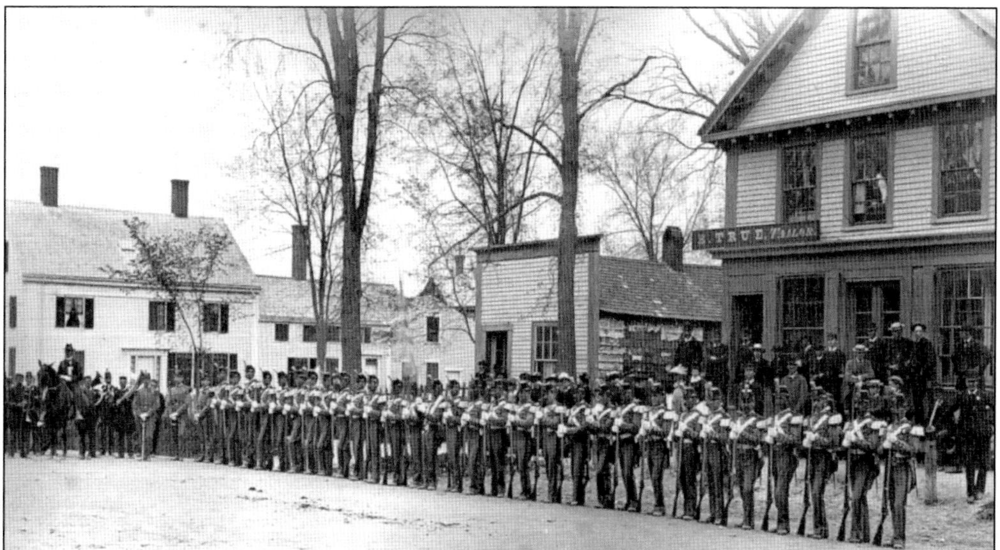

From the earliest days of its colonial settlement, the town organized militia companies for its defense. In the peaceful years following the Civil War, these companies were primarily ceremonial. The Yarmouth Rifles, who were active between 1883 and 1897, purchased lavish uniforms and perfected elaborate drill routines. In this image, they are in formation along Main Street in the Lower Village, probably as part of a Memorial Day parade in the 1880s. (Collection of Lois Rogers Lippincott.)

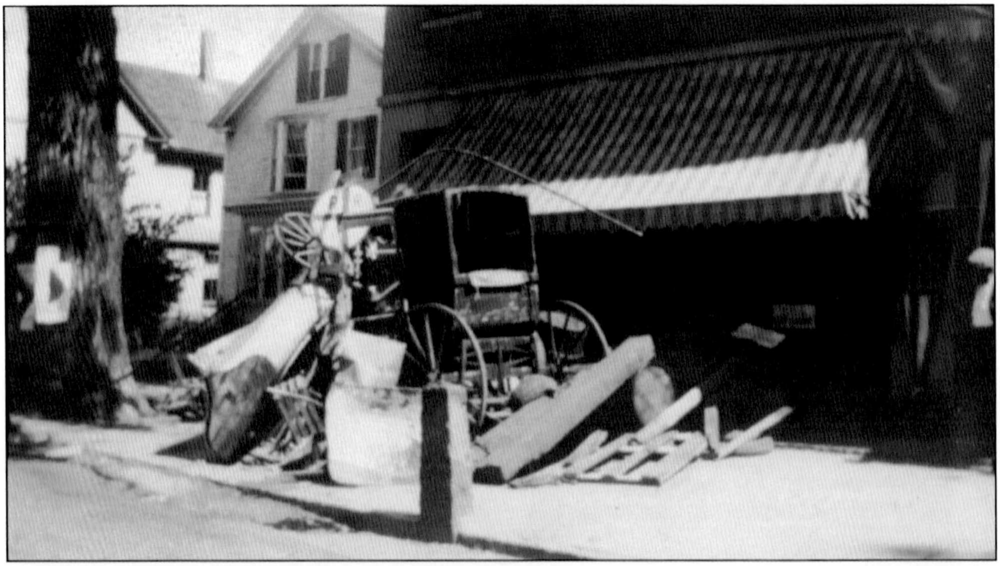

While the citizens of Yarmouth were very serious about Memorial Day, the Fourth of July was another story, especially between 1890 and World War I. The unusual celebration often started before dawn with pranks such as this pile of junk in front of Harry Marston's store. That would be followed by an early-morning parade known as the Yarmouth Horribles, which featured irreverent portrayals of community groups. The rest of the day usually involved firemen's musters, a merchants' parade, neighborhood picnics, and fireworks. (Collection of the Yarmouth Historical Society.)

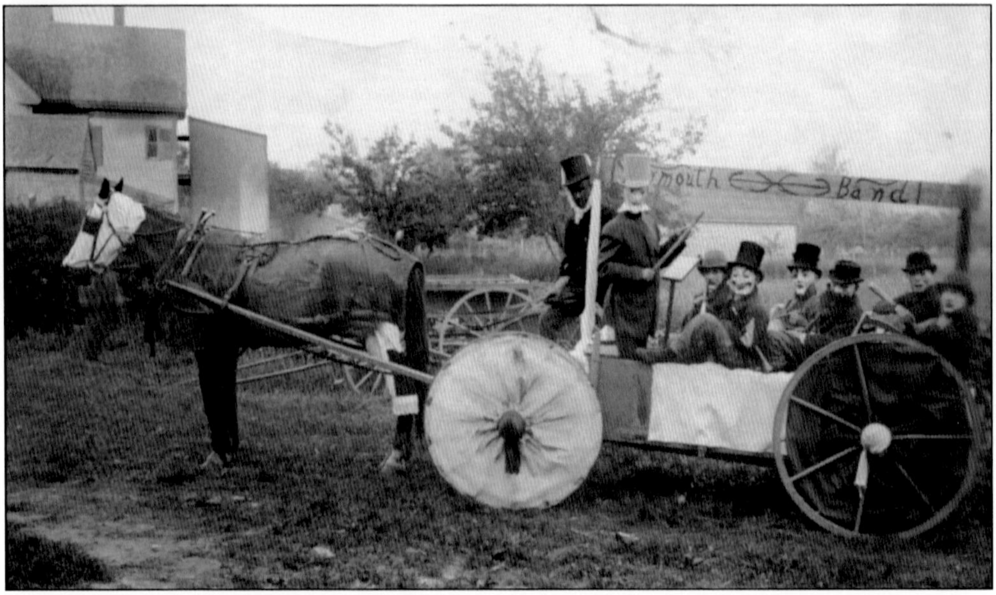

Seen in this wagon *c.* 1904, the Yarmouth Horribles have painted their faces and are using noisemakers as instruments in a parody of the Yarmouth Band. When the Village Improvement Society was organized in 1911, it was immediately mocked by a float that had a strange-looking horse labeled "Society Goat." The board of trade eventually took offense and pushed the town to enact rules "for the observance of a saner Fourth of July." (Collection of the Yarmouth Historical Society.)

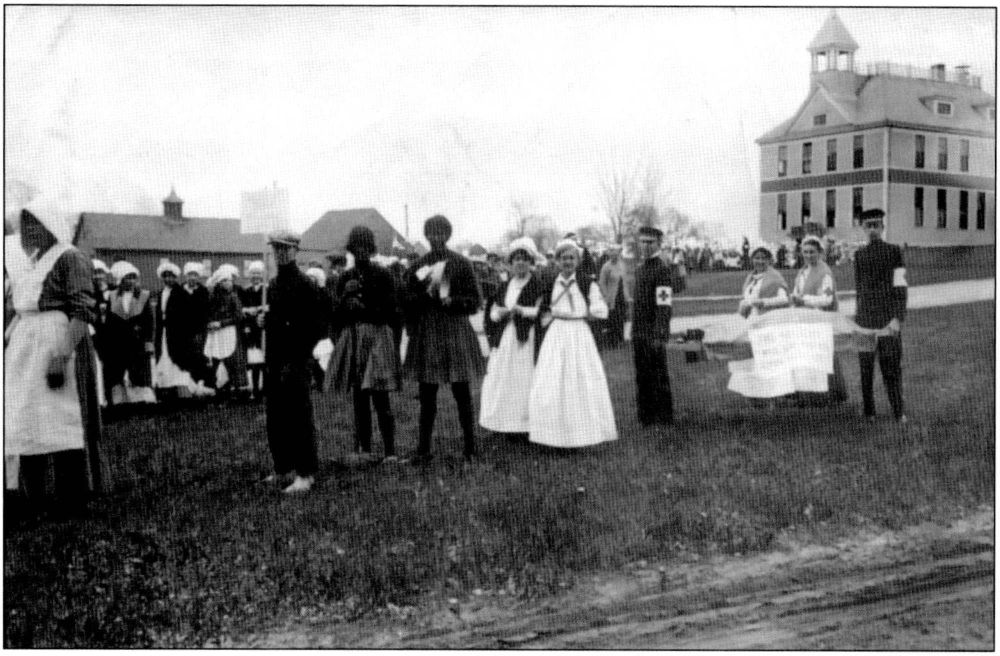

In its campaign to tidy up the town, the Village Improvement Society initiated an annual Clean-Up Parade in 1914. A procession of schoolchildren started in front of the old high school and marched back and forth to the Upper and Lower Villages. A few years later, World War I influenced these North Yarmouth Academy students to dress as nurses and medics. Two young men in the center have dressed in skirts to symbolize the cleaning power of Spic and Span. (Collection of the Yarmouth Historical Society.)

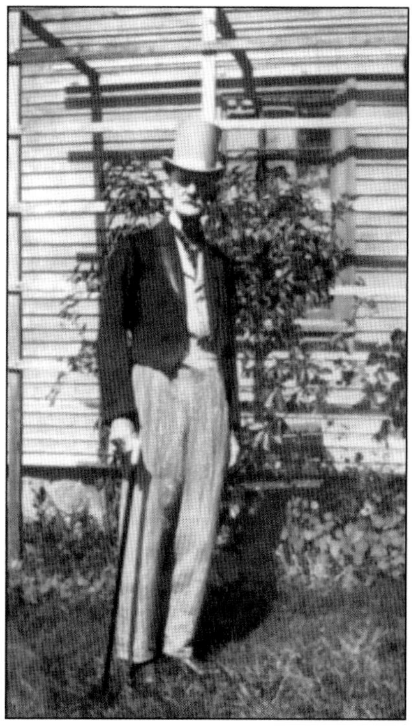

In an effort to encourage civic pride and raise money for Village Improvement Society projects, the organization started a celebration known as Old Home Week in 1911. Beginning with fairs, suppers, and auctions, the event expanded to include parades, concerts, and even a show of antique wedding dresses in 1939. During the fancy dress parade in 1921, Walter B. Allen won first prize for this Uncle Sam outfit. (Collection of Lois Rogers Lippincott.)

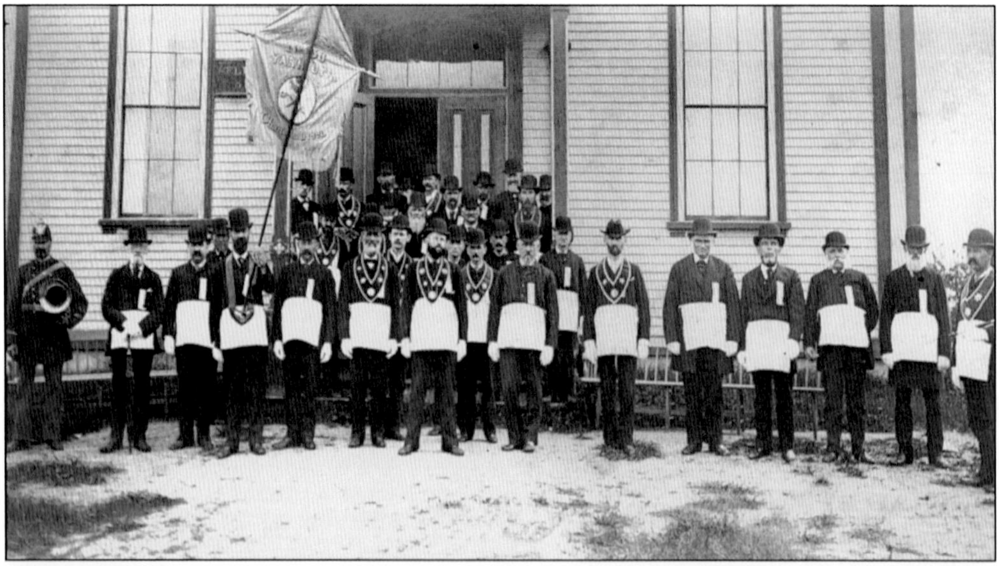

The oldest fraternal organization in Yarmouth is the Casco Lodge, which dates back to 1820. On June 23, 1890, many of the town's prominent men were photographed in their Masonic regalia. The owner of the cotton mill, L.L. Shaw, is the third man from the right in the front row. The men on either side of him are sea captains David Lawrence (left) and Joseph Young. John Greely, on the far left, is wearing the band uniform. (Collection of Lois Rogers Lippincott.)

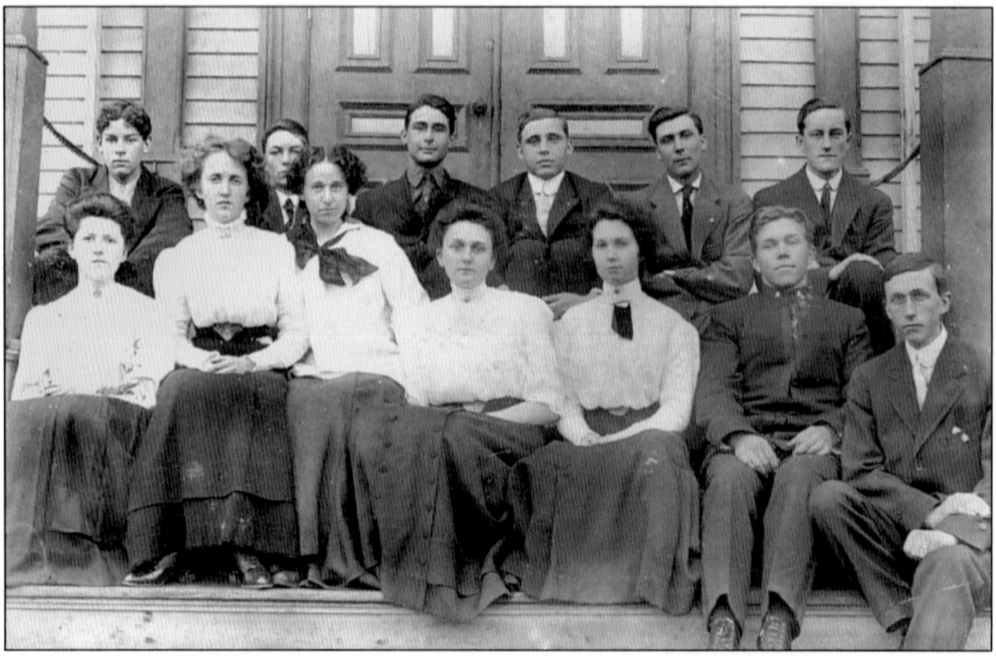

With a real stage, kitchen facilities, and a large seating capacity, the Masonic Hall became the town's unofficial civic center after 1875. Concerts, minstrel shows, and graduation ceremonies were also held there. In 1910, these Yarmouth High School students posed on the steps before performing *The Country Minister*. Between 1895 and 1909, the selectmen also maintained an office in the building. (Collection of Lois Rogers Lippincott.)

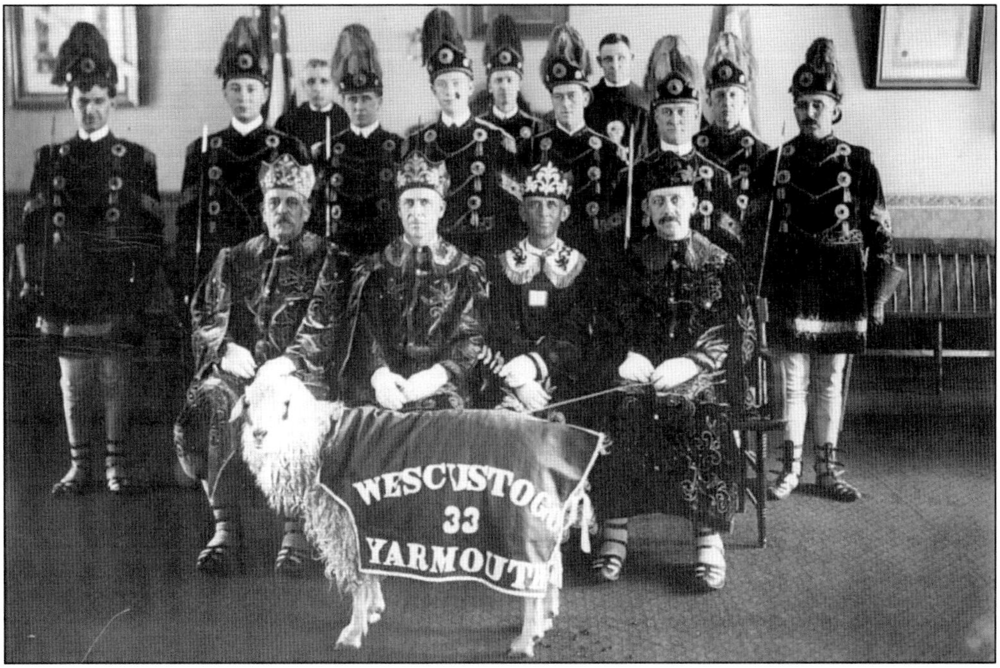

The end of the 19th century was the great age of fraternal organizations in the United States. These men are from the Yarmouth chapter of the Knights of Pythias, which was organized in 1882. Their mascot, Billy, may not be housebroken, but at least he is well dressed and looking at the camera. (Collection of Lois Rogers Lippincott.)

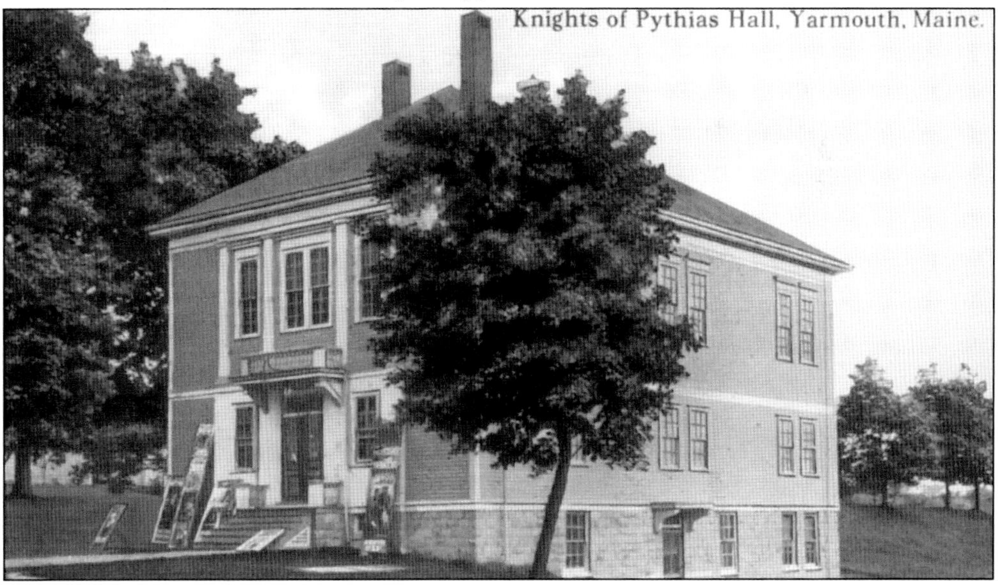

By 1904, the local membership in the Knights of Pythias had increased to more than 200 men. As a result, they erected this large building across from the Masonic Hall. The movie posters propped in front reveal that the building was also used to show films. Called the Pastime Theater in the 1920s, it became the Yarmouth Theater from 1942 to 1956. The hall was last used as a hardware store before being torn down to make space for Key Bank's drive-through window. (Collection of the Maine Historic Preservation Commission.)

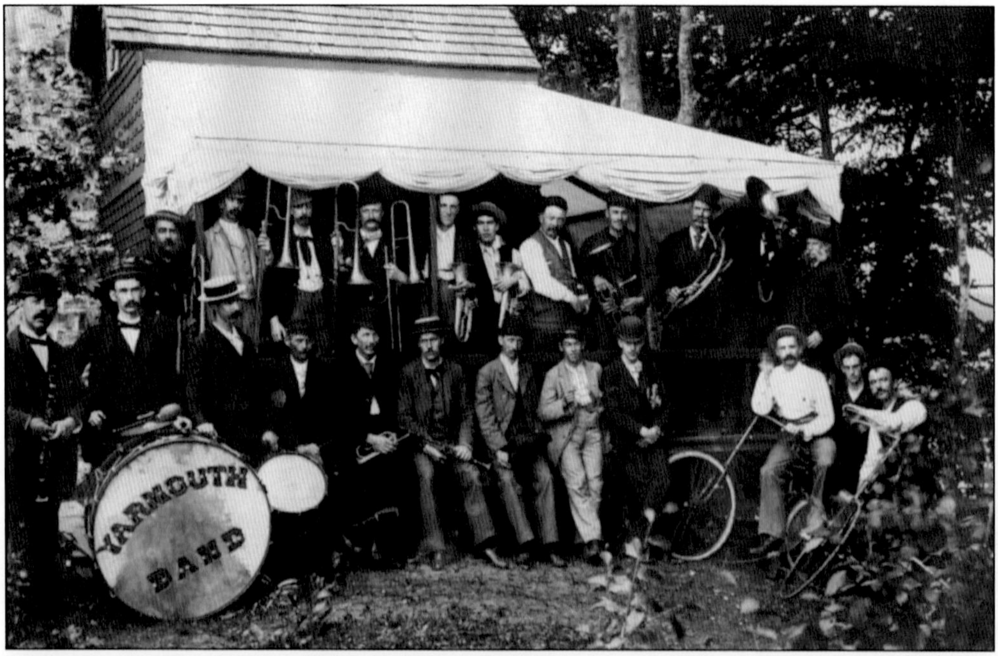

With its roots going back to 1847, the Yarmouth Band was one of the best in the state. It was in great demand for concerts, parades, and political rallies. The band preferred Republican parades. This group portrait from the 1890s was taken at Charles Blake's cottage on the shore at White's Cove. Blake is the second from the left in the back row. The man with the muttonchops in the back row on the far right is Joseph Raynes, the band's business manager. (Collection of the Yarmouth Historical Society.)

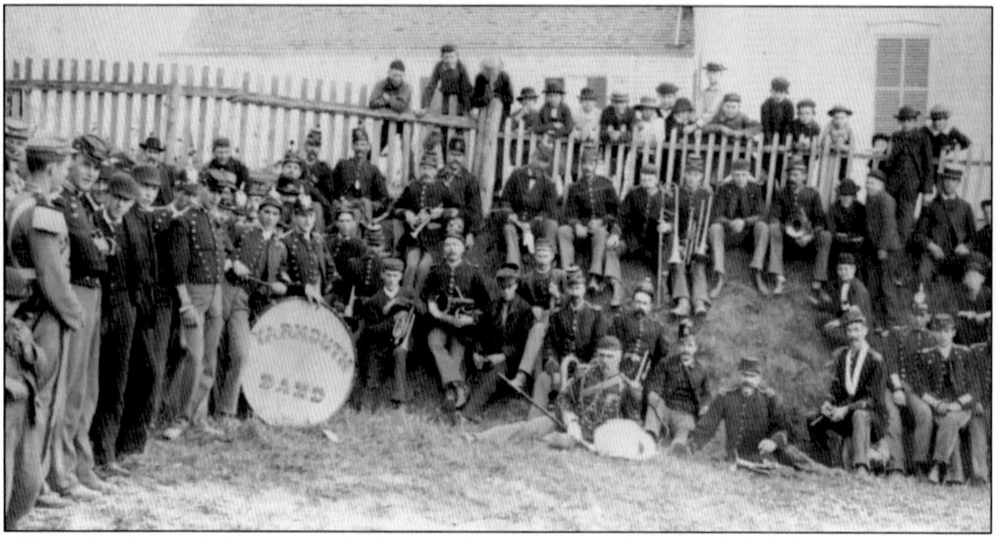

These members of the Yarmouth Band are resting beside the Masonic Hall, probably on Memorial Day in 1895. Beginning at 8:00 a.m., they led the veterans' parade to Riverside Cemetery to decorate the graves. Marching back to town, they paused for lunch at the Masonic Hall. At 1:30 p.m., they proceeded to the Baptist Cemetery on Hillside Street and then marched back to the First Parish Church for an oration by Reverend Reynolds. (Collection of Lois Rogers Lippincott.)

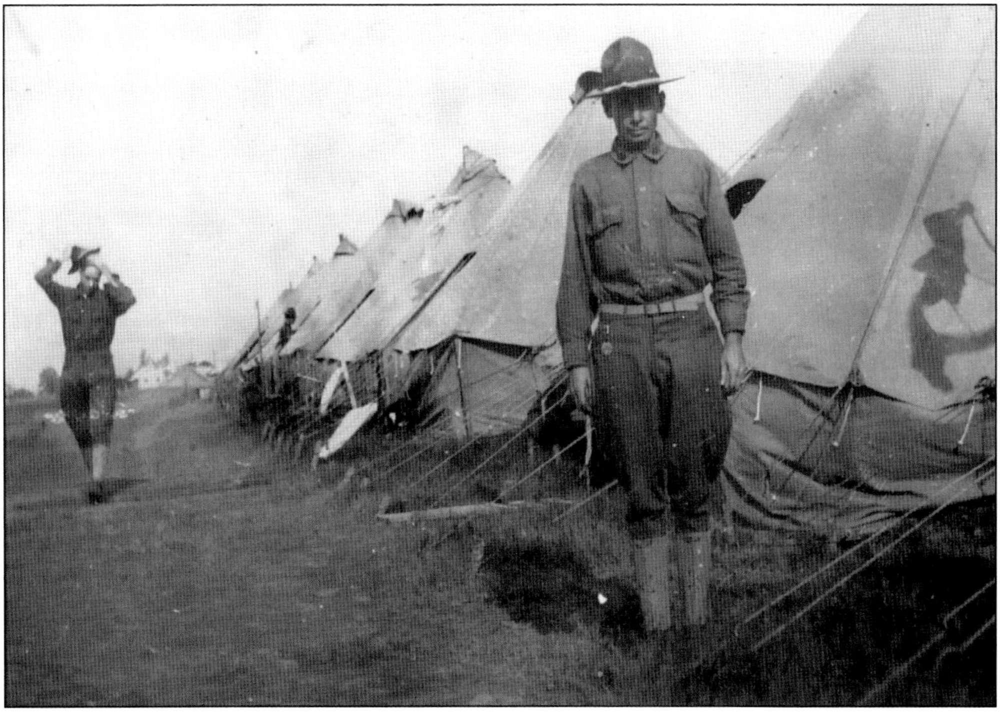

Although most Yarmouth men received military training at Fort Williams or Fort Devens, Eddie Adams was sent to Indiana, where he was photographed in 1917. In France, Adams was severely wounded and lost his right leg. He eventually returned to Yarmouth, where he found peace and quiet at his summer cottage on Cousins Island. In the bottom photograph, he is leaning against the right side of Rent's store *c.* 1930. (Collection of Alfreda Drinkwater Thurston.)

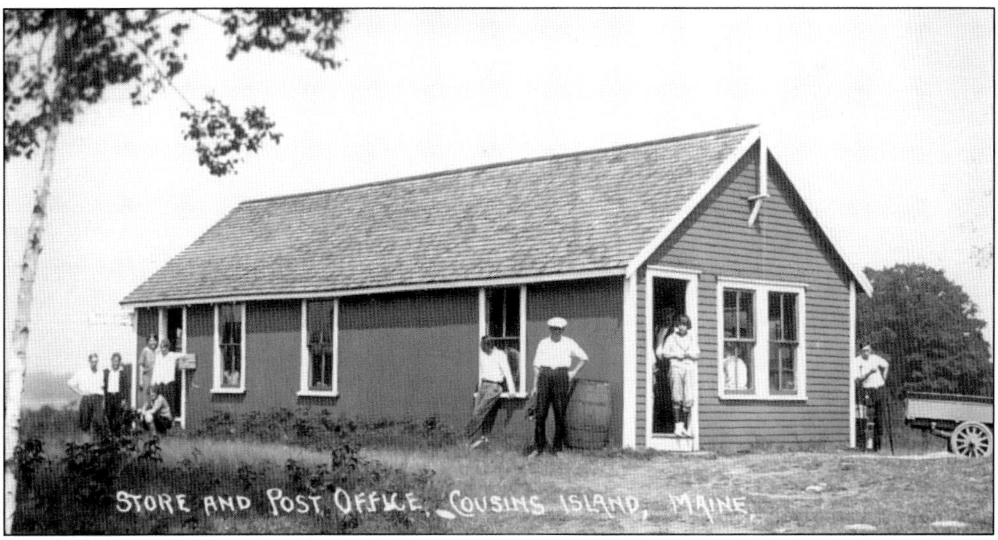

World War I had a deep impact on the lives of Yarmouth citizens. In addition to the 107 men who enlisted, the war demanded sacrifices at home, including meatless and wheatless days and conservation of fuel. When the war was finally over, church bells rang and a torchlight celebration snaked through the streets. One Yarmouth soldier, Ernest Storer, was wounded in action only hours before the armistice took effect on November 11, 1918. (Collection of Mildred Kinney.)

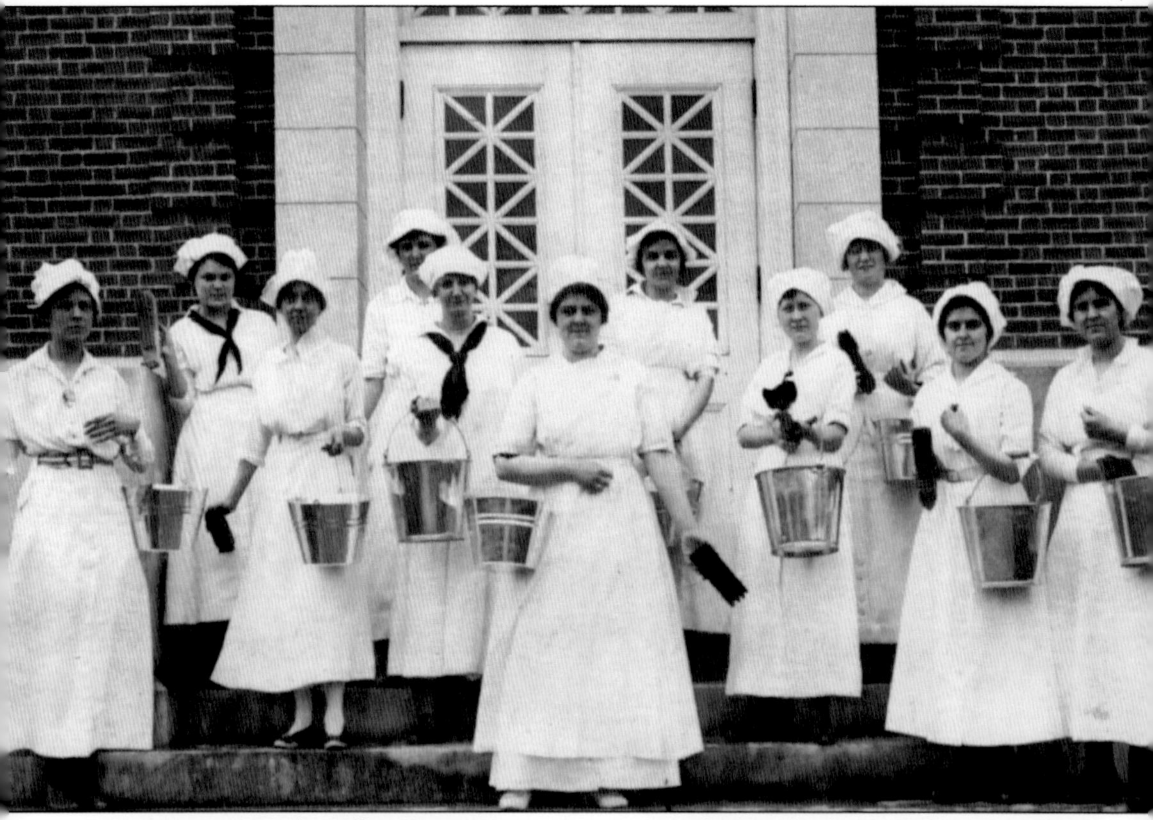

On May 4, 1916, the Village Improvement Society launched its third annual Clean-Up Week by having these young women scrub the steps of the Merrill Memorial Library. The symbols of nurses' uniforms and spotless buckets serve also as reminders of the town's frightening struggle with epidemics, including 22 cases of smallpox in 1914. That outbreak of smallpox in 13 different homes closed the library, schools, churches, and all public meetings while the local board of health fought the disease by vaccinating the whole town, quarantining affected families, fumigating homes, and burning infected household goods. As a result of these heroic efforts, no one died from that deadly outbreak.

Unfortunately, there was a tragic postscript to this story when one of these "nurses," Elsie Wellcome (front row, center), died two years later in an even greater epidemic that ravaged the town. Between September 15, 1918, and January 4, 1919, Spanish influenza hit Yarmouth in two waves, resulting in 370 cases and 17 deaths. William Rowe, who was then one of the town's pharmacists, later declared that "fear stalked the streets." He described the somber tolling of church bells as the bodies of two Yarmouth servicemen were returned from Fort Devens, where they had died during the epidemic. Yarmouth's American Legion post was later named for these two men, Edgar Anderson and Edwin Mayberry. (Collection of the Yarmouth Historical Society.)

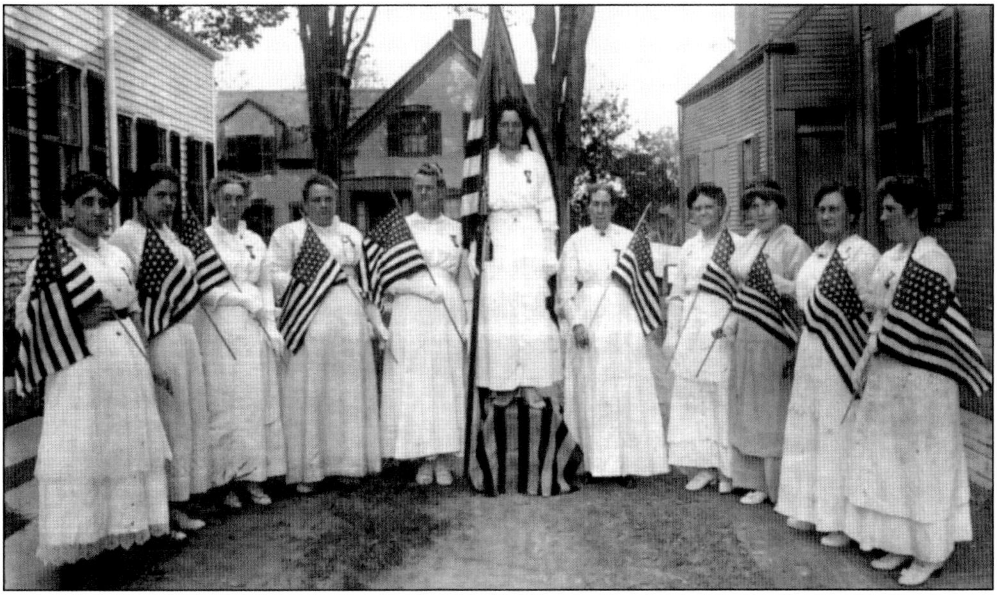

Women's groups in Yarmouth responded energetically to the crises of war and epidemic. These Daughters of the American Revolution seem to be literally rallying around the flag held by "Grannie Thurston." They are standing in front of 87 Main Street, which is across from Goff's Hardware. The event is unidentified but is probably linked to the grand victory parade in May 1919. As patriotism swept the town, a special appropriation was added to the 1919 school budget to purchase American flags. (Collection of the Yarmouth Historical Society.)

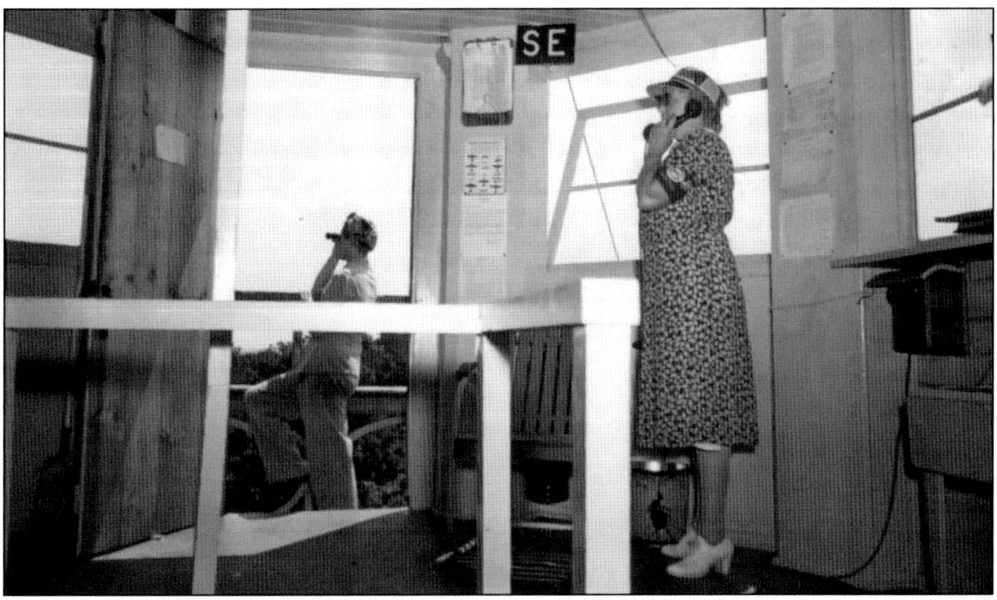

From 1942 to 1944, Yarmouth women served as plane spotters 24 hours a day in the belfry of the old Baptist meetinghouse. Guarding the eastern defenses of Portland Harbor, Yarmouth was particularly important to the U.S. Army's Anti-Aircraft and Searchlight Division. Reports from observers like Edna Webber and Martha Allen (right) were coordinated by telephone with the searchlights and guns on Princes Point and the islands. (Collection of the Yarmouth Historical Society.)

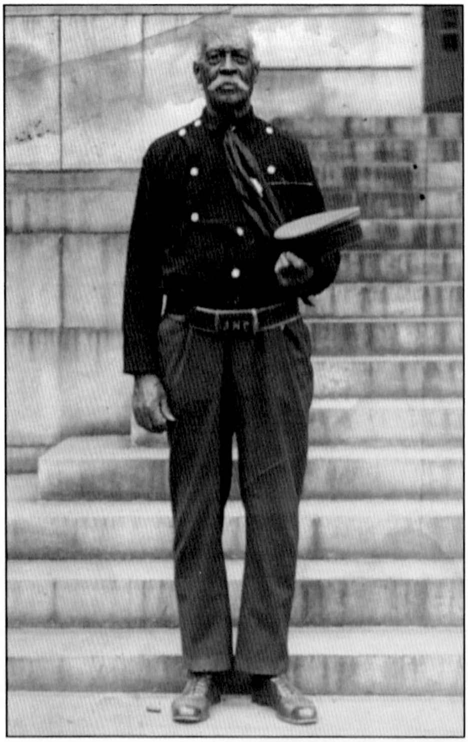

An imposing John Henry Carter stands before Portland City Hall, perhaps wearing the uniform of Yarmouth's Pumgustuk Fire Company. Born in 1857, he was the son of John and Nancy Carter, who owned a farm on West Elm Street. John Henry worked in Thomas Brown's stables as a hostler, a job that his own son carried on for George Hammond and others. His name appears frequently on the rolls of the fire company c. 1900. He died in 1927. (Collection of the Yarmouth Historical Society.)

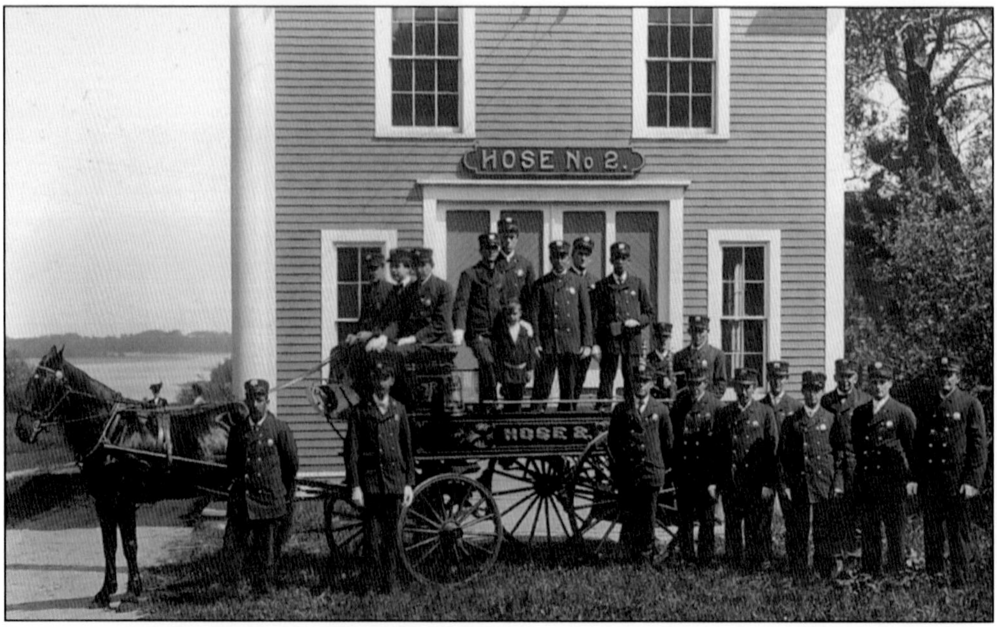

During a training exercise in 1893, the local fire company's "apparatus" burst its hoses and frightened a horse, which took off with the machine. Shortly thereafter, a reorganization created the Yarmouth Fire Department. In 1900, just after Hose No. 2 was built at the Lower Falls, a fire near the depot burned the corn factory and ignited 22 buildings in the Upper Village. Ironically, the town's new electric alarm system was lying unpacked at the depot during the fire. (Collection of the Yarmouth Fire Department.)

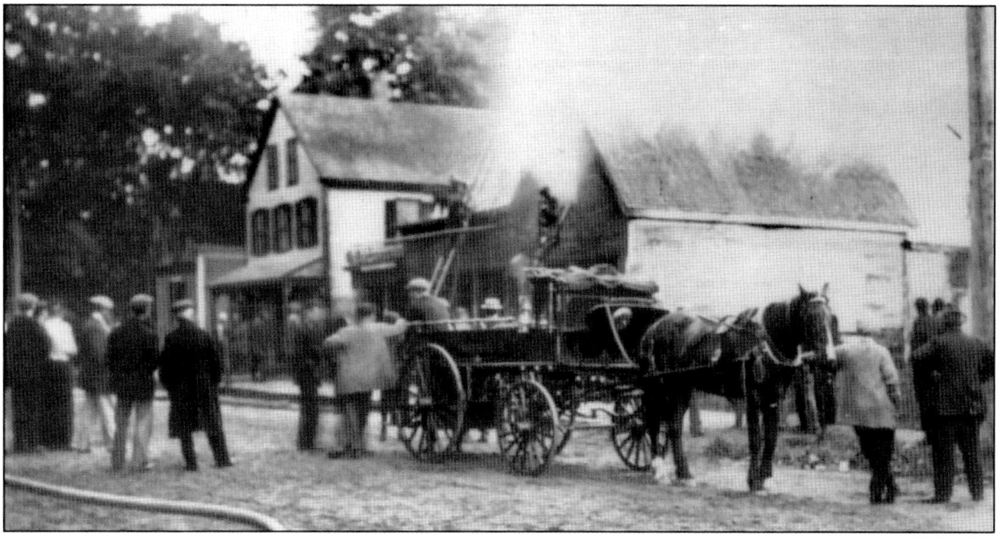

Bernstein's clothing store, located on Main Street near the railroad tracks, burned on July 13, 1913. Firemen responded by horse and wagon, but the costly fire underscored their need for a motorized vehicle. In 1921, the town purchased a new Reo combination fire truck, which Chief Charles Greeley quickly pointed out "saved more property value than the machine cost." (Collection of the Yarmouth Historical Society.)

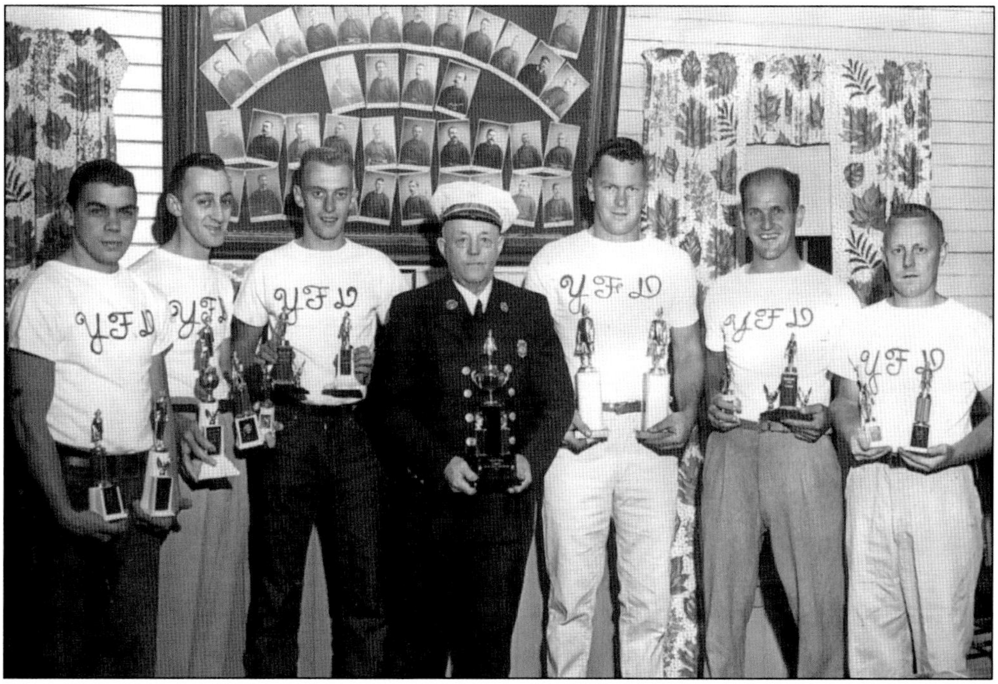

Clutching their trophies, the muster team of the Yarmouth Fire Department poses c. 1960. From left to right, they are Danny Reynolds, Arthur Desroche, Bud Reynolds, Ray Smith, Arthur Fox, Norm Christopher, and George Smith. For many years, Ray Smith coached the teams and operated the last general store on Main Street. From that location, he manually operated the town's fire signals and sometimes ran into the middle of street to tell volunteers where to find the fire. (Collection of the Yarmouth Fire Department.)

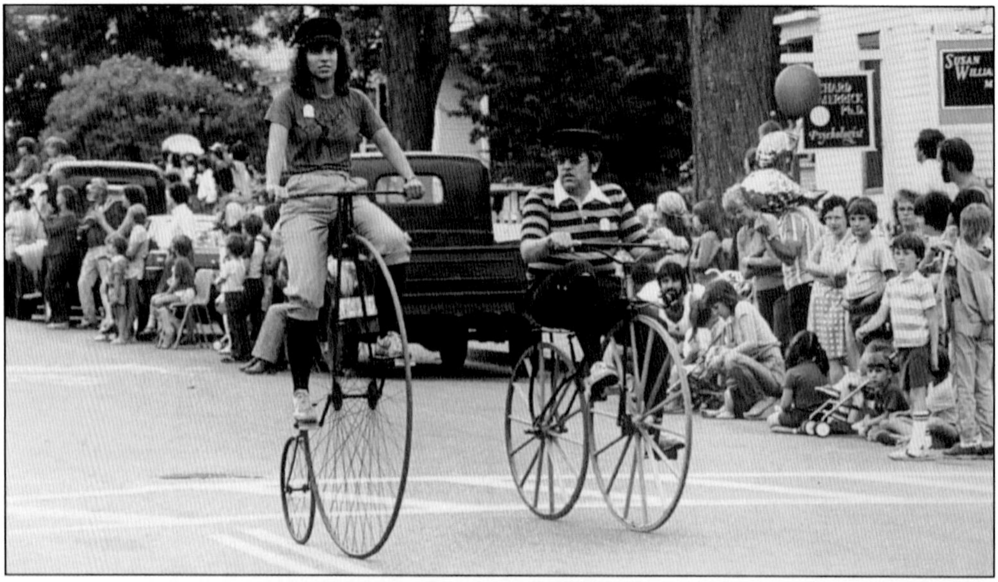

Every year in July, the town of Yarmouth cheerfully inflicts upon itself an extravaganza known as the Clam Festival. Although residents argue about who specifically started it in 1965, the festival definitely grew out of the town's traditions of holding musters and Old Home Week. As far back as 1817, booths and tents were set up on muster day to sell refreshments to the large (and somewhat inebriated) crowds who converged to watch the local militia companies clash in mock battles. (Collection of Virginia Turner.)

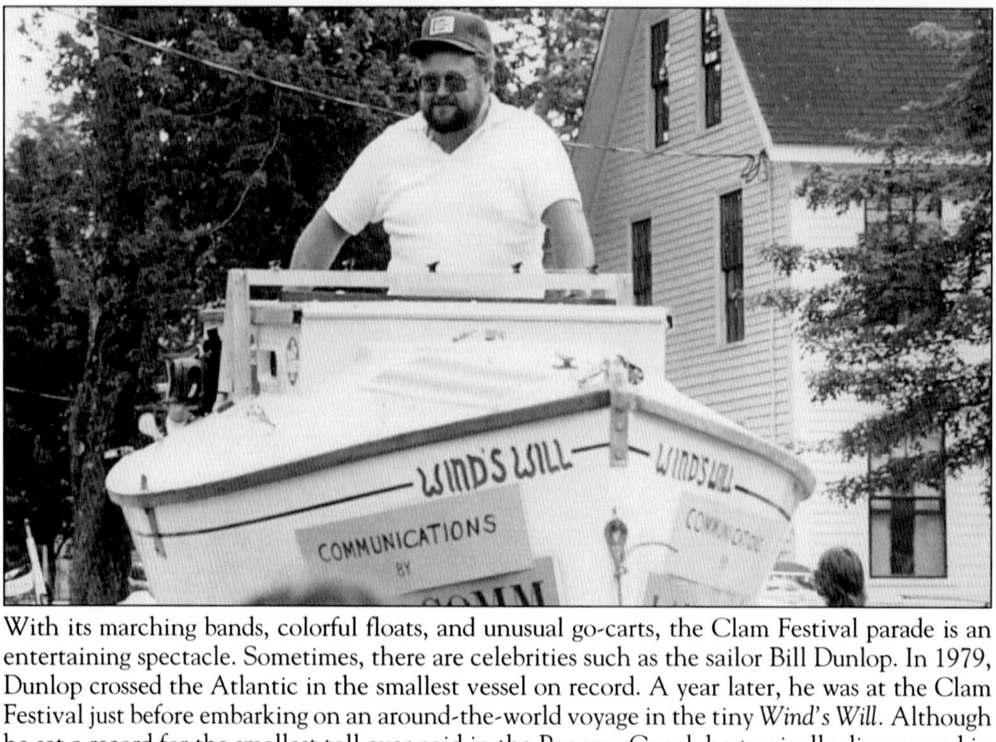

With its marching bands, colorful floats, and unusual go-carts, the Clam Festival parade is an entertaining spectacle. Sometimes, there are celebrities such as the sailor Bill Dunlop. In 1979, Dunlop crossed the Atlantic in the smallest vessel on record. A year later, he was at the Clam Festival just before embarking on an around-the-world voyage in the tiny *Wind's Will*. Although he set a record for the smallest toll ever paid in the Panama Canal, he tragically disappeared in the Pacific. (Collection of Virginia Turner.)

Seven

AT WORK

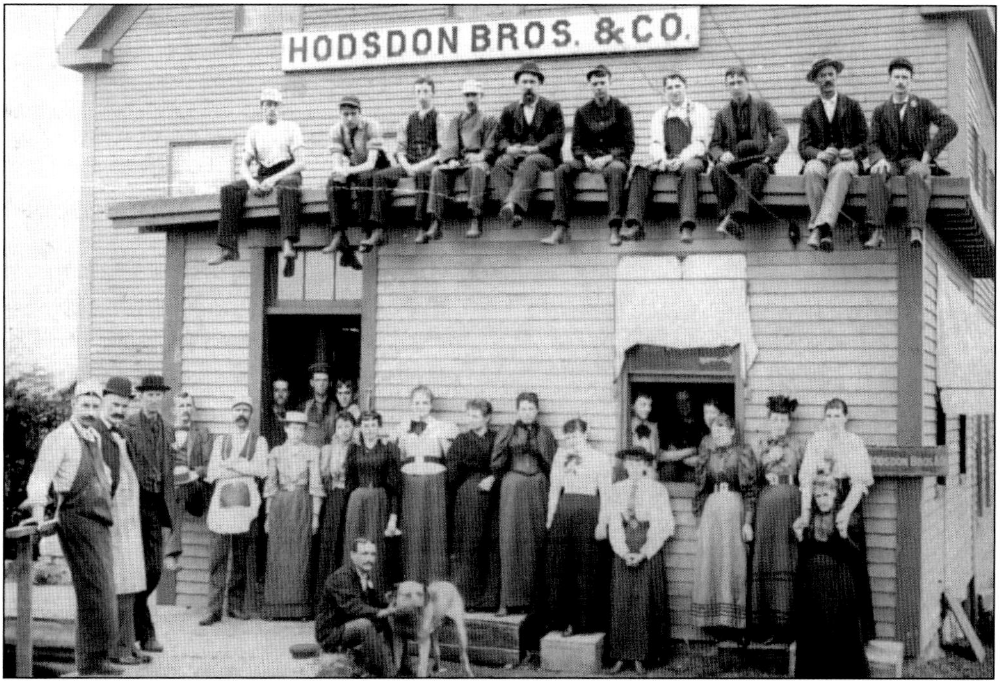

Despite its waterfalls, railroads, and direct access to the sea, Yarmouth never became a classic New England mill town. Even at its industrial peak in 1910, Yarmouth's cotton mill, shoe factory, and pulp mill employed fewer than 400 people. Instead of grim rows of tenements, the town's industrial legacy is surprisingly scenic: a riverside park on the site of several mills, a cannery transformed into shops and offices, and a cotton mill that now produces software rather than grain bags. The shoe industry arrived in Yarmouth in 1880 when the Hodsdon Brothers established this factory at the fourth falls for "ladies' and misses' boots and shoes." The company maintained a showroom and office in Boston, Massachusetts, and it fired all the workers who tried to unionize in 1888. Photographed a year later, the remaining employees seem rather cheerless, even the irrepressible Ella Woods (lower right), who often played practical jokes on her friends. (Collection of the Yarmouth Historical Society.)

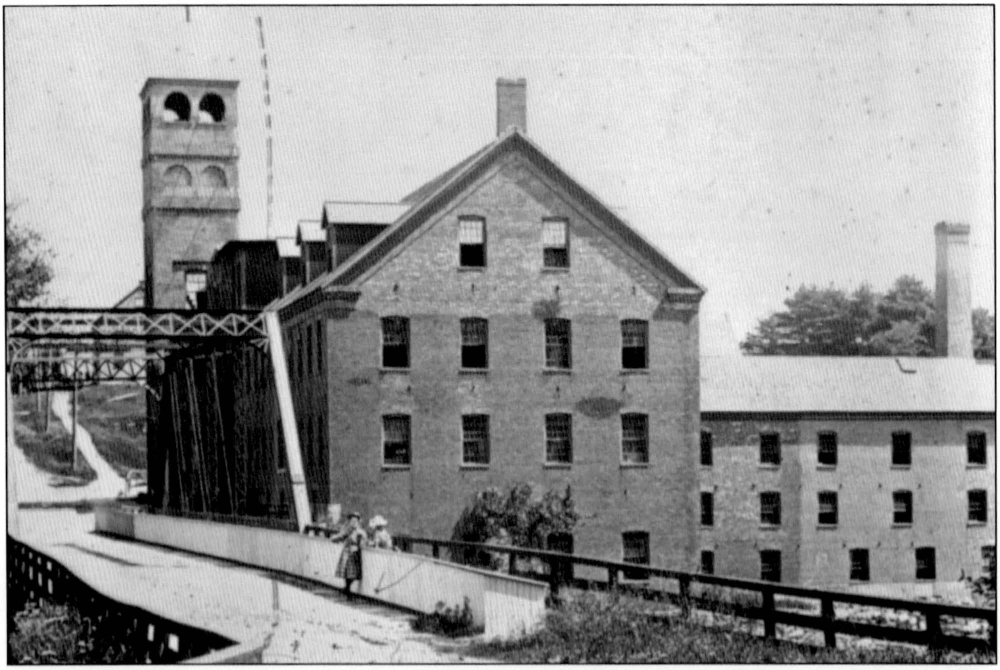

It is no accident that Yarmouth's cotton mill and railroad both arrived in 1849. With a dependable means of transportation and an adequate supply of water, the mill prospered. In this view from the 1890s, the lighter bricks in the gable suggest the reconstruction that occurred after a fire in 1855. When the mill was rebuilt, the company shrewdly focused on warp yarns and grain bags instead of textiles. This niche market kept the business going well into the 20th century. (Collection of the Yarmouth Historical Society.)

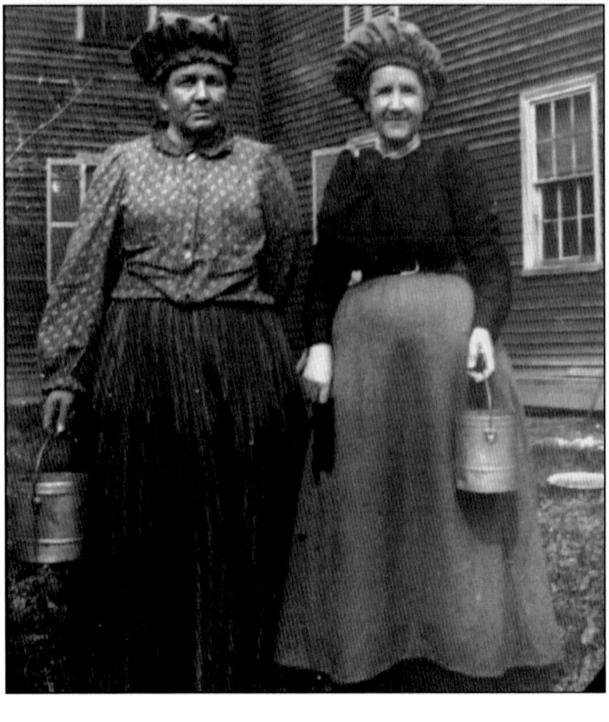

When the cotton mill was first established, it followed the pattern initiated at Lowell, Massachusetts, by providing housing for the young women who tended the mill's 2,500 spindles. The boardinghouse, which is now an apartment building on Bridge Street, can be seen beyond the bridge in the top photograph. These two women with their lunches in lard buckets may have been photographed behind that boardinghouse. (Collection of the Yarmouth Historical Society.)

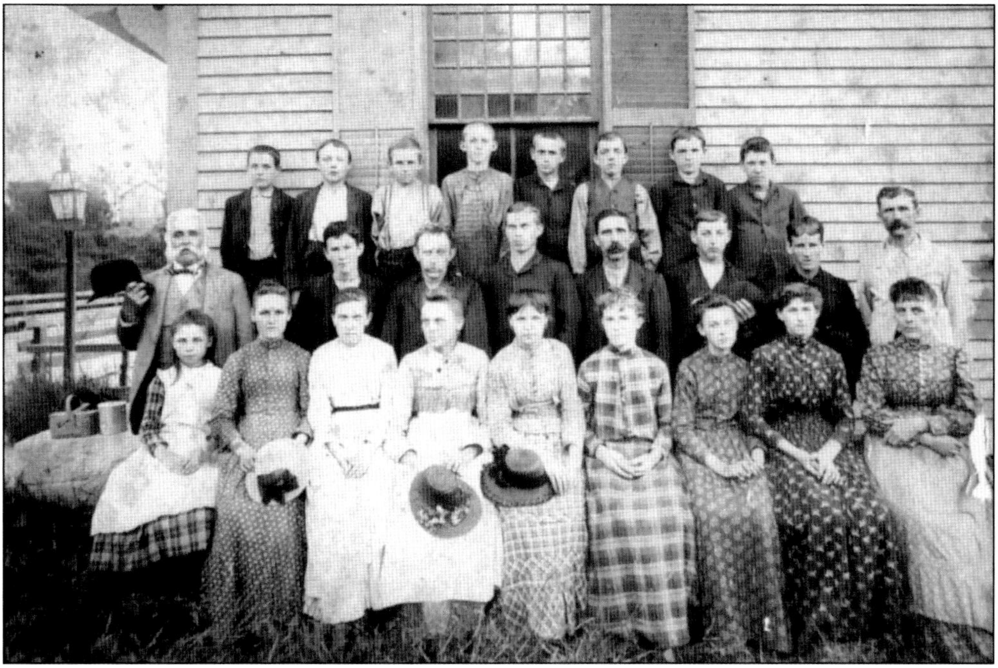

Working at the cotton mill in the 1870s, bobbin boys were paid as little as 25¢ for a 12-hour day. In 1889, when this photograph was taken, women usually received a dollar a day, a third of which was remitted to the company if they lived at the boardinghouse. The workers are flanked on the left by the white-haired owner, L.L. Shaw, and on the right by their overseer, Monroe Stoddard. A few years later, the factory started to hire French Canadian immigrants from Prince Edward Island. (Collection of the Yarmouth Historical Society.)

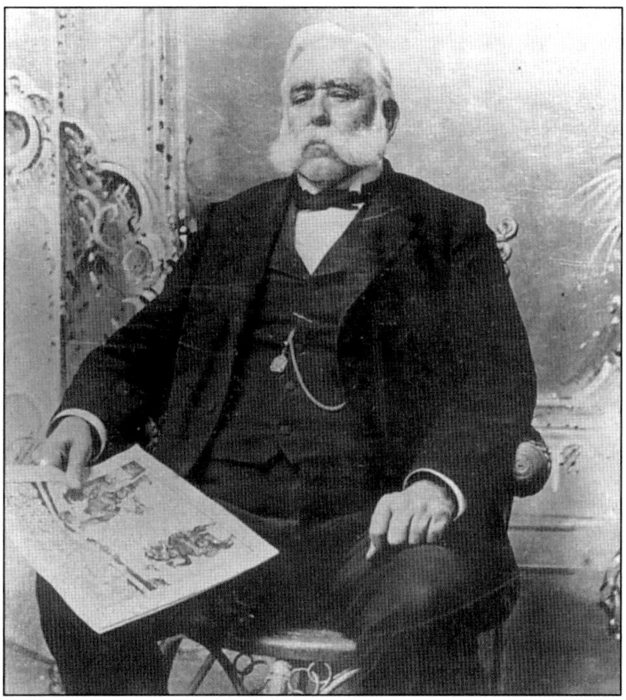

After a textile career that began in Lowell, Massachusetts, as a bobbin boy, L.L. Shaw arrived in Yarmouth in 1871 to form a partnership with a local lawyer, Barnabus Freeman. In 1888, Shaw bought out Freeman and ran the cotton mill until his death in 1906. Shaw's house stood on the corner of Bridge and Main Streets until it was destroyed by fire in 1967. His stylish carriage house has been turned into offices at 121 Main Street. (Collection of Lois Rogers Lippincott.)

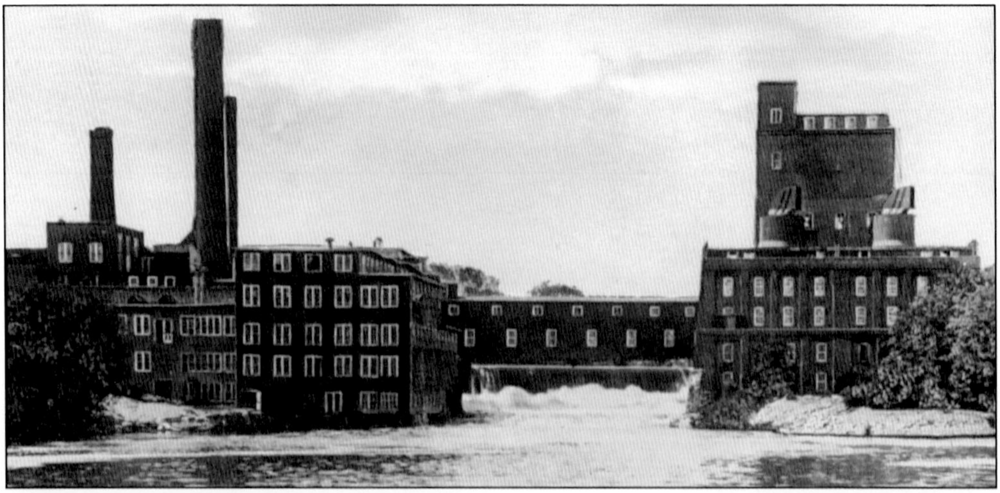

Although Yarmouth had a rag paper mill as early as 1816, the Forest Paper Company was revolutionary in the 1870s for using trees as the source of fiber for papermaking. The S.D. Warren Company obtained its first wood pulp from this mill and liked it so much that Warren bought and dramatically expanded the Yarmouth facility. Installed in 1901, the 12-story vertical digesters on the right were pressure cookers for the wood pulp. By 1906, the mill provided nearly one quarter of the town's tax revenue. It closed abruptly in 1923 and burned in a spectacular fire in 1931. (Collection of the Maine Historic Preservation Commission.)

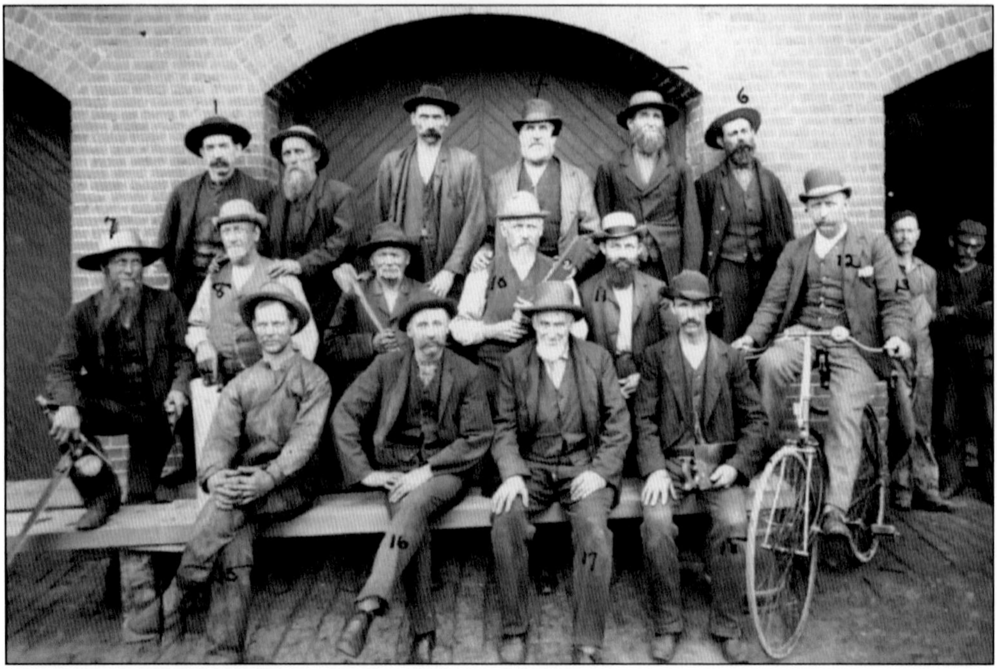

The paper mill was always in a state of reconstruction as its managers tried to keep up with new chemical processes and the rapid shift from waterpower to steam and electricity. The saws, mallets, and levels clutched by these men reveal that they were part of the mill's construction crew. A civil engineer named Ferdinand Merrill helped to coordinate the construction, and Frederick Gore, a trained chemist from the Massachusetts Institute of Technology, was overseer of the production processes. (Collection of the Yarmouth Historical Society.)

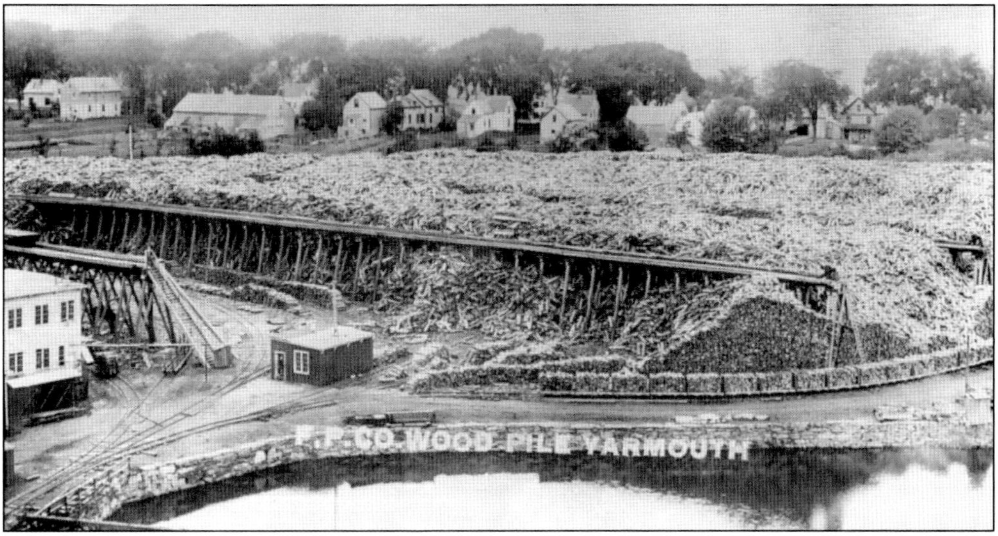

The scale of the Forest Paper Company's operation can be measured against the length of East Elm Street. Unloaded from railroad cars, a mountain of logs provided the 15,000 cords of poplar used by the mill each year. Additional trestles were built for the 10,000 tons of coal that fired its steam boilers. A separate spur delivered the tons of caustic soda and chlorine used to break down and bleach the wood fiber. (Collection of the Maine Historic Preservation Commission.)

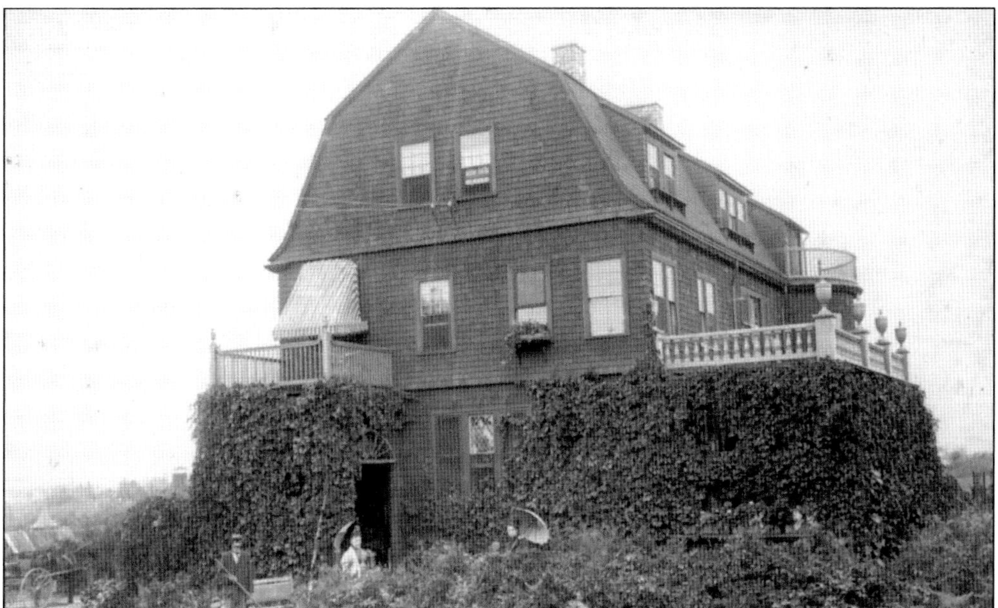
Today, the most visible monument to the Forest Paper Company is George Hammond's unusual Camp Hammond, which was built in 1889. Beneath its Shingle-style exterior, the house was constructed of slow-burning solid timber walls. The baronial interior includes 18th-century bedposts for newels and a huge stone fireplace. When Frederick Law Olmsted's firm designed the landscaping, they apparently underestimated the ability of Hammond's gardener to make things grow. That gardener, a Scotsman named Daniel Burns, is standing on the left. The cover photograph for this book was taken at the far end of the porch on the right. (Collection of Lois Rogers Lippincott.)

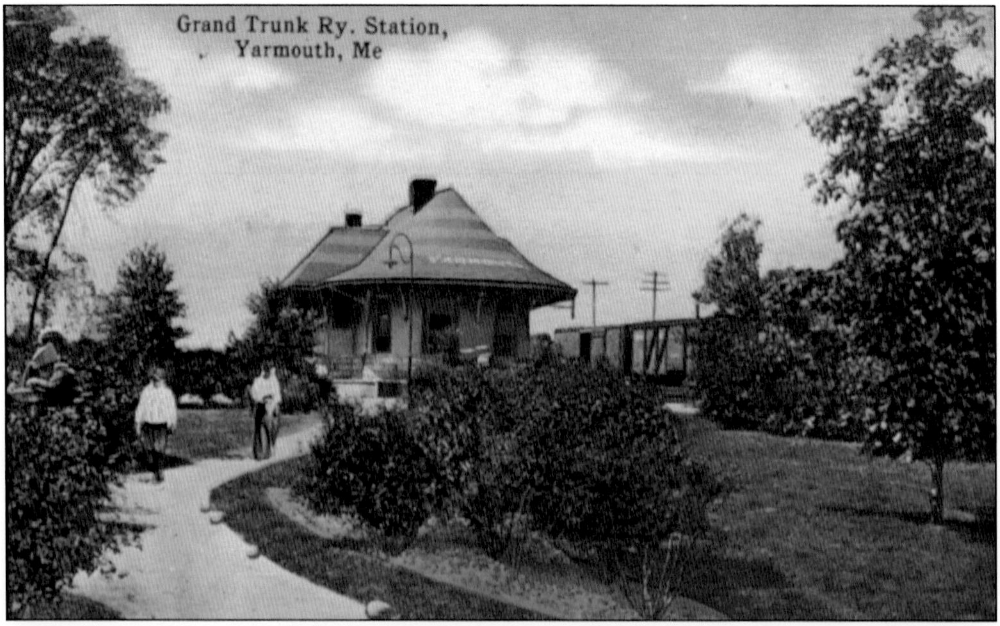

Yarmouth industries grew because two railroads intersected in town: the Grand Trunk and Maine Central. Ship timbers, horses, bales of cotton, and even Bert Coombs's new Fords all arrived by train. The original Grand Trunk station was completed in October 1848 and replaced by the current building in 1906. Four years later, Carl Rust Parker was asked by Harriet Bird and others to design this small park as a gateway to the town. Bird's father had been Yarmouth's first daily commuter to Portland in the 1870s. (Collection of Brenda Roy.)

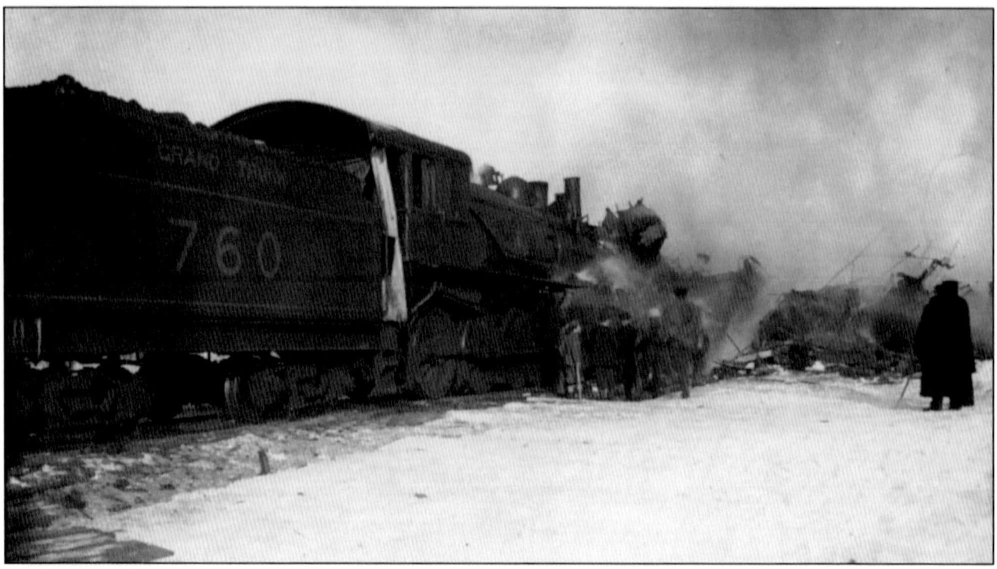

A memorable train wreck occurred at 5:20 a.m. on February 15, 1912, near Dunn's Corner. A westbound freight was backing its 25 cars onto a siding when a freight train bound for Portland ignored orders to slow down. The collision drove both engines 30 feet into the air and ignited tons of wheat and wooden boxcars. Three men were killed and several others were seriously injured. Despite this tragedy, Yarmouth was the last stretch of the Grand Trunk to receive automatic block signals in 1924. (Collection of the Yarmouth Historical Society.)

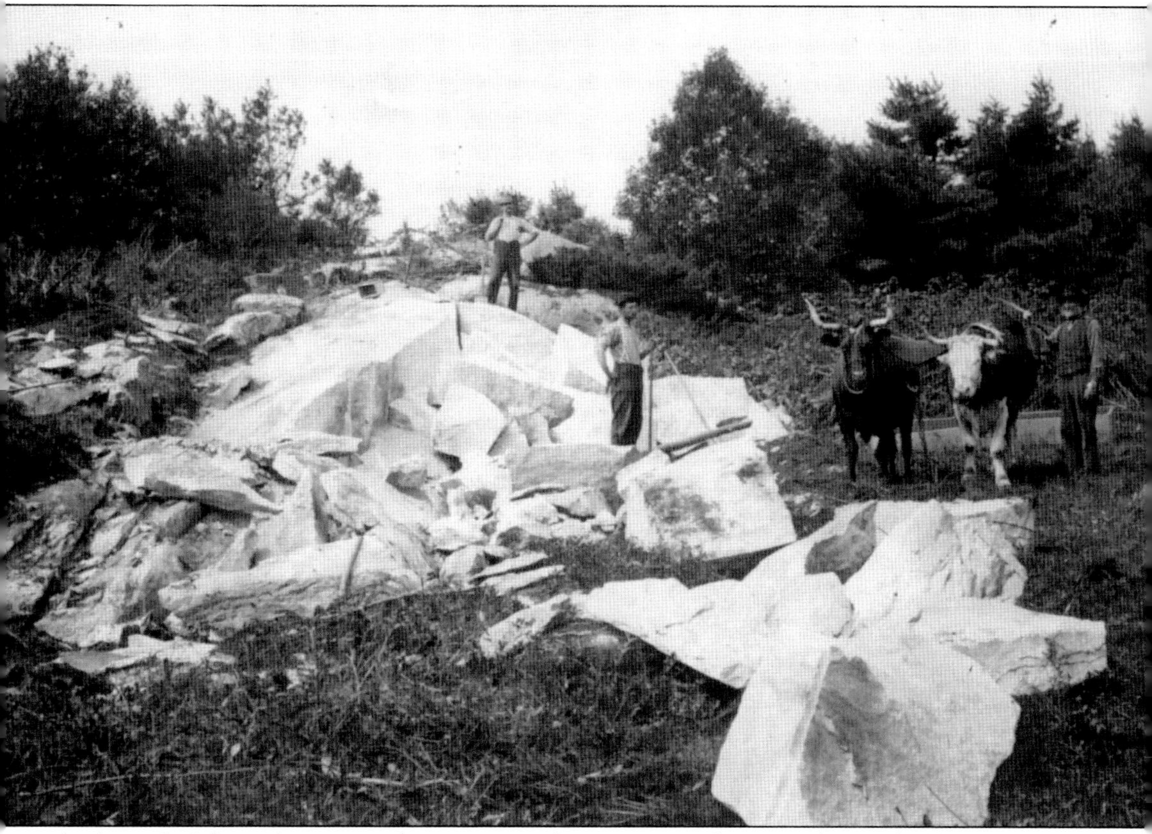

At the end of the 19th century, the quarrying of granite was a dangerous but profitable business in the towns of Yarmouth, Pownal, and North Yarmouth. Several quarries near Ledge Road and Granite Street supplied the stone for local buildings such as the Catholic church and also for mills, dams, and water projects all over the eastern United States. It took Charles Knight two years to cut the granite that formed the latticework foundation of Bailey Island's unique cribstone bridge. In 1901, a scheme was developed to construct a railroad along Granite Street to transport the stone to a landing on the Cousins River, but it was never built. The quarry in this photograph is very likely the one that Charles G. Gooding opened in 1890 on the western end of Pleasant Street. When the town was seeking granite to rebuild a culvert on Pleasant Street, Gooding contracted to supply the stones. Oliver Jordan did the actual quarrying, and he is probably one of the two men standing on the pile of rocks. (Collection of Lois Rogers Lippincott.)

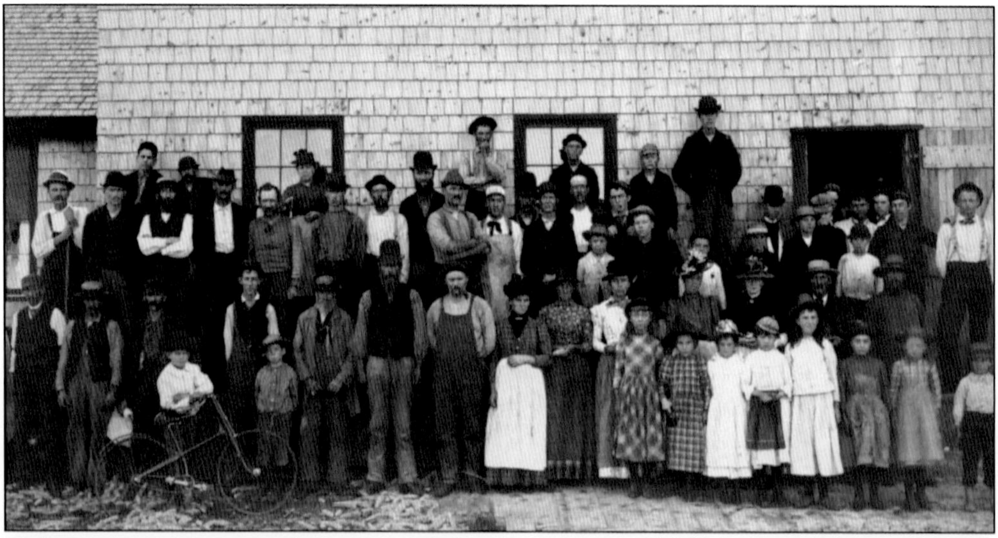

Husking sweet corn was a democratic activity for workers of both sexes and all ages. At Asa York's packing plant near the Grand Trunk depot, 50 huskers were typically employed during the brief harvest season in early September. York had another 40 employees who specialized in tasks like sealing the lids. As a result, the factory could process 16,000 cans per day. In 1900, York's cannery was destroyed in a fire, but corn packing was continued in Yarmouth until World War II. (Collection of Lois Rogers Lippincott.)

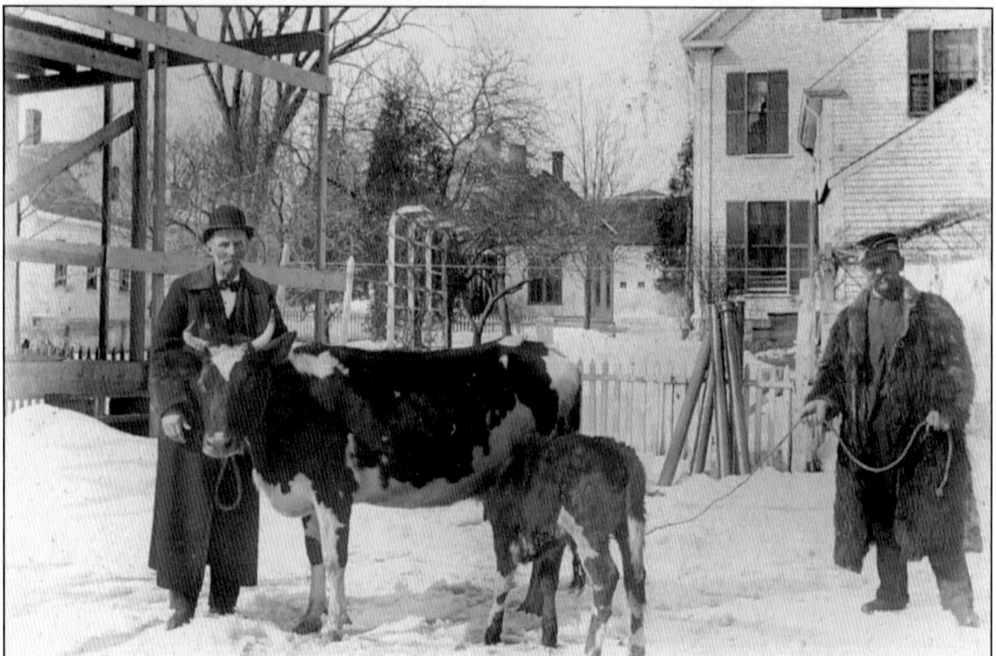

Farming was part of Yarmouth's way of life well into the 20th century. As late as 1910, a third of Yarmouth's schoolchildren lived on farms, and many families in the village kept both a milk cow and a horse. In the 1890s, local cattle dealer J.D. Rogers (left) regularly shipped cows and calves to the Brighton stockyards near Boston, Massachusetts. The Gothic-style house under construction on the left is now owned by Ben Soule. (Collection of Lois Rogers Lippincott.)

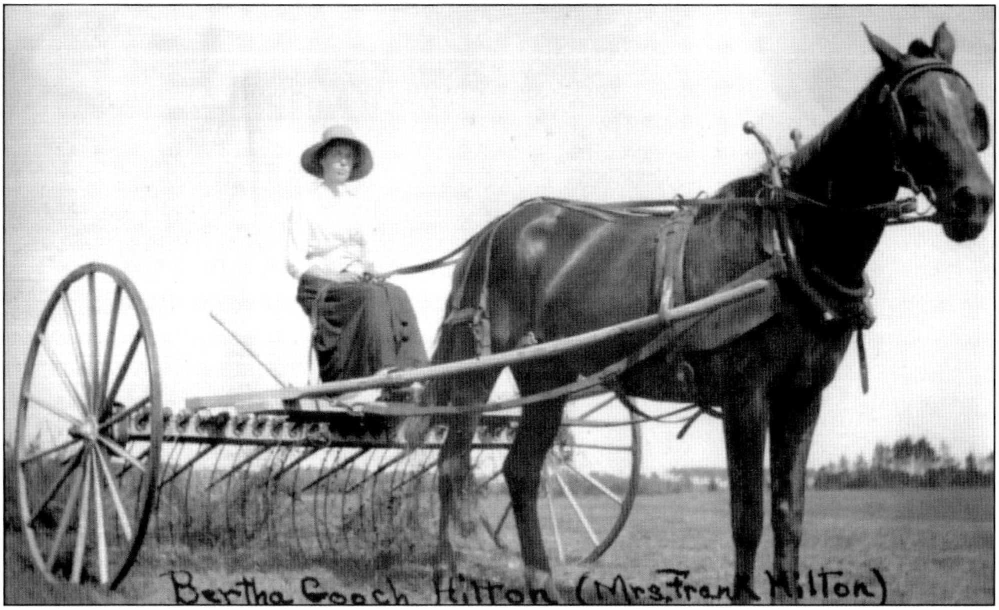

In 1820, when Maine became a state, Yarmouth and Cumberland were still part of the original town of North Yarmouth. The farms of the North Yarmouth area dominated Maine agriculture with the most barns, horses, pigs, acres of corn, and upland hay. When Bertha Hilton was photographed on this hay rake, probably along Ledge Road c. 1915, corn and hay were still the leading crops produced on Yarmouth farms. (Collection of the Yarmouth Historical Society.)

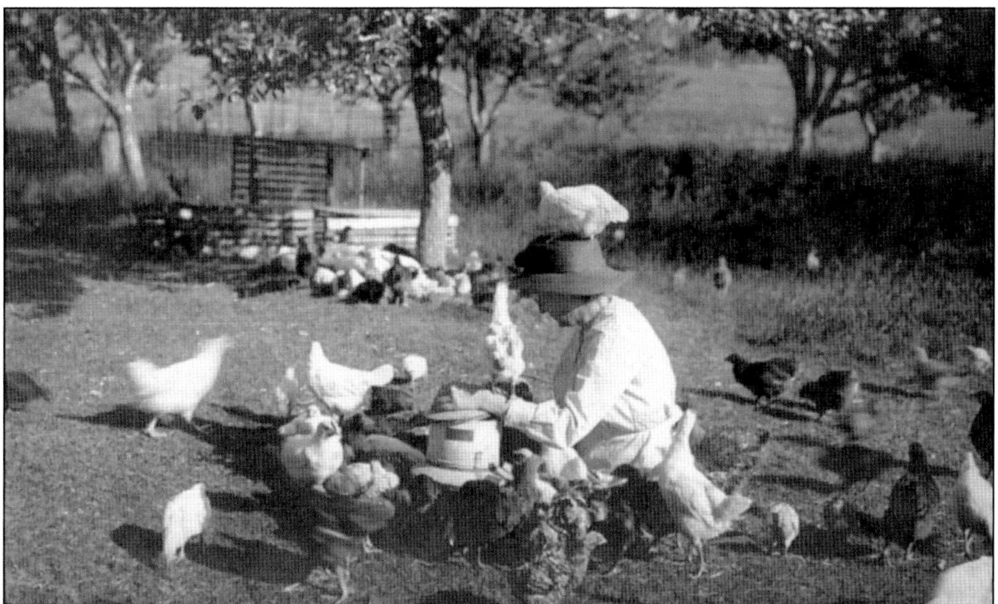

From 1880 until shortly after World War II, many Yarmouth families raised poultry either for market or home use. In this image, a Mrs. Hunt is surrounded by her appreciative flock in her backyard. Druggist L.R. Cook raised fancy fowl such as Rose Comb Brown Leghorns and served as president of the local poultry association in 1890. Other popular varieties included Rhode Island Reds, buff Plymouth Rocks, and white Wyandottes. (Collection of Lois Rogers Lippincott.)

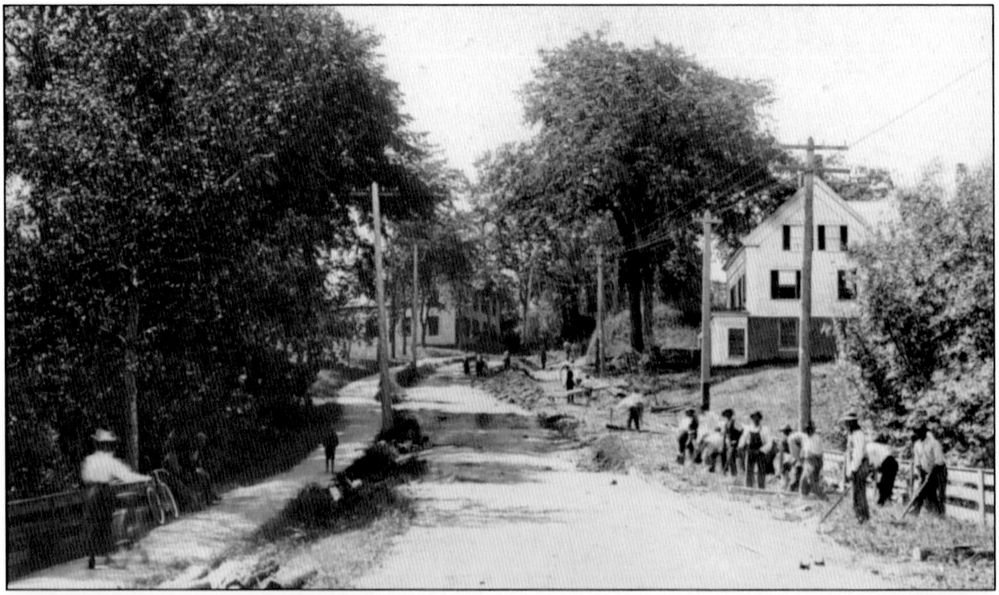

In 1893, L.R. Cook, Yarmouth's representative to the legislature, filed a petition to establish an electric street railway from Portland to Yarmouth. By the summer of 1897, these Italian laborers were laying tracks along Pleasant Street. It took another year to finish the project, including the overhead wires and a carbarn and battery house at Brickyard Hollow. While the trolley service was being extended to Brunswick, the workers, armed with knives and revolvers, staged a nasty strike. (Collection of Alan M. Hall.)

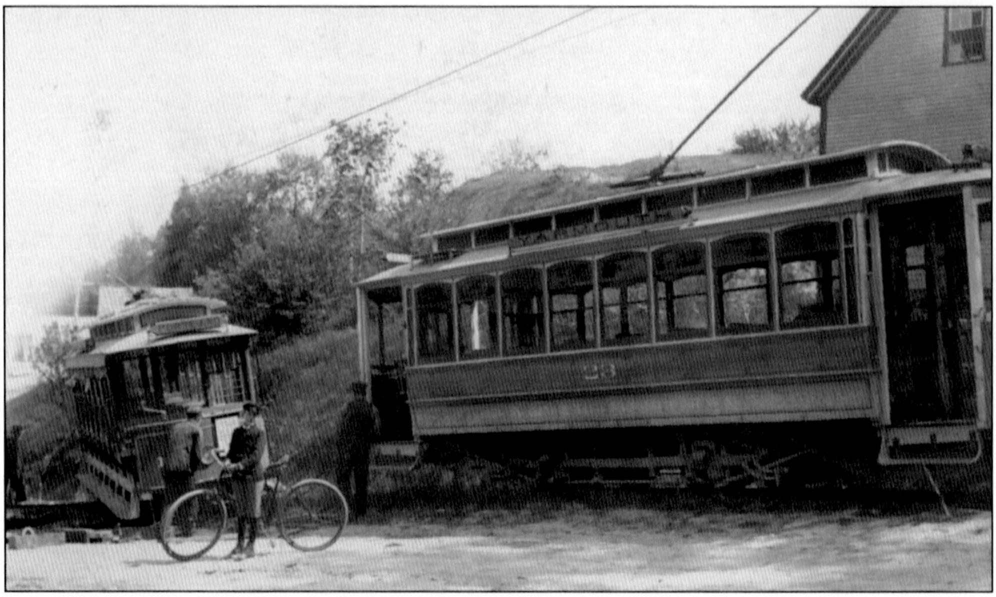

In 1906, a trolley bridge was built over the Royal River exactly where the walker's path now crosses the river beside U.S. Route 1. This allowed the Brunswick and Portland trolleys to connect at a new waiting station near Yarmouth's Grand Trunk depot. In the first years of operation, collisions between Yarmouth cows, trolleys, and carriages were not uncommon. This derailment occurred c. 1910 at the lower end of Main Street near Rocky Hill Road. (Collection of the Yarmouth Historical Society.)

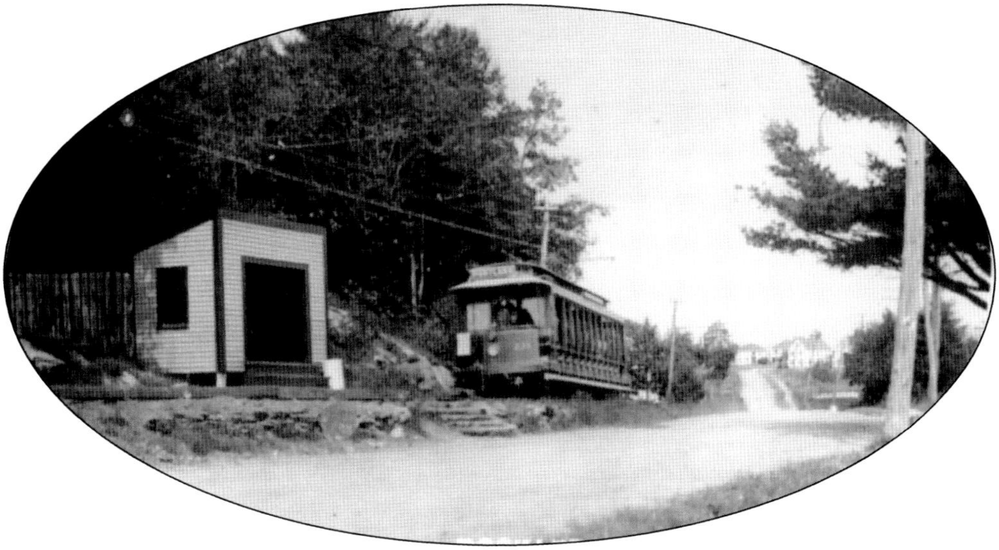

Trolley passengers waited in this little shed at the sharp curve where Route 88 now meets the western end of Pleasant Street. Because it was necessary to lean far out to see if the trolley was approaching, Rock Ledge Station was commonly known as Rubberneck. Capt. Sumner Drinkwater, who lived near this spot, gave up the sea to become motorman No. 704 on the electric railroad, retiring shortly before the trolley service ended in 1933. (Collection of the Maine Historic Preservation Commission.)

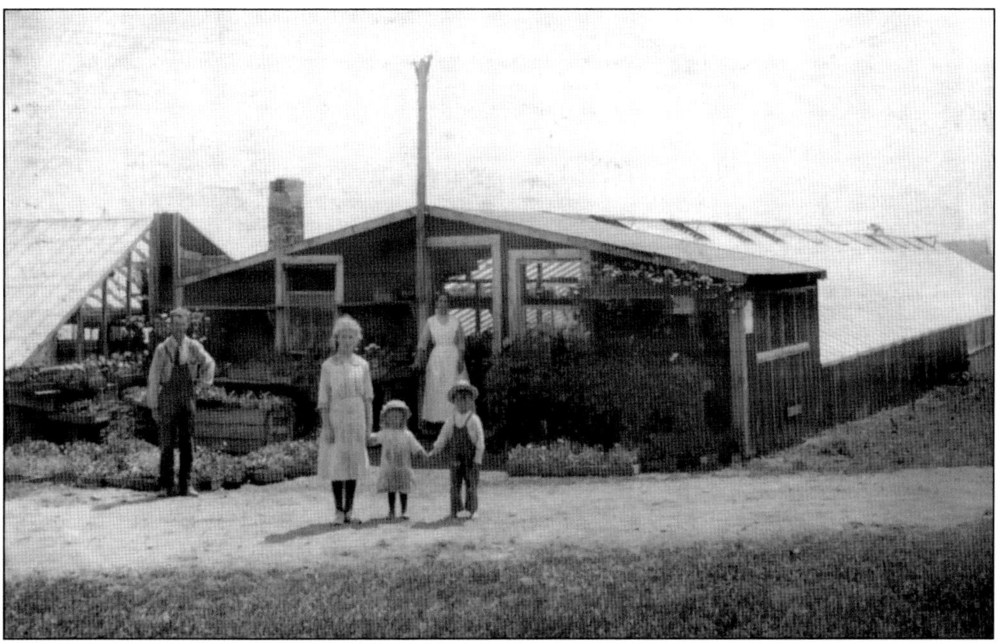

Bert Winslow (left) and his wife, Clara (in the doorway), established this greenhouse on Pleasant Street *c.* 1913. By 1933, Yarmouth had five retail florists and one wholesale operation. Although many Yarmouth flowers were shipped to distant locations by rail, the Winslows did a thriving business as wholesalers to Portland florists. Their son Ernest, the little boy with the straw hat, later ran the business and served as the town's fire chief. (Collection of the Yarmouth Historical Society.)

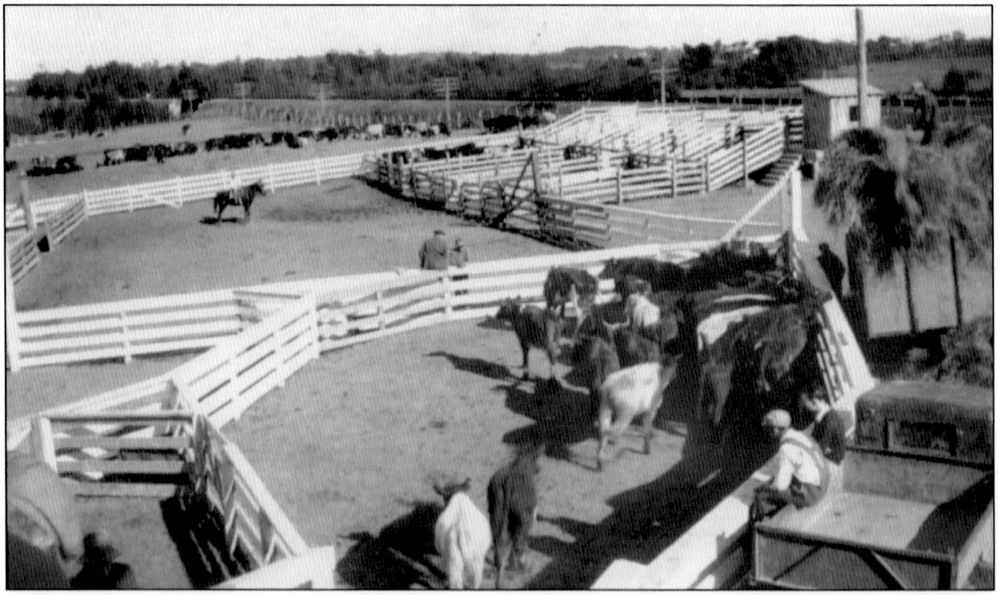

The image of cowboys rounding up thousands of head of cattle seems a little out of sorts with Yarmouth's clam-digging heritage. During World War I, the demand for horses and mules in Europe was so great that a New York company purchased a 40-acre farm on Sligo Road to gather animals from the west for shipment overseas from Portland. Granaries, stables, pens, and a hospital were constructed. After the war, Patrick Ward continued the operation as the Yarmouth Stock Yards, shipping thousands of head of cattle to market. (Collection of the Yarmouth Historical Society.)

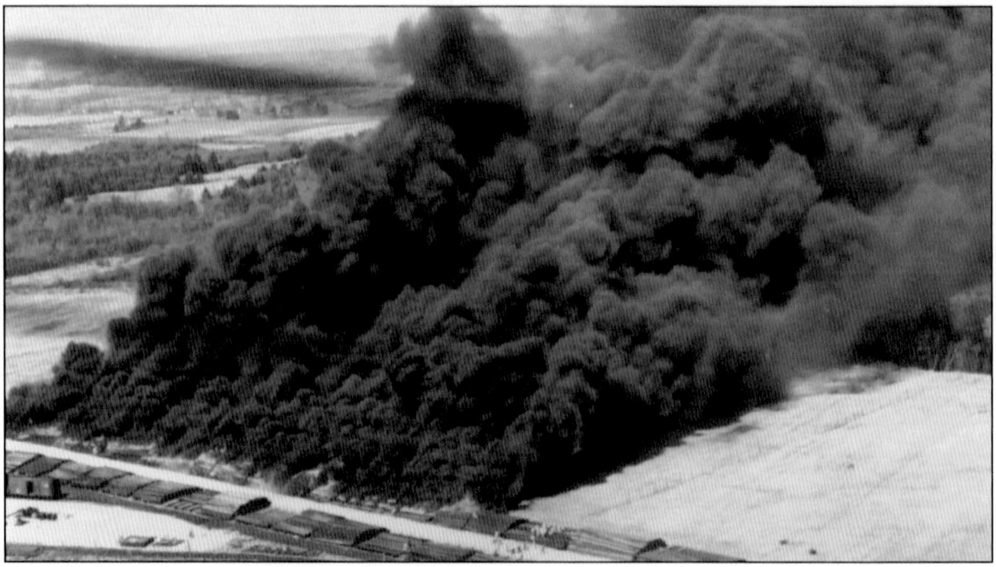

The stockyards were eventually sold to the New England Pole and Treating Company in the late 1920s. By the 1950s, the Koppers Company used the facility to creosote utility poles. On May 8, 1957, a fire broke out among the huge stacks of poles and was quickly spread by gusty winds. It jumped the Royal River and threatened homes along North Elm Street and North Road before a wind shift helped to contain the spectacular blaze. (Collection of the Yarmouth Historical Society.)

Eight

At Play

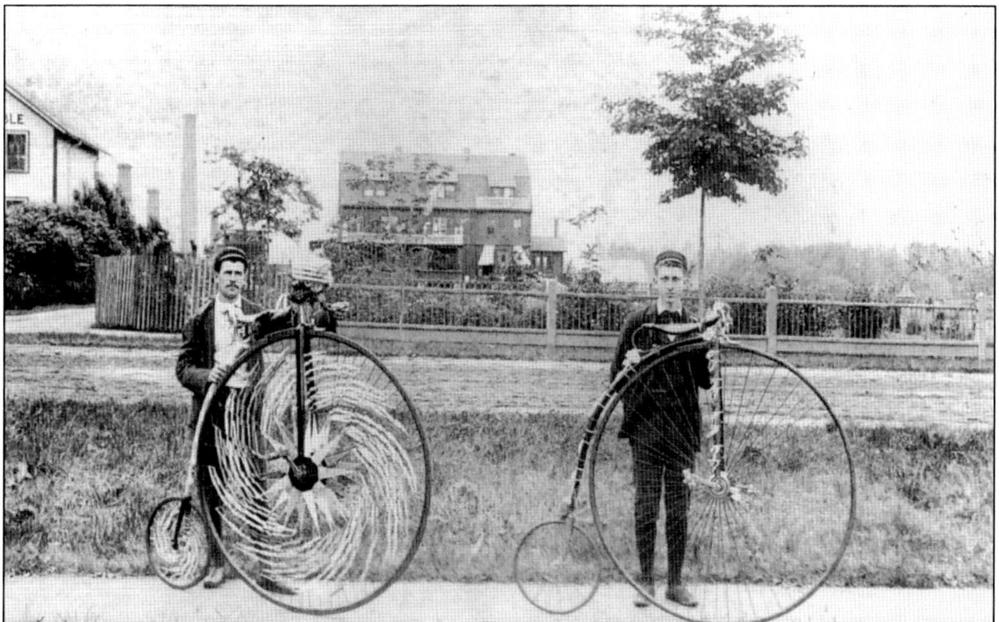

There is a nice juxtaposition between the worlds of work and play in this photograph. Harry Storer (left) and J. Carswell Lane pose with their high-wheeled bikes as the paper company's smokestacks loom in the background. Camp Hammond, the mill owner's estate, is behind the ornate fence on the other side of Main Street. The landscaping at Camp Hammond and the patriotic decorations on the bikes suggest that this photograph was taken on the Fourth of July in 1894. The oversized wheels allowed these cyclists to travel farther on each rotation of the pedals. Unfortunately, riders frequently pitched forward, coining the expression, "taking a header." (Collection of the Maine Historic Preservation Commission.)

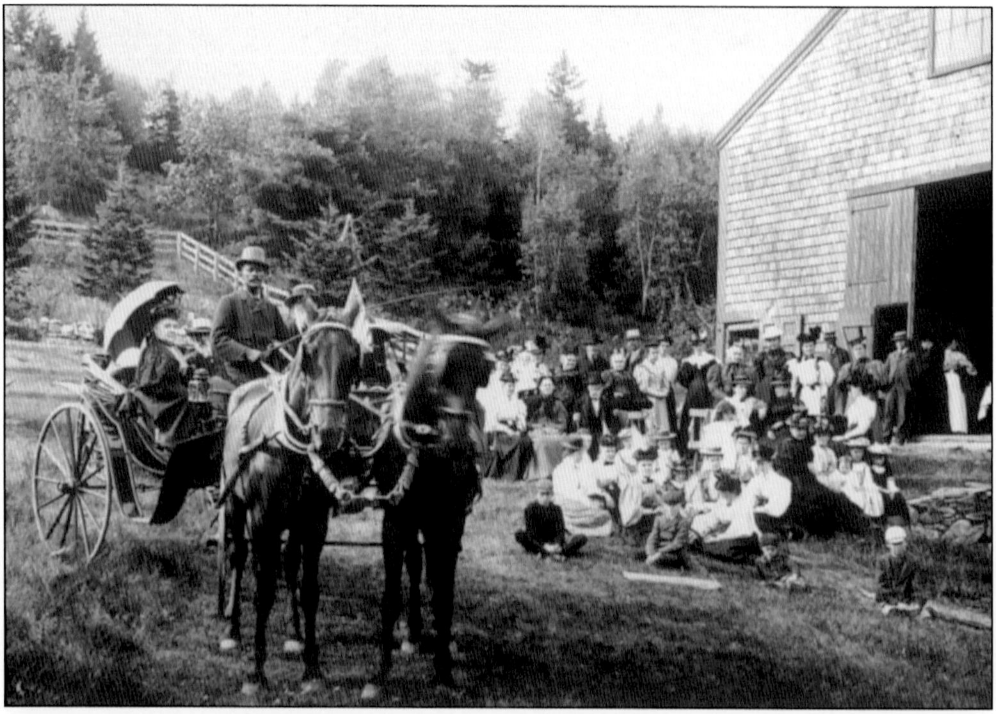

Leisure activities in 19th-century Yarmouth usually meant doing things with groups of people. This picnic at the old Gilman farm was a very stylish affair *c.* 1890. It appears that two of Yarmouth's retired sea captains, possibly Alfred Small and Richard Harding, have just arrived in the elegant carriage on the left. (Collection of Lois Rogers Lippincott.)

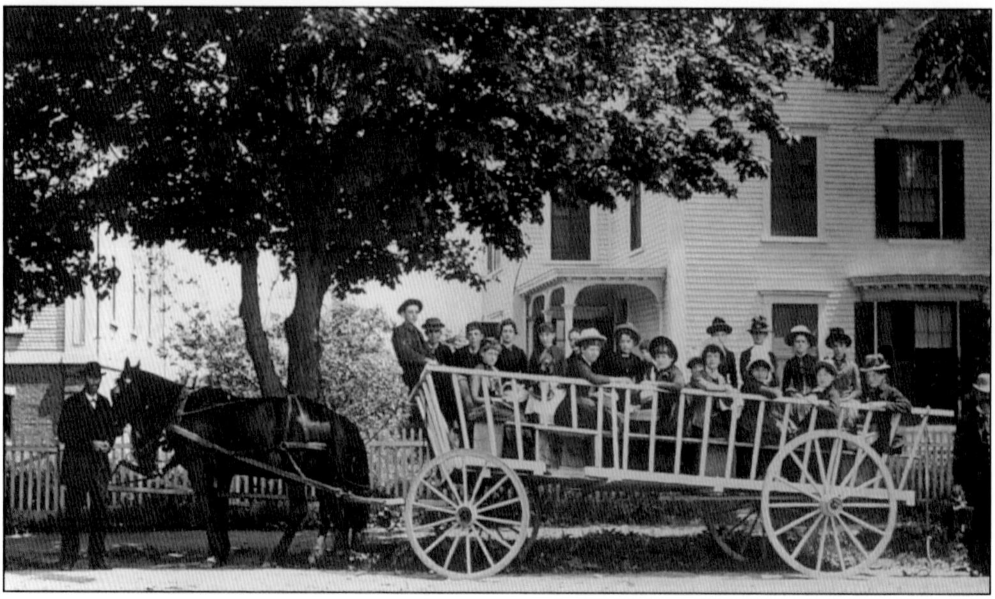

The Unitarians chose a hay wagon for their Sunday school picnic. In the background are the old Central Parish church and parsonage, which were turned over to the Unitarian Universalists in 1885. This picnic occurred after that change, probably *c.* 1888. (Collection of Lois Rogers Lippincott.)

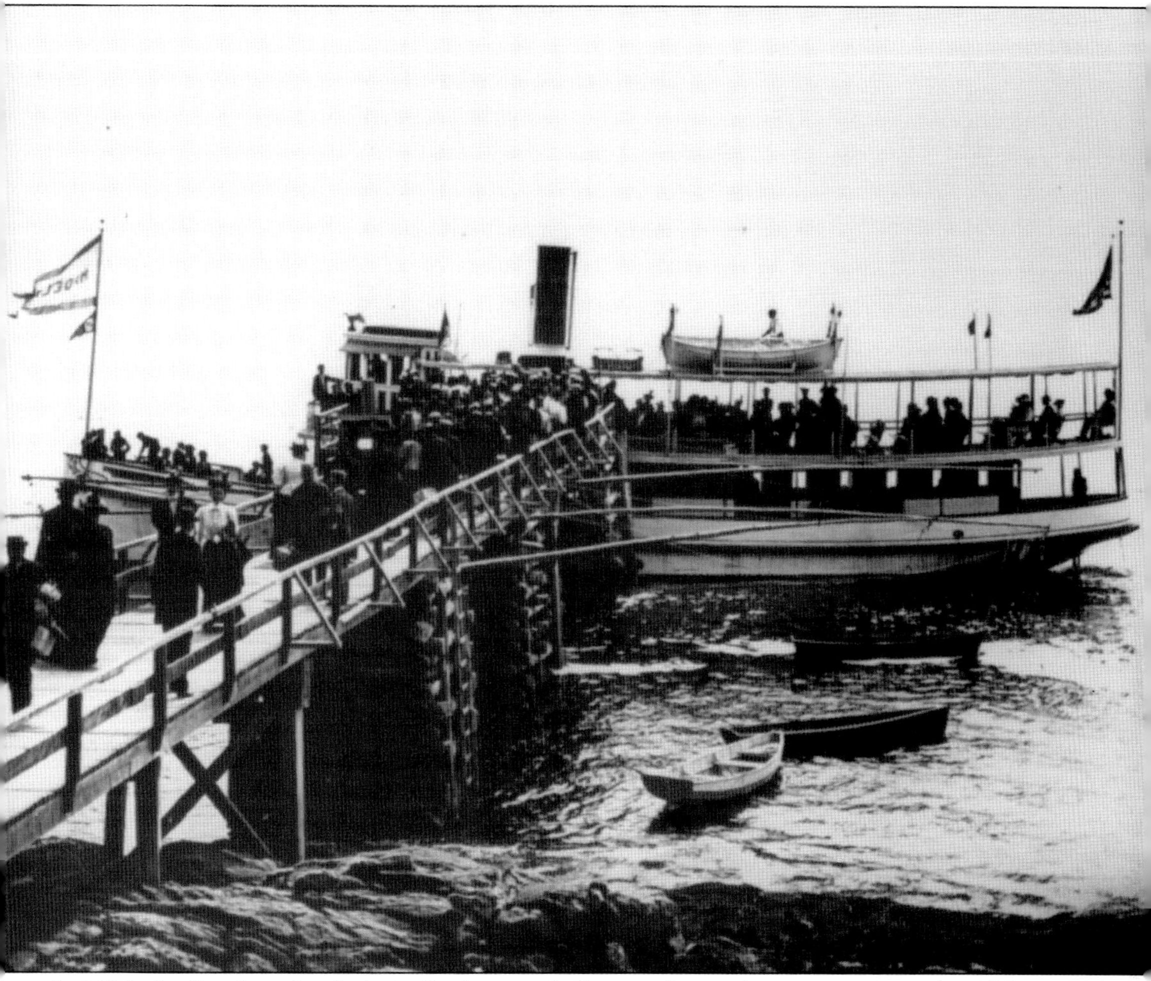

In 1898, the Sunday school picnic for the town's Baptists featured an excursion on the 86-foot steamer *Madeleine*. With activities such as this, it is little wonder that Rev. Herbert Caulkins greatly increased the attendance at the Baptist Sunday school. Although Madeleine Point, on Cousins Island, was apparently named for this steamboat, the picture was probably taken at Princes Point. (Collection of the Yarmouth Historical Society.)

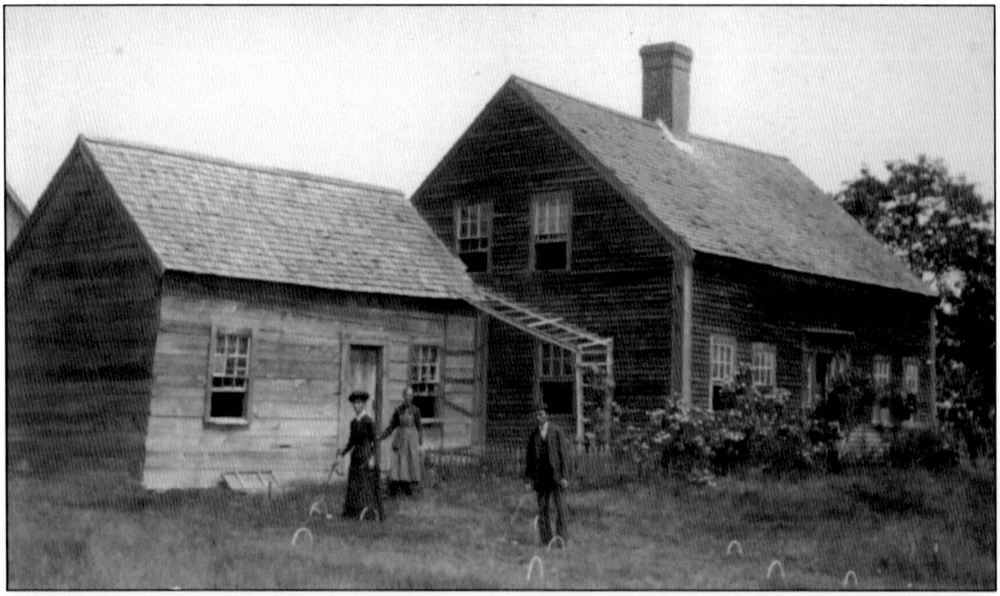

The game of croquet was democratized when it arrived in the United States after the Civil War. Lightweight inexpensive equipment and new rules allowed it to be played by men and women alike on rough turf like this unidentified farm yard. In the spring of 1890, L.R. Cook advertised that he had "a full line of croquet sets" for sale in his Yarmouthville store. (Collection of the Yarmouth Historical Society.)

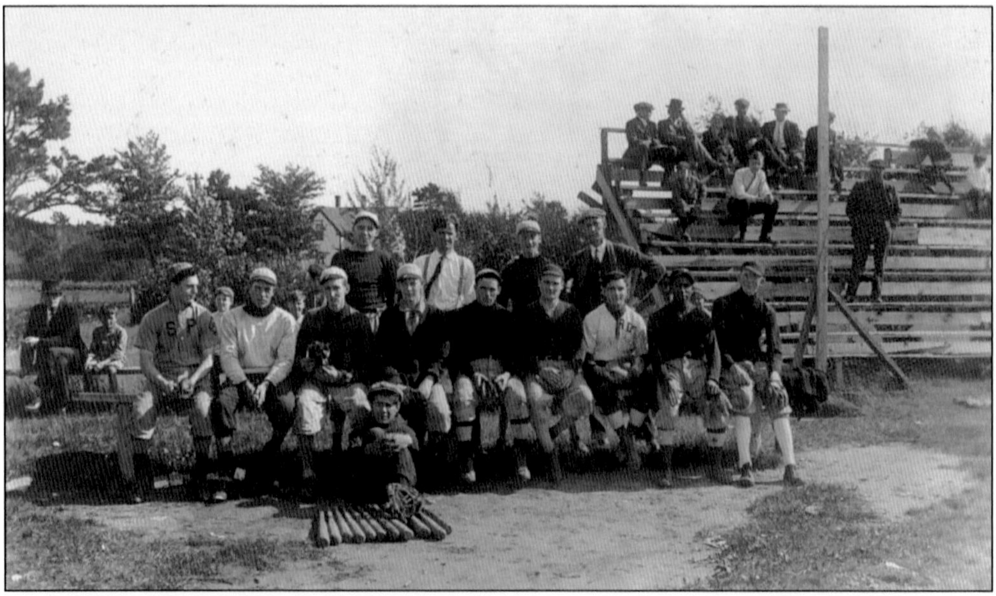

Baseball has a long heritage in Yarmouth. Before the Civil War, games of bat and ball were so popular that the town passed rules to keep them off the streets. Those rules were ignored by local boys who played a version of baseball in the 1870s called round ball. It had the key elements of the modern game, including four goals, a yarn ball, a pitcher, and a batter. Ferdinand Corliss took this photograph of the Yarmouth town team *c.* 1909. They are very likely using the North Yarmouth Academy's new field with its commodious grandstand, which was donated by Joseph Merrill in 1907. (Collection of Lois Rogers Lippincott.)

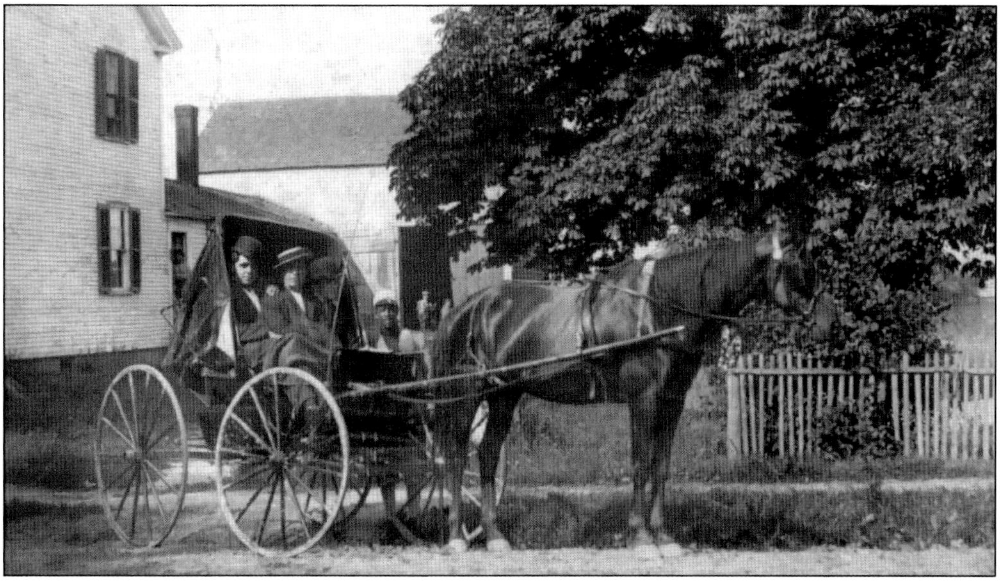

With their rakish hats and buggy whip at hand, Mike Beote, Percy Adams, and Tom Perry do not look as though they intend to observe the town's six-mile-per-hour speed limit. Fred Carter, who is standing beside the buggy, trained horses and drove for a variety of Yarmouth families. In the winter, Carter sometimes raced a sulky at high speed on the ice of the Royal River. (Collection of the Yarmouth Historical Society.)

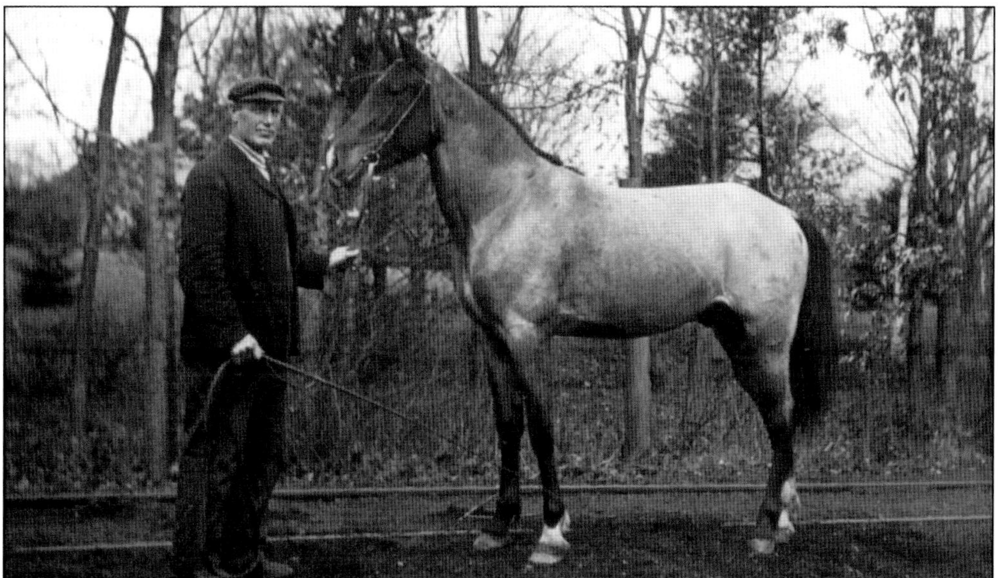

Dr. Charles W. Gerow also loved fast horses. After establishing a lucrative dental practice, he purchased a mansion on Main Street and soon put a large billboard over the stable, announcing that it was the home of his famous stallion, Roan Wilkes. In Gerow's capacity as the town's part-time chief of police, he proudly rode his horses in the Memorial Day parades. He is pictured here with his horse Summe Wilkes. Behind him are the tracks of the Brunswick trolley line that ran beside his stable and now form the walkers' path to the Rowe School. (Collection of the Yarmouth Historical Society.)

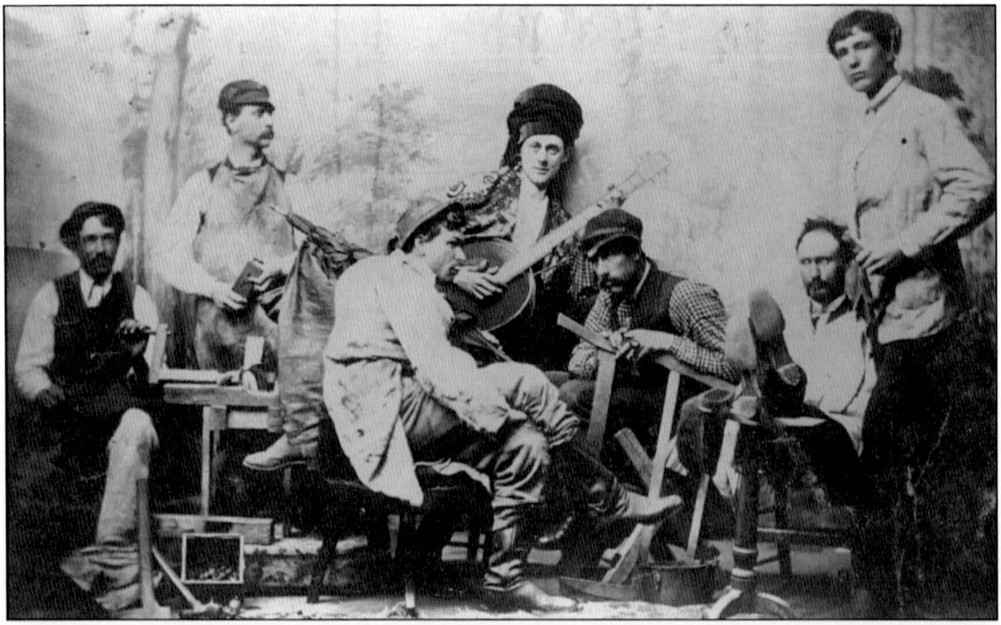

The name of this dramatic tableaux from 1870 has been lost, but its performers include several of the town's leading figures, such as Walter B. Allen. A century ago, local performances of music, dance, and theater played a much larger role in the town's popular culture than they do today. Church groups, fraternal organizations, and schoolchildren all sponsored events, including talent shows, dramatic productions, fan dances, and band concerts. Even the shoe workers, known as the "Happy Lasters," organized a quadrille at the Masonic Hall in 1893. (Collection of Lois Rogers Lippincott.)

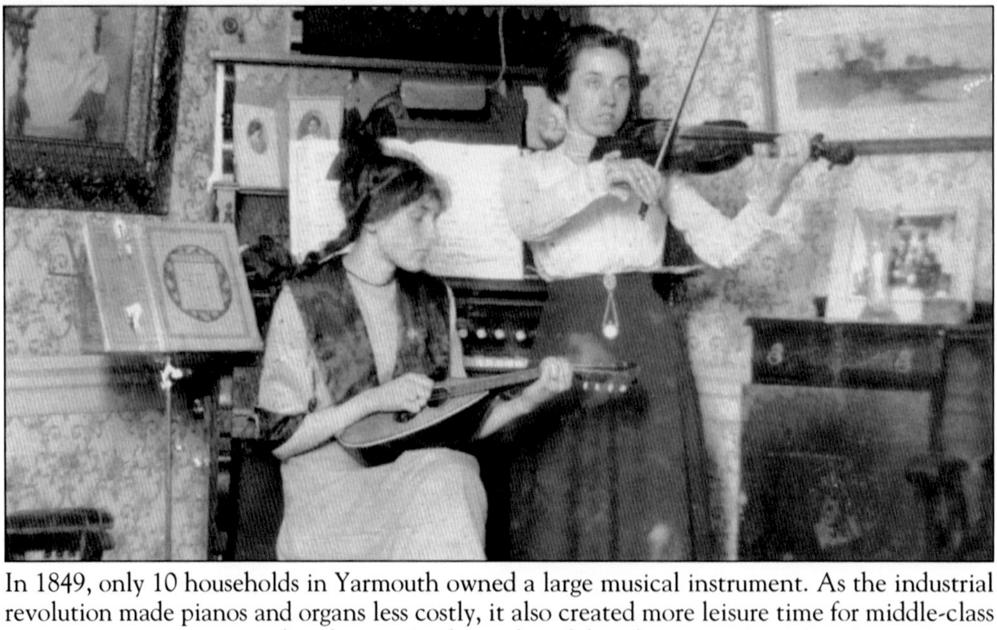

In 1849, only 10 households in Yarmouth owned a large musical instrument. As the industrial revolution made pianos and organs less costly, it also created more leisure time for middle-class citizens to enjoy music in their homes. In the parlor of their house on East Main Street, Louise (left) and Annie May Rogers play a duet using a mandolin and a violin. The stops and keyboard of a small parlor organ are visible behind them. (Collection of Lois Rogers Lippincott.)

Like the Yarmouth women who had to choose between a factory job or teaching, Yarmouth's black males were expected to be either horse trainers or barbers. William Freeman chose the latter. His shop was over Doughty's hardware store in the Lower Village, but his heart was always with his music. An outstanding cornet player in the Yarmouth Brass Band, Freeman tried to make a name for himself on the local band circuit. He even printed up special stationery to advertise his talents. (Collection of Lois Rogers Lippincott.)

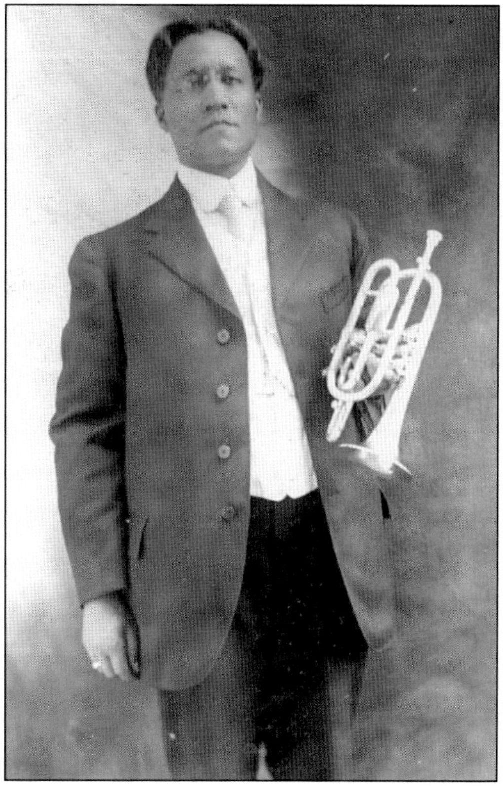

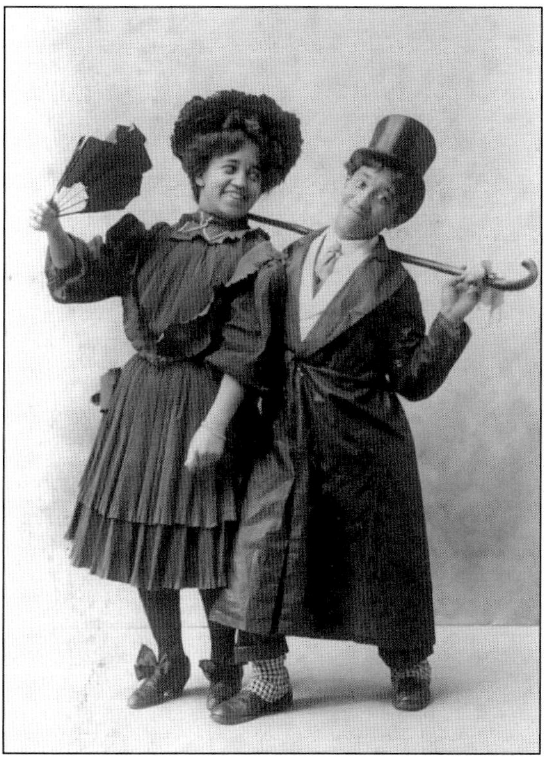

Throughout the 19th century, most of Yarmouth's African Americans, including the Freeman family, had lived on West Elm Street near the Cumberland line. William Freeman chose to live on Lafayette Street, which was closer to his barbershop. This song-and-dance routine suggests that his children, William and Jennie, were talented performers like their father. (Collection of Lois Rogers Lippincott.)

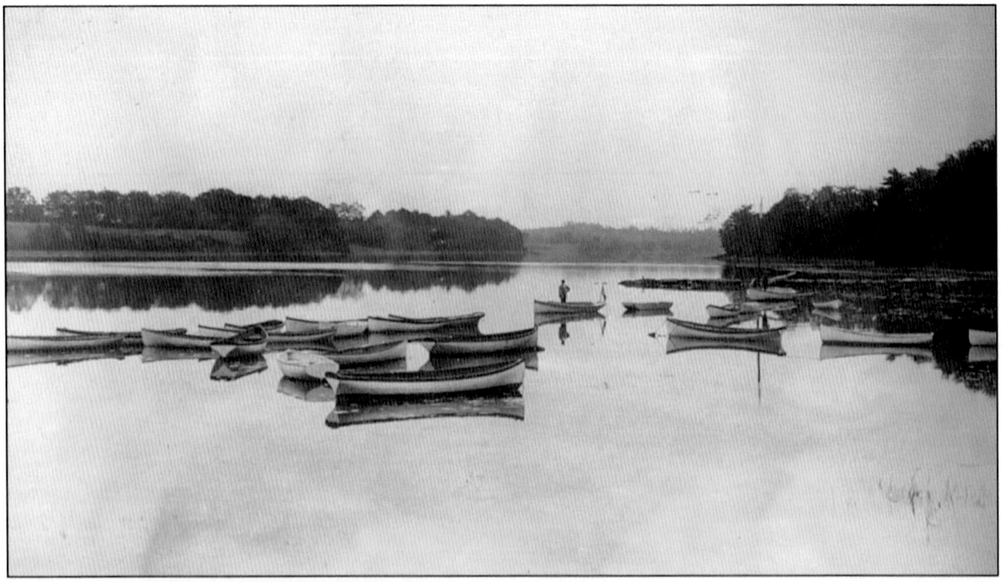

John A. Drinkwater realized *c.* 1905 that many of Yarmouth's new summer residents wanted to be able to use boats without having to buy them. He offered more than 30 rowboats for rent, complete with moorings and a delivery service. By 1919, he was weary of doing all the maintenance and agreed to let his young cousin Alfred Drinkwater store the boats in a barn on Cousins Island. Unfortunately, the barn and all but three of the boats were destroyed by fire during the winter. (Collection of Alfreda Drinkwater Thurston.)

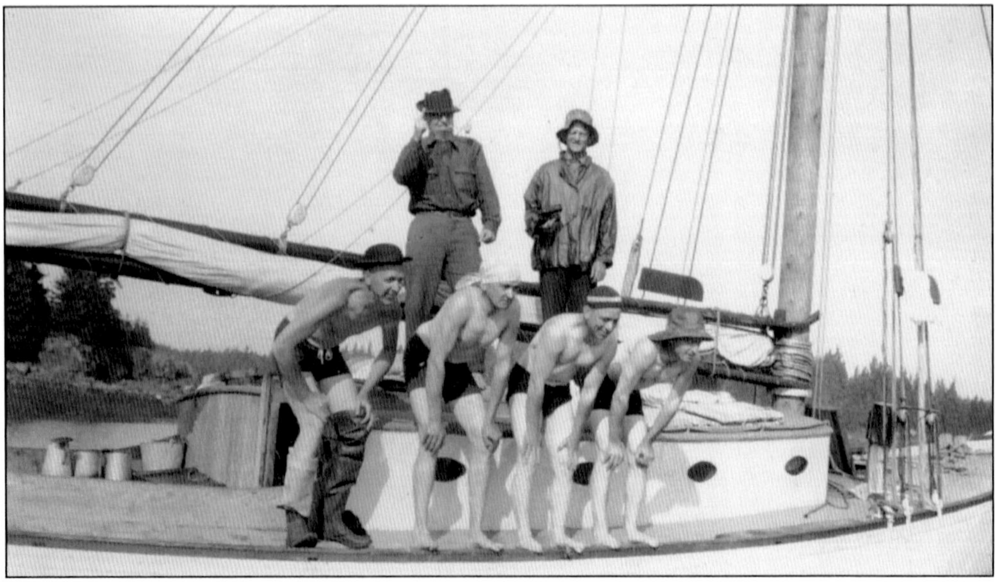

As a small boy, Alfred Drinkwater sometimes accompanied his sea captain father on coastal voyages. Always restless with life on the shore, Alfred often skippered his own sailboat for charter parties. Leaning against the boom of his sloop *Wanderlust* in 1923, Alfred was probably wondering if these men from Rhode Island were really going to dive in while wearing hats and boots. (Collection of Alfreda Drinkwater Thurston.)

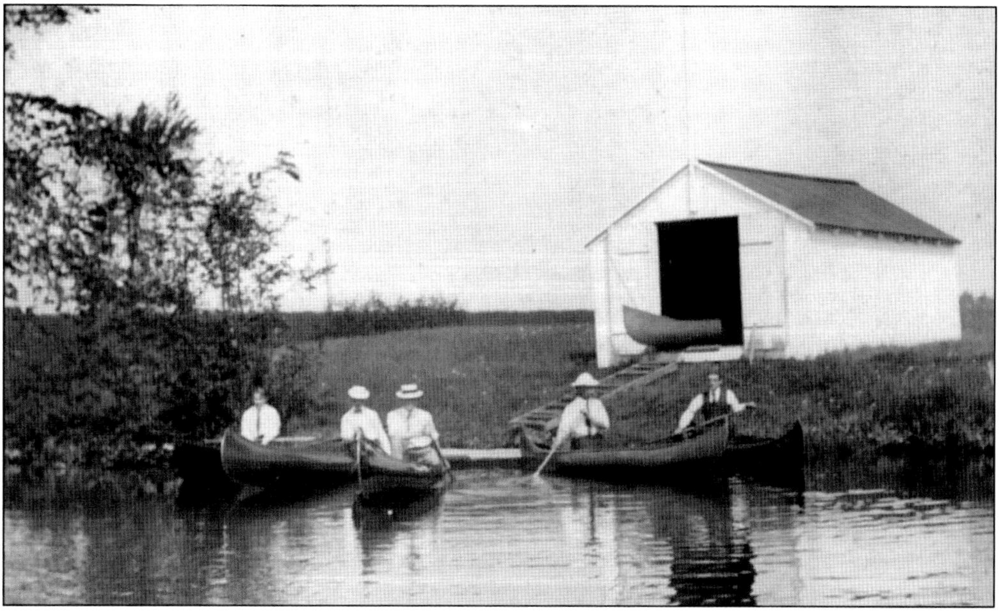

There is an Edwardian elegance to this image as five men, smartly dressed in ties, go canoeing on the Royal River c. 1912. The boathouse was located across from what is now the Yarmouth Water District office near the Grand Trunk trestle. In 1892, a small steamer named the *Hoyt* ferried guests from this spot to a mineral springs hotel in North Yarmouth owned by Giles Loring. (Collection of the Yarmouth Historical Society.)

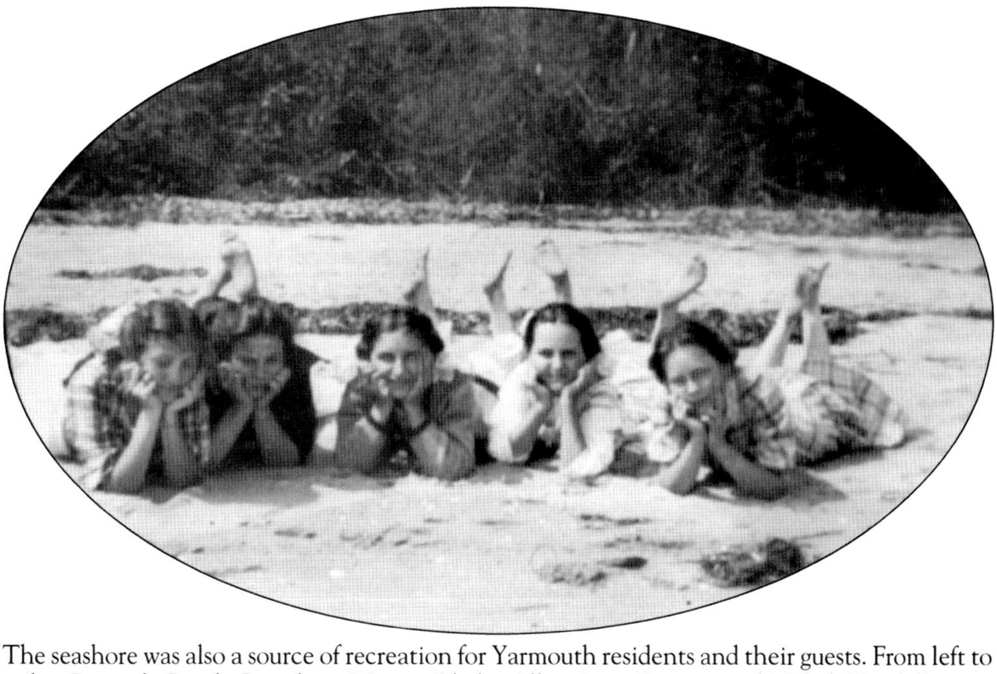

The seashore was also a source of recreation for Yarmouth residents and their guests. From left to right, Gertrude Smith, Josephine Moxie, Gladys Allen, Irma Sawyer, and Mabel Wendell enjoy a trip to the beach. Although the town of Yarmouth includes 30 miles of coastline, most of it is rock or alluvial mud, with only a few hundred yards of somewhat sandy beaches. (Collection of the Yarmouth Historical Society.)

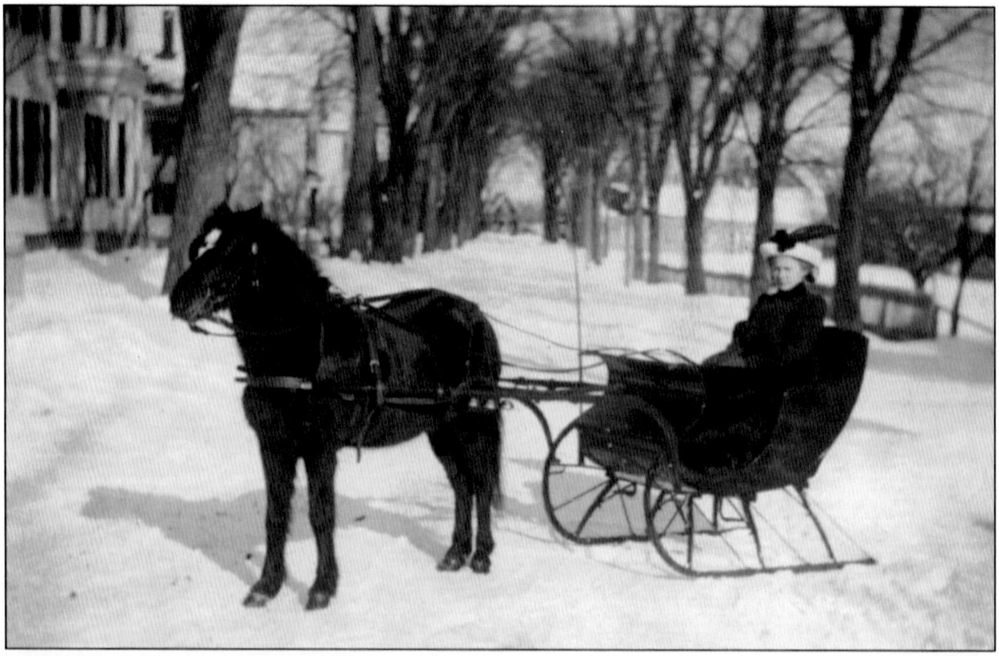

Winter recreation in Yarmouth traditionally involved skating and sleigh riding. Rena Blanchard was enjoying a sleigh ride with her pony on South Street when this picture was taken c. 1912. Exceptionally cold winters in the late 19th century regularly froze the bay, allowing Edwin Hamilton in 1874 to skate all the way from Cousins Island to Portland to buy a gift for his parents. He repeated his feat the next day when he had to exchange the gift. (Collection of the Yarmouth Historical Society.)

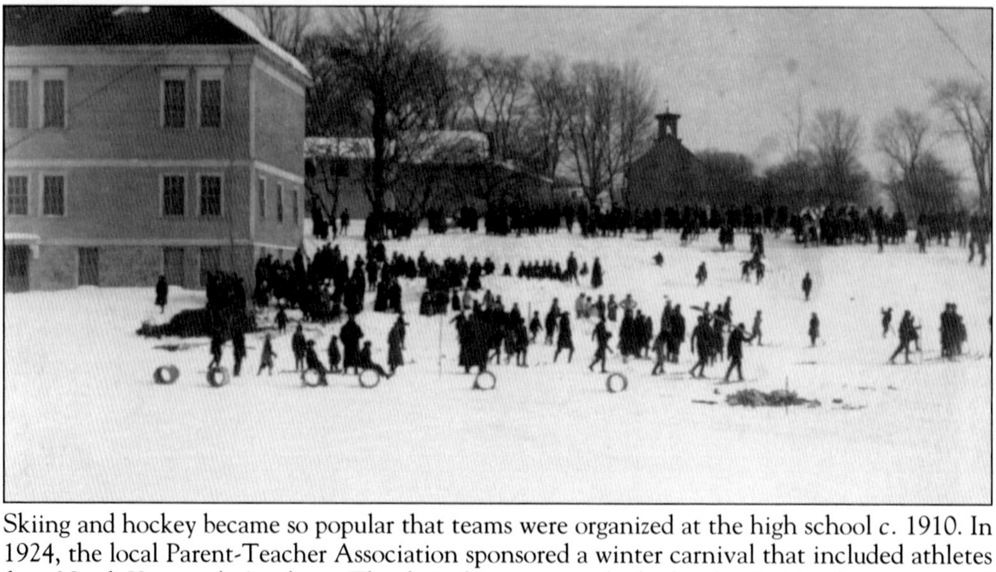

Skiing and hockey became so popular that teams were organized at the high school c. 1910. In 1924, the local Parent-Teacher Association sponsored a winter carnival that included athletes from North Yarmouth Academy. Thanks in large part to the high-school girls who won several races, Yarmouth High School won the competition. A freshman named Ralph Kinghorn captured the ski jump by soaring just 25 feet. This photograph was taken approximately where the town hall now stands, looking toward the academy. The building with the tower was the old Yarmouth Institute. (Collection of the Yarmouth Historical Society.)

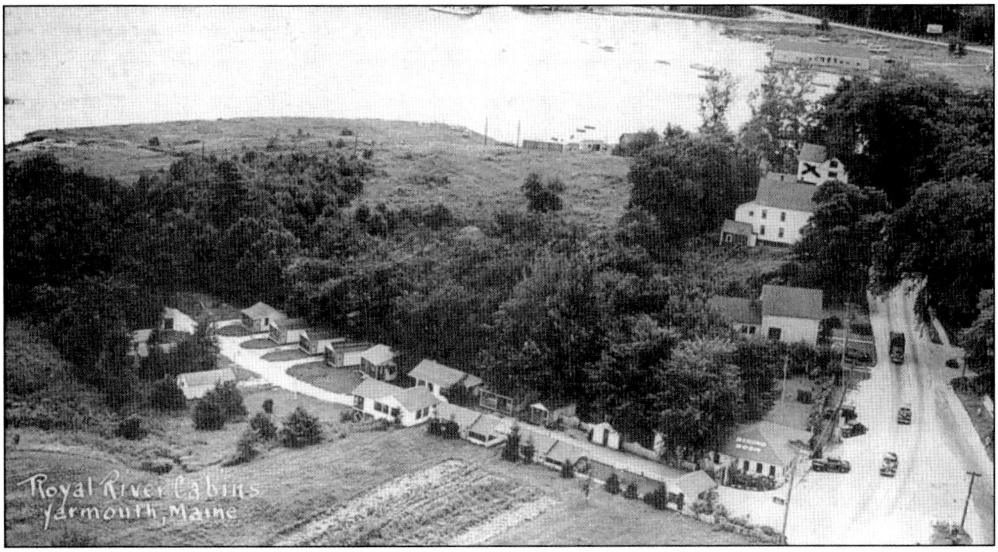

Paved roads and automobile tourism came to Yarmouth in 1914. The new federal highway from Portland to Bath included four miles from Pleasant Street to the Freeport line. Gas stations, tourist cabins, tea shops, and seafood places soon opened along this stretch, offering much needed employment after the pulp mill closed in 1921. The Royal River Cabins actually started as an inn on East Main Street. That building, which now houses Schwinds' antique shop, is marked with an X, thanks to the person who sent this postcard to Brunswick in 1941. (Collection of Frank Witkowski.)

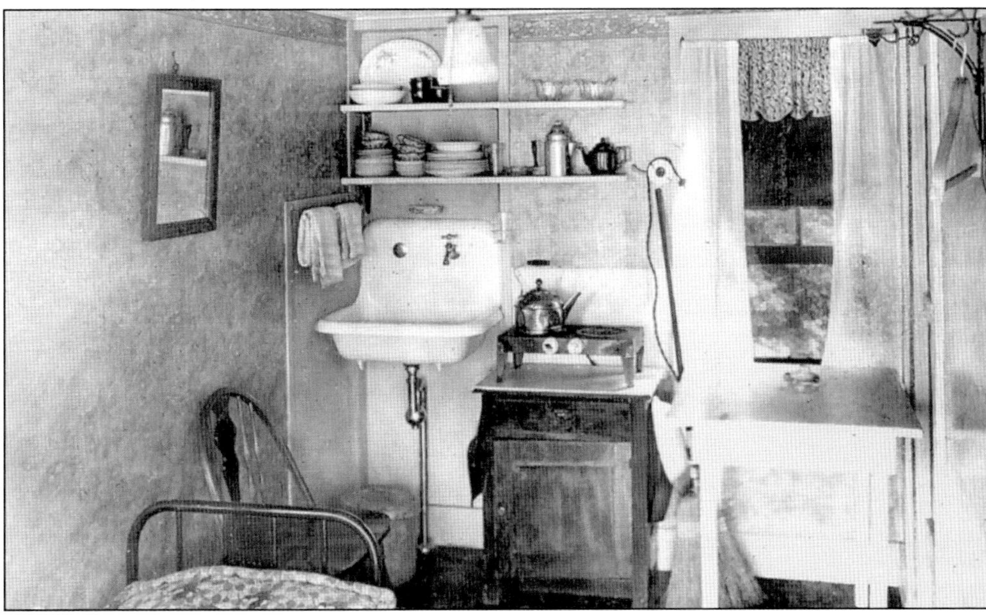

The Royal River Cabins flourished between 1934 and 1950. Although a later owner declared that these units were the very first tourist cabins built in Maine, that claim is doubtful. Guests could dine at the coffee shop or prepare their own meals using the kitchenette in each cottage. Eleanor Roosevelt and her entourage once stayed overnight because the Eastland Hotel in Portland banished her dog Fala. The president's wife chose to dine at the Westcustogo Inn. (Collection of Alan M. Hall.)

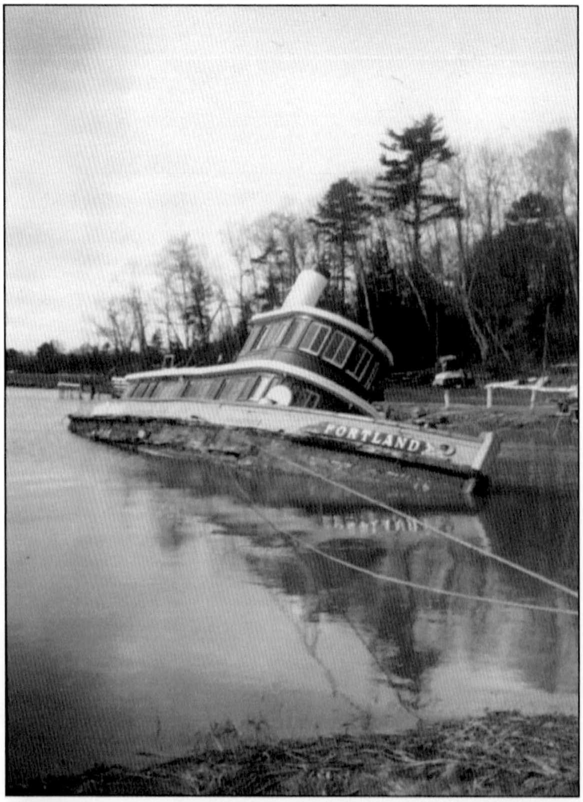

The citizens of Yarmouth were persistent and ingenious in their efforts to sell seafood to tourists. Shortly after World War II, Clarence "Mit" Collins brought the 1902 tug *Portland* up the Cousins River to make a restaurant near the highway. Although ice in the river eventually sank this venture, the incident provided the Muddy Rudder restaurant with its name. (Collection of Virginia Turner.)

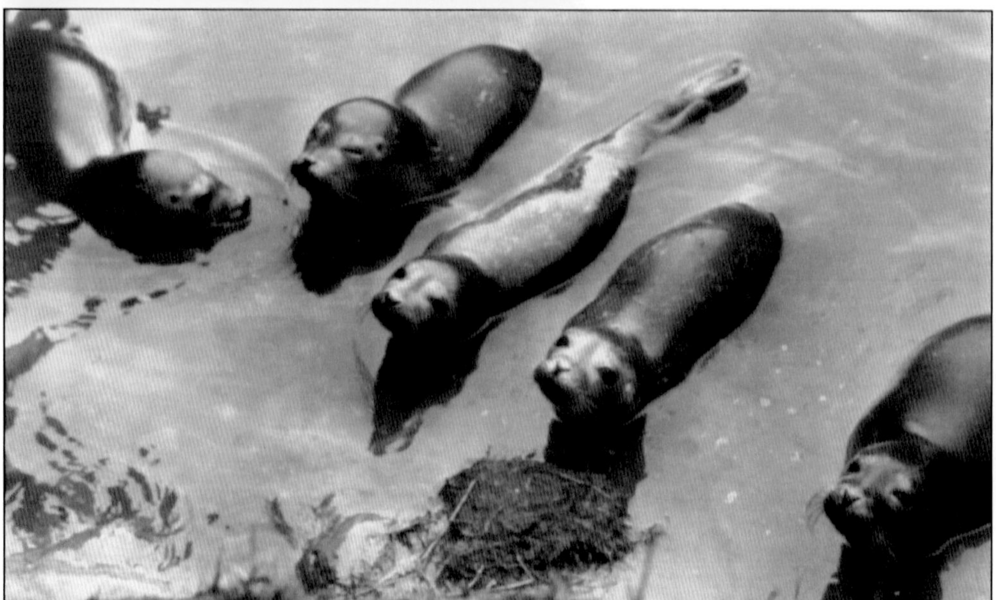

To be absolutely certain that motorists would stop at his tugboat, Collins added pens of live seals. He named the enterprise the Treasure Island Seal Pound and declared it was "fine entertainment for young and old." The seals were probably grateful that the business did not prosper. (Collection of Richard Thoits.)

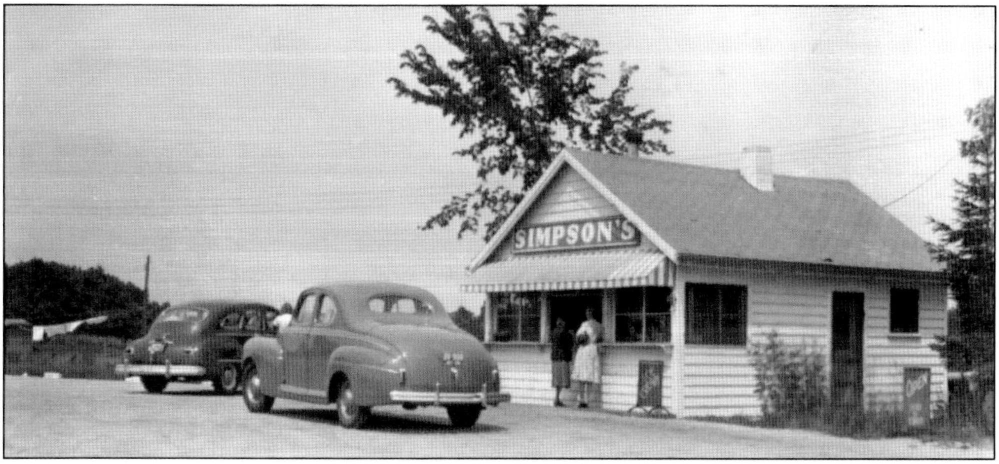

Before the arrival of fast-food chains in the 1960s, Simpson's drive-ins were well known in the greater Portland area for their tasty hamburgers. In the 1940s, this one was located on what is now Route 88, not far from the Riverside Cemetery. It closed *c.* 1952 when U.S. Route 1 was relocated through the middle of town. Before Simpson's was built, a dairy bar called the Buttermilk Bar was operated on the site by Old Tavern Farm. (Collection of Alan M. Hall.)

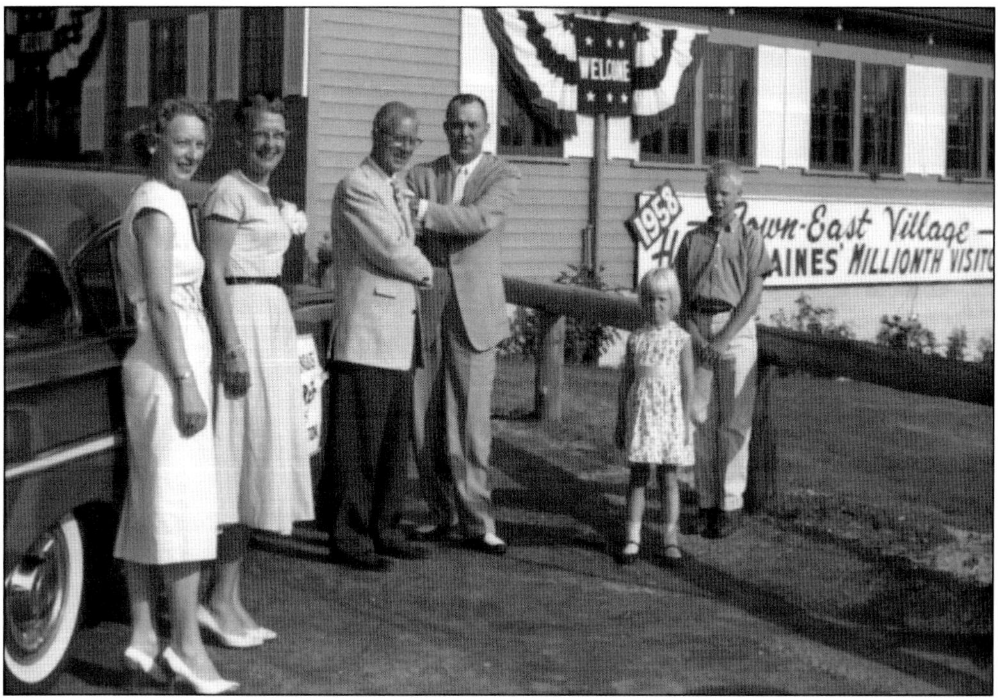

Delayed by World War II, the U.S. Route 1 bridge over Main Street was quickly completed in the late 1940s. New gas stations, restaurants and motels replaced the old tourist cabins that were bypassed on Route 88. Sensing a good investment, a Wall Street broker named E.V. Yeager bought a large tract of land near the Royal River and built a restaurant and motel complex, which is now known as Downeast Village. In this 1958 photograph, the Summerill family—"Maine's millionth visitors"—receives royal treatment from the Ferrells, who still operate Downeast Village. The current owner, Ed Ferrell, is the grandson of E.V. Yeager. (Collection of the Yarmouth Historical Society.)

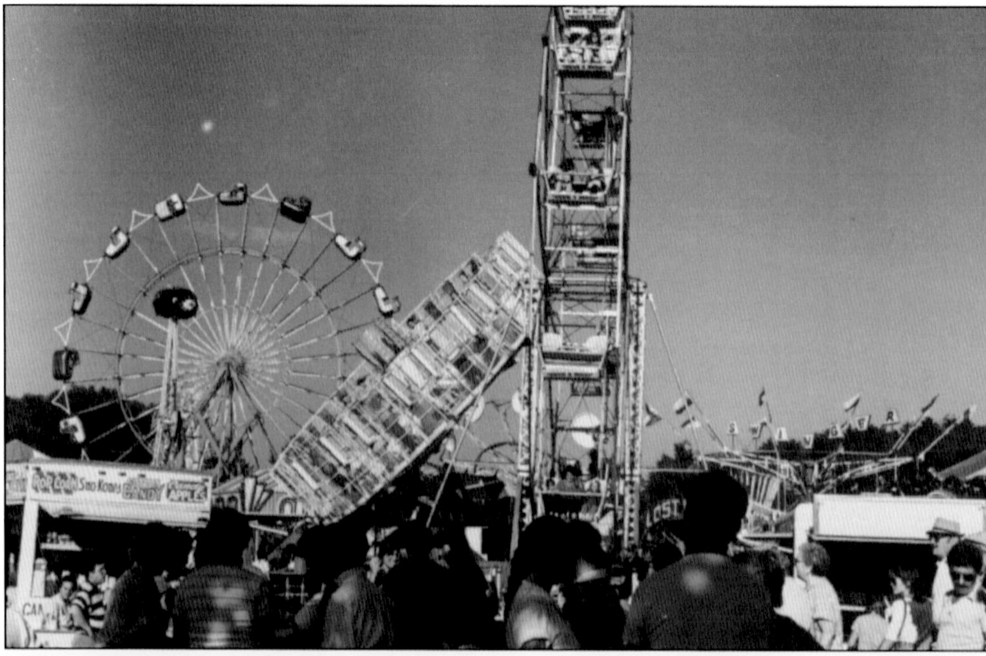

In the previous photograph, the Summerhill family was staying in Yarmouth to attend the town's Old Home Week in late August. In 1965, this annual activity was reinvented as the Clam Festival and moved to the middle of July. Despite the fact that 150,000 people usually attend the event, the Clam Festival has managed to preserve its small-town heritage by including such attractions as a firemen's muster and outdoor band concerts. The popular carnival rides are kept apart from these activities, which helps to spread out the crowd. (Collection of Virginia Turner.)

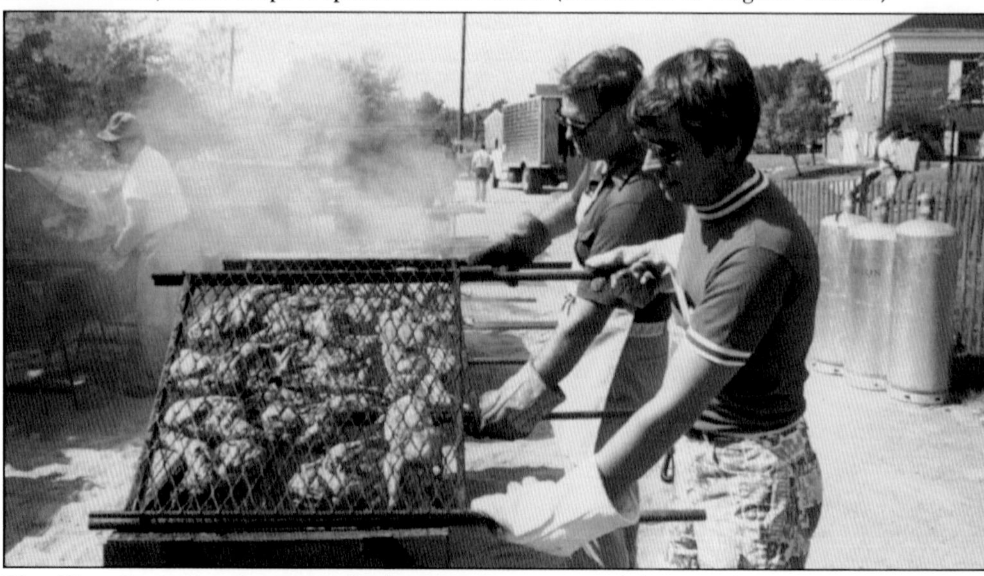

The Clam Festival is the major fundraising opportunity of the year for scores of civic groups in Yarmouth. Over time, each organization has acquired the right to sell a particular type of refreshment. Only the firemen, for example, can offer the popular fried clams. In this c. 1981 photograph, Charlie Mansfield (front) and Art Vanderburg grill chickens for the Yarmouth Lions Club. (Collection of Virginia Turner.)

Nine

Life on the Shore

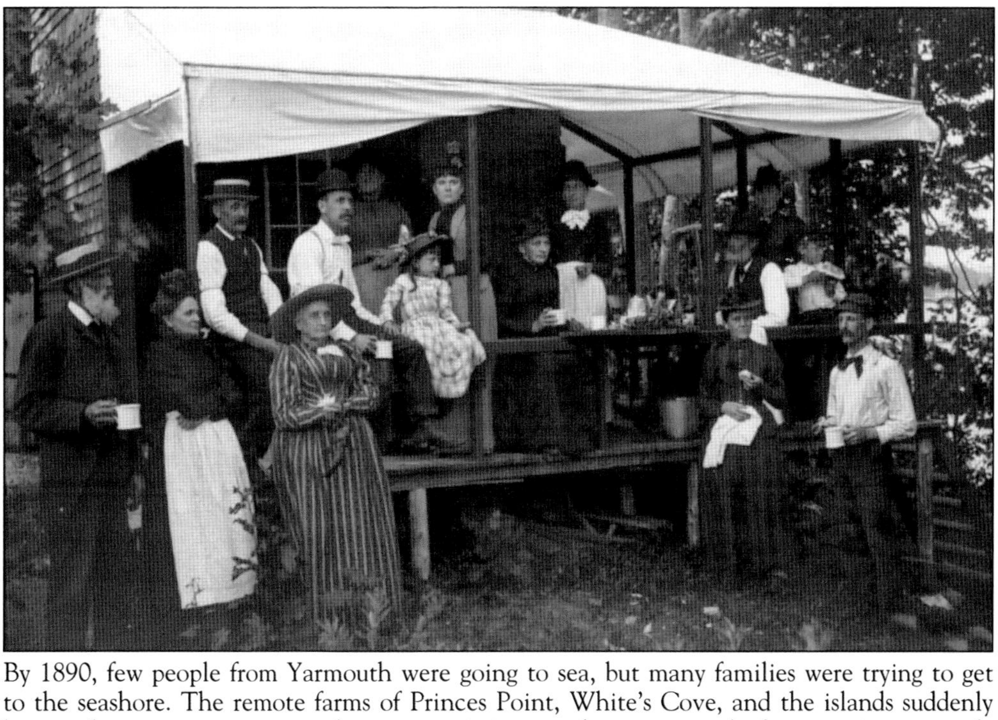

By 1890, few people from Yarmouth were going to sea, but many families were trying to get to the seashore. The remote farms of Princes Point, White's Cove, and the islands suddenly became hot properties as speculators, associations, and cottagers rushed to acquire oceanside lots. The boardinghouses, summer cottages, and hotels brought with them a relaxed and rustic lifestyle that local boosters touted as "away from the noise and tumult of the city and yet within such easy reach." That, of course, is the premise on which Yarmouth would build its future as a seaside suburb. Year-round homes now occupy the sites of Victorian cottages, such as C.L. Blake's Tablerock, which was located in White's Cove. In the 1890s, summer residents such as these could purchase six lobsters on Princes Point for as little as a quarter. Notice that the woman in the striped dress is holding a lobster. (Collection of Lois Rogers Lippincott.)

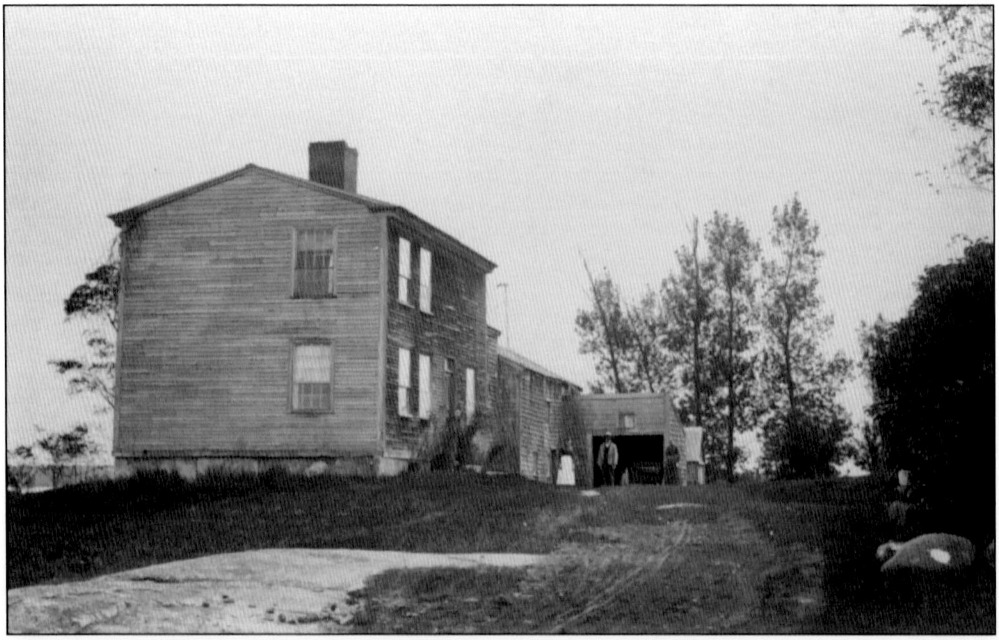

When Yarmouth voted to secede from North Yarmouth in 1849, the residents of Princes Point and the islands identified with the inland farmers and firmly opposed the idea. Coastal farms, such as the Nicholas Drinkwater homestead on Princes Point, were often perched on more ledges than topsoil, a fact that nudged many Drinkwaters into a life at sea. Capt. Sumner Drinkwater, who was born in this house, once complained to his father that it was hard to hoe because there "ain't much soil." (Collection of Alan M. Hall.)

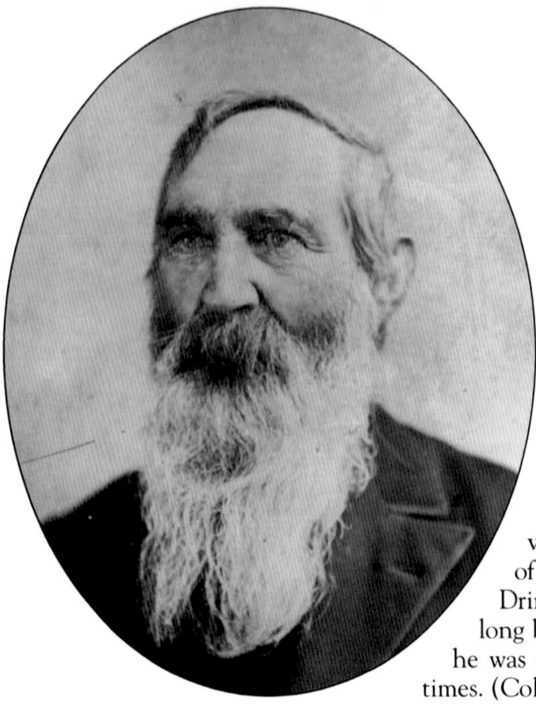

The saltwater farms of Princes Point and the islands produced many sea captains, such as Nicholas Drinkwater. By taking short voyages carrying coal, lumber, and sugar along the East Coast, they were able to maintain their farms, although coasting trips made less money than deepwater voyages with grain and guano. The flexibility of the short voyages also allowed Nicholas Drinkwater to be active in community affairs long before he ended his seafaring. Even though he was a Democrat, he was elected selectman 11 times. (Collection of Lois Rogers Lippincott.)

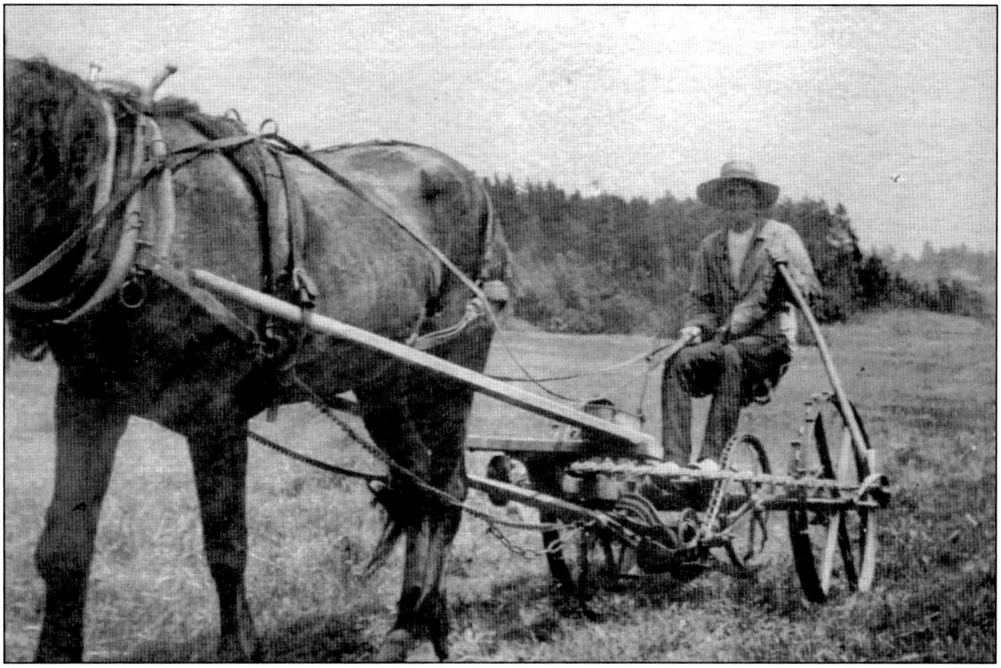

Even as full-time farming declined along the shore, fields were mowed to provide hay for the horses and to keep open some of the views. In this 1909 photograph, Alfred Drinkwater is cutting hay on Cousins Island. Although he preferred to be on his sailboat, he was a skilled mason and carpenter who helped to build several of Yarmouth's summer cottages. (Collection of Alfreda Drinkwater Thurston.)

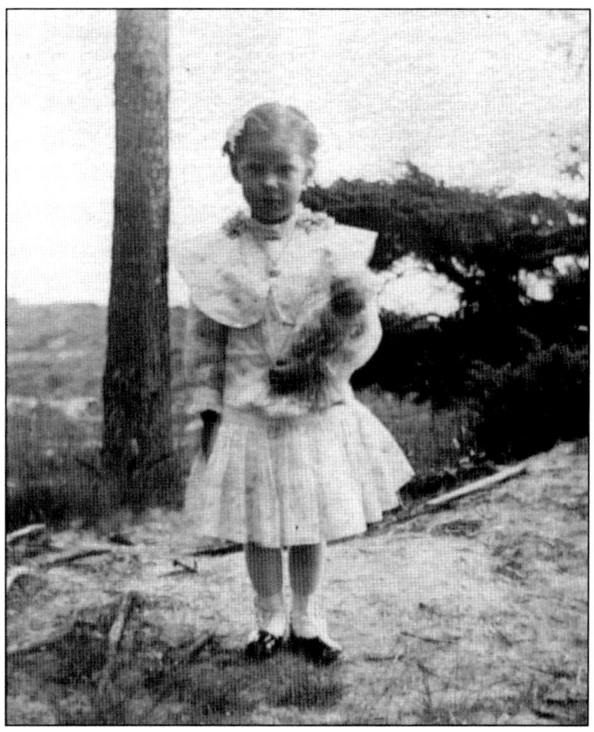

In August 1906, Nicholas Drinkwater's four-year-old granddaughter Elizabeth poses with her teddy bear along the shore. Although two of the old captain's sons also went to sea, Elizabeth's father, Joshua Drinkwater, became an independent-minded postman and farmer. Elizabeth later married Alfred Drinkwater (above), who tragically died just before their daughter Alfreda was born. Still living in the 171-year-old family home on Princes Point, Alfreda Thurston keeps the Drinkwater heritage alive with delightful stories. (Collection of Alfreda Drinkwater Thurston.)

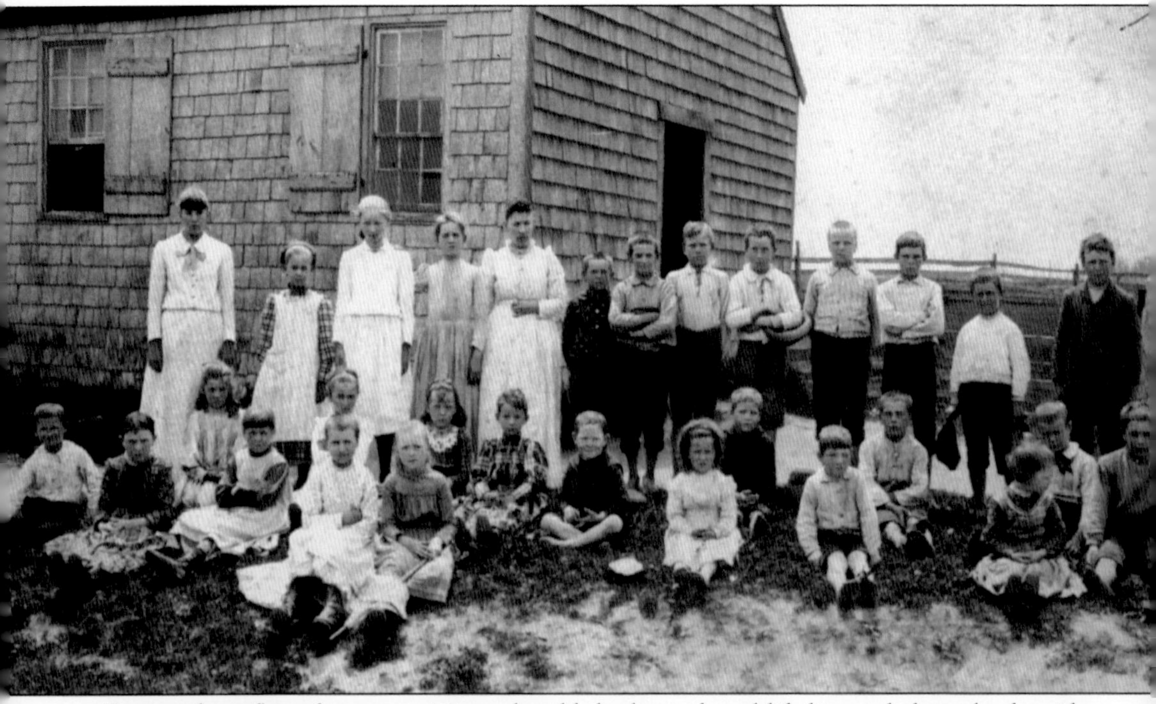

Despite the influx of summer visitors, the old rhythms of rural life lingered along the foreside. The Old Ledge School was almost 150 years old when this photograph was taken in 1886. Fifteen years later, the building had been replaced and one of the girls in this picture was now the teacher. Bertha Drinkwater (back row, third from left) was paid $6.50 per week in 1901. However, the number of students had declined by a third, alarming the superintendent, who said that the school was becoming too small to create "a healthy rivalry between pupils." He said that more large families ought to move into the vicinity of the Old Ledge School to increase its population. (Collection of the Yarmouth Historical Society.)

In the 1880s and 1890s, Charles Gooding captured many of the images used in this book and somewhat immodestly styled himself as "the Photographer." Although he was born into a local family of boatbuilders, he opened his first photographic studio in Augusta during the Civil War and later moved back to Yarmouth. He was the brother-in-law of James Durgan, who was another superb Yarmouth photographer in the 1860s and 1870s. (Collection of Alan M. Hall.)

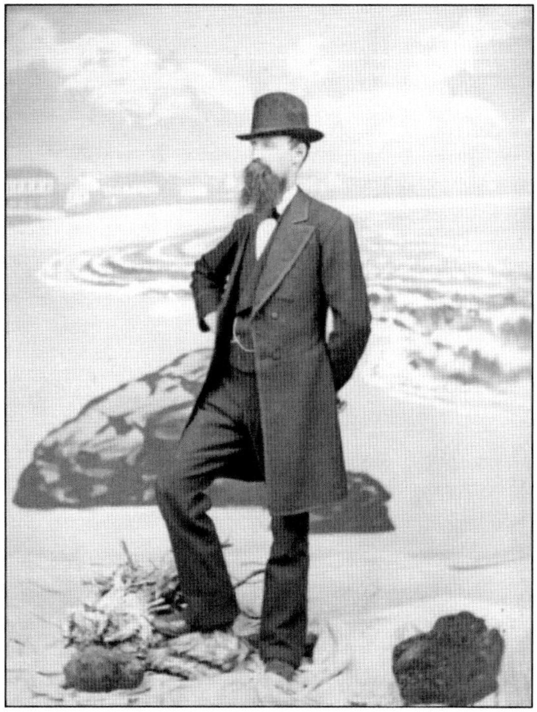

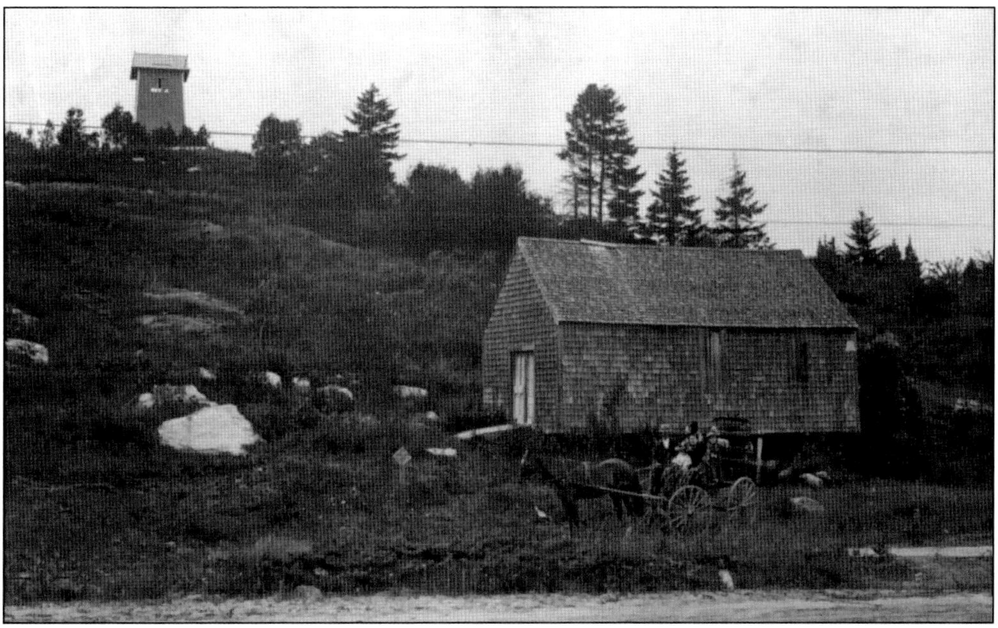

Although Charles Gooding was gifted as a photographer, he was an inept entrepreneur. Anticipating a flood of tourists along the trolley line, he built a viewing tower and historical park near Pleasant Street. On the road going up the hill, he had names and dates from Yarmouth history carved in granite. Tourists could buy his homemade elderberry tonic at the Old Ledge School, examine the weathervane of the first meetinghouse, and view an "Indian footprint" carved in the ledge. The ocean view from his tower was lovely but not a commercial success. (Collection of Lois Rogers Lippincott.)

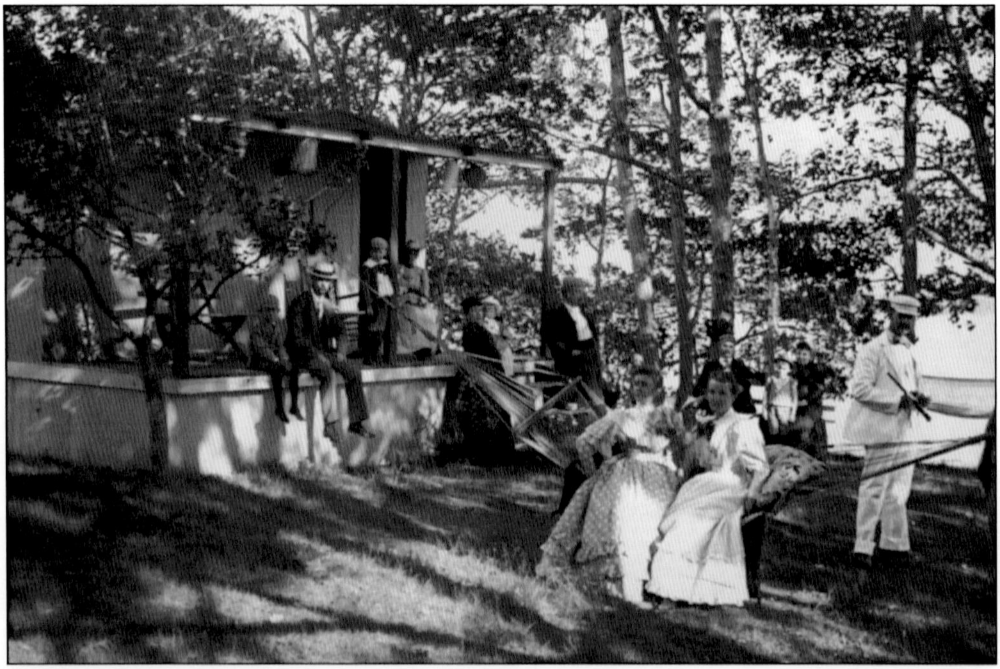

Charles Gooding's tiny cottage on Bucknam's Point may have been the same small studio he once kept by the Grand Trunk depot. To achieve this idyllic family portrait, he has carefully staged their relaxation. If the man with the spyglass actually had a chance to use it, he had a fine view of Yarmouth's main shipping channel, which then ran along Princes Point, not out toward the east as it does today. (Collection of Lois Rogers Lippincott.)

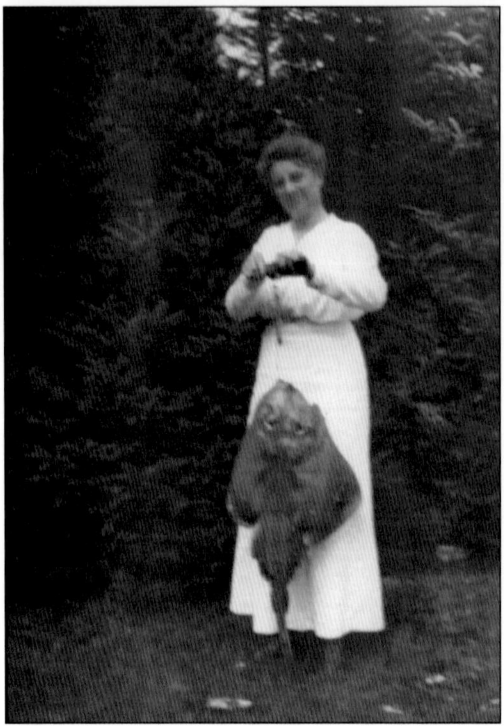

The informality of this c. 1914 snapshot provides a sharp contrast with the Victorian view of cottage life that is shown in the previous picture. The woman holding this skate is a Mrs. Proctor, who was probably married to one of the Proctor brothers that ran a dry goods store in the Upper Village. (Collection of the Yarmouth Historical Society.)

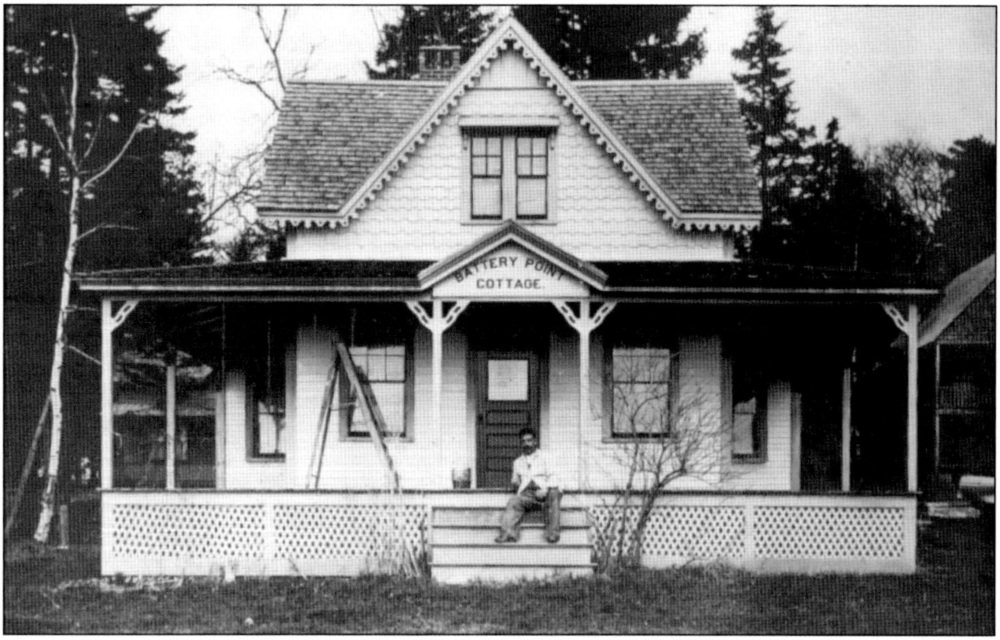

Erected for eight members of the Yarmouth Band in 1884, this cottage was the first one built on Princes Point. By 1908, when Leon Collins was photographed painting the building, it was known as Battery Point Cottage. Ferdinand Corliss took this picture while standing on the historic earthworks used to defend the town during the Revolution and the War of 1812. (Collection of Richard Thoits.)

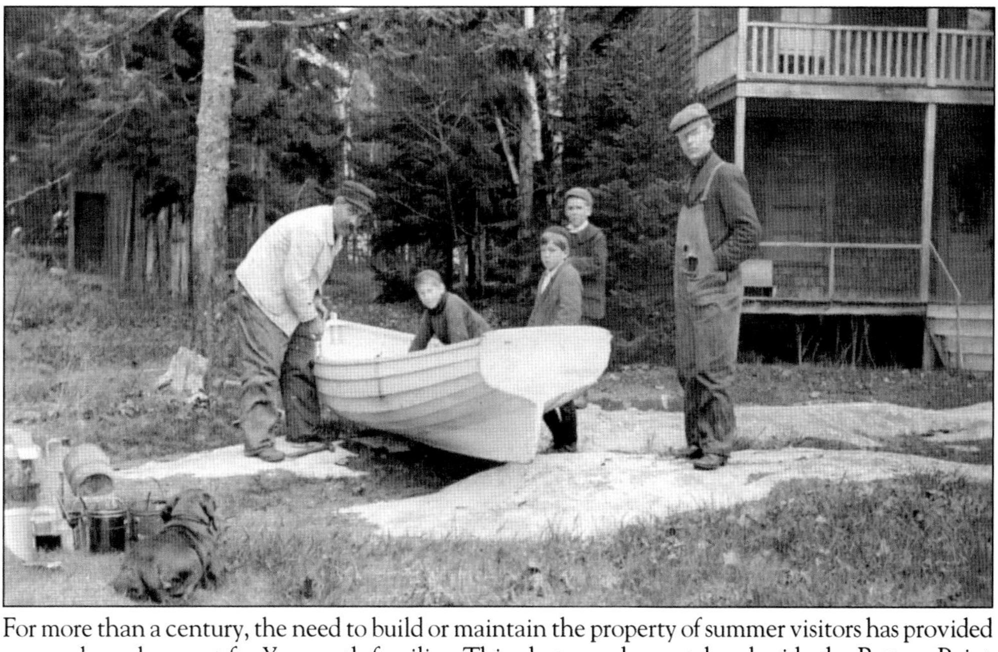
For more than a century, the need to build or maintain the property of summer visitors has provided seasonal employment for Yarmouth families. This photograph was taken beside the Battery Point Cottage on the same day as the previous image. From left to right are Leon Collins, Bob Collins, Ed Collins, Clarence "Mit" Collins, and Bert Corliss. Bob Collins later recalled that this was his very first lesson in how to paint a boat. (Collection of Richard Thoits.)

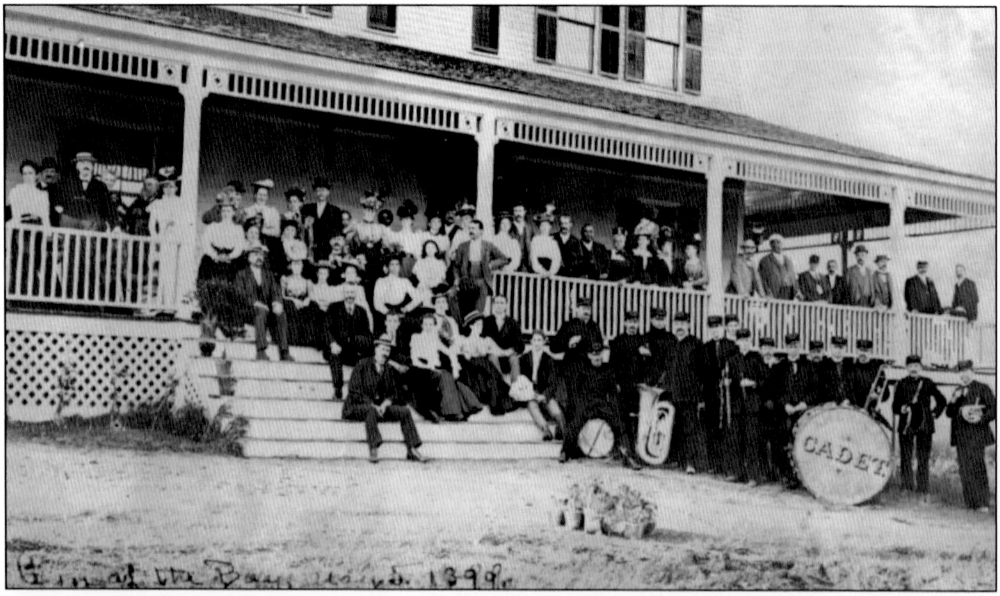

The grand opening of Yarmouth's first big summer hotel was captured in this photograph on May 5, 1899. Four stories high and perched on a hill, the Gem of the Bay dominated the skyline of Princes Point. With steam heat, several telephones, and electric bells in each room, the resort was very luxurious. When it burned in October 1900, a local girl lamented, "When with reel and hose they reached the shore, a heap of ruins and nothing more." (Collection of Lois Rogers Lippincott.)

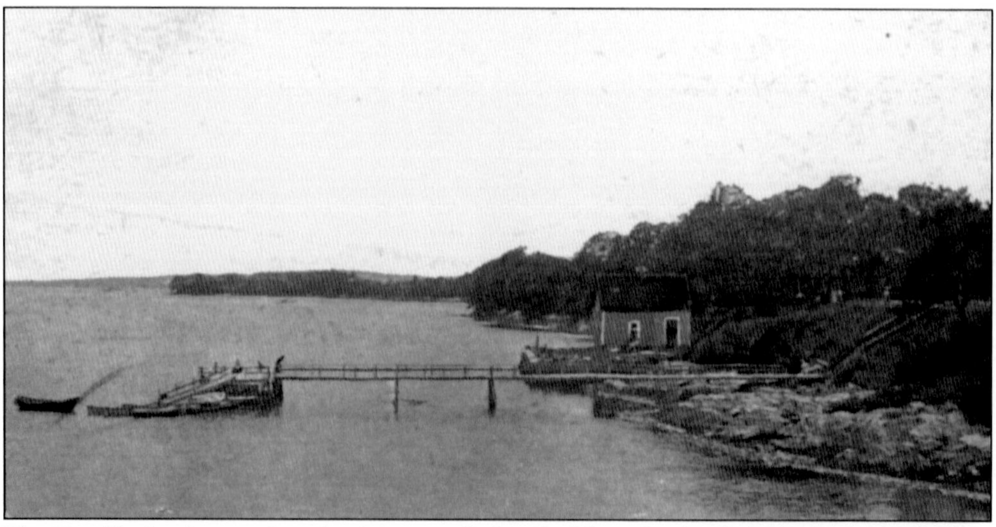

The Trimble family ran a boardinghouse at the head of this wharf and also operated a quarry in Whites Cove for paving stones c. 1905. The little house in this picture was later transformed into Tides, one of the 12 guest cottages associated with Homewood Inn. Damaged by ice, the wharf was later relocated, creating a spot on the shore for another popular Homewood Inn cottage called Houseboat. (Collection of Chris Havey.)

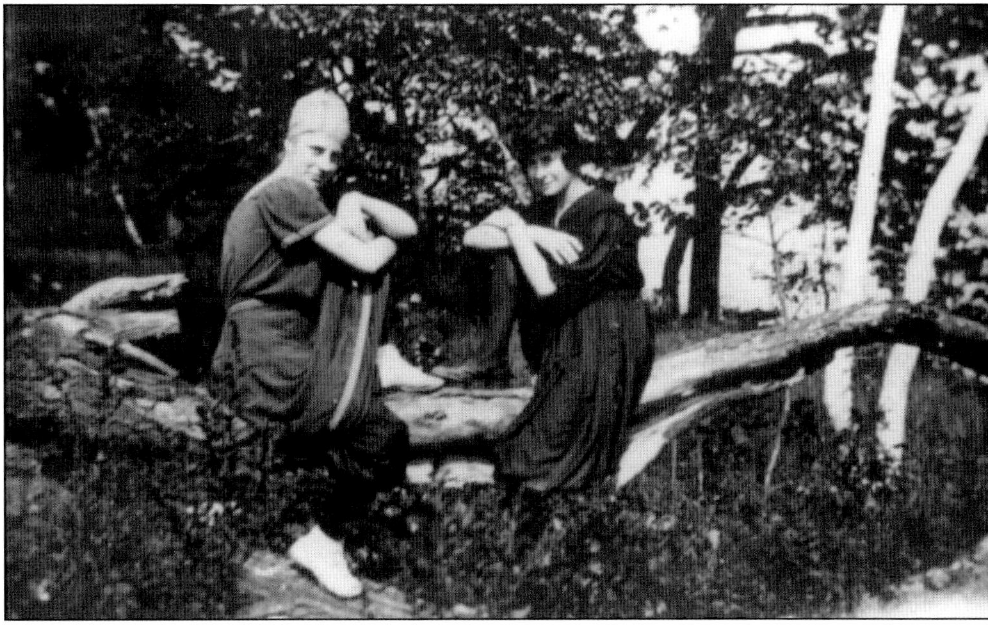

During a break from work in the summer of 1918, two of the waitresses at Homewood Inn pose for this swimsuit picture. While working at the inn, Edna Marston (left) stayed in a room over the garage. In 1919, she was hired as a teacher for Yarmouth's most rural school—the Pratt School, located on North Road. Four years later, she married George Lombard. (Collection of the Yarmouth Historical Society.)

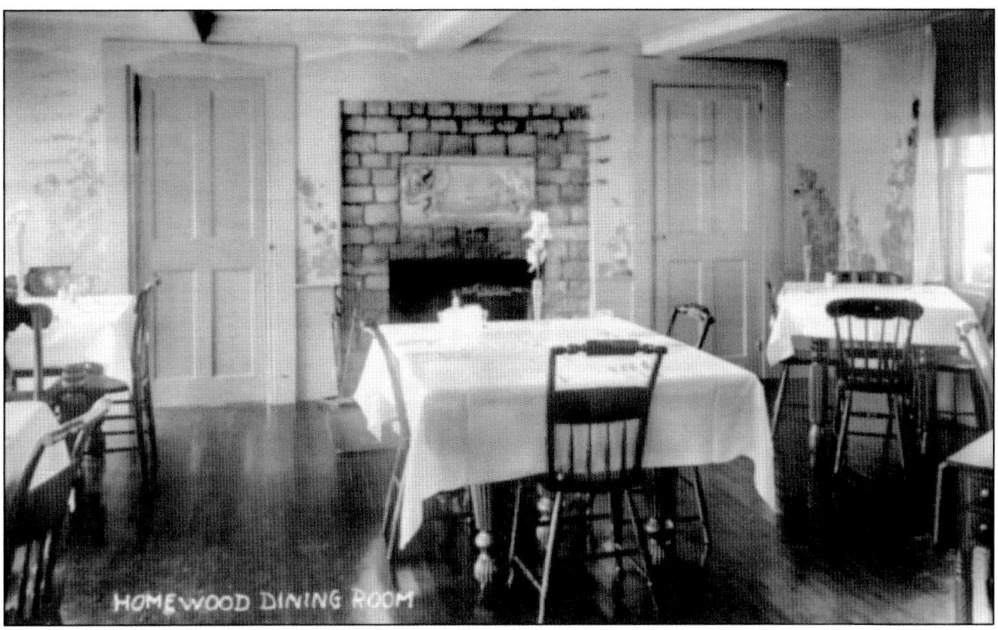

With its restaurant, swimming pool, gift shop, and relaxed style, Homewood Inn attracted guests from 1912 to 1992 and became the last survivor of Yarmouth's many seaside tourist havens. When Mabel Knight sent this postcard in 1934, she asked her friend Bertha, "Can you picture us at the center table eating good food and having a fine view of Casco Bay?" (Collection of Frank Witkowski.)

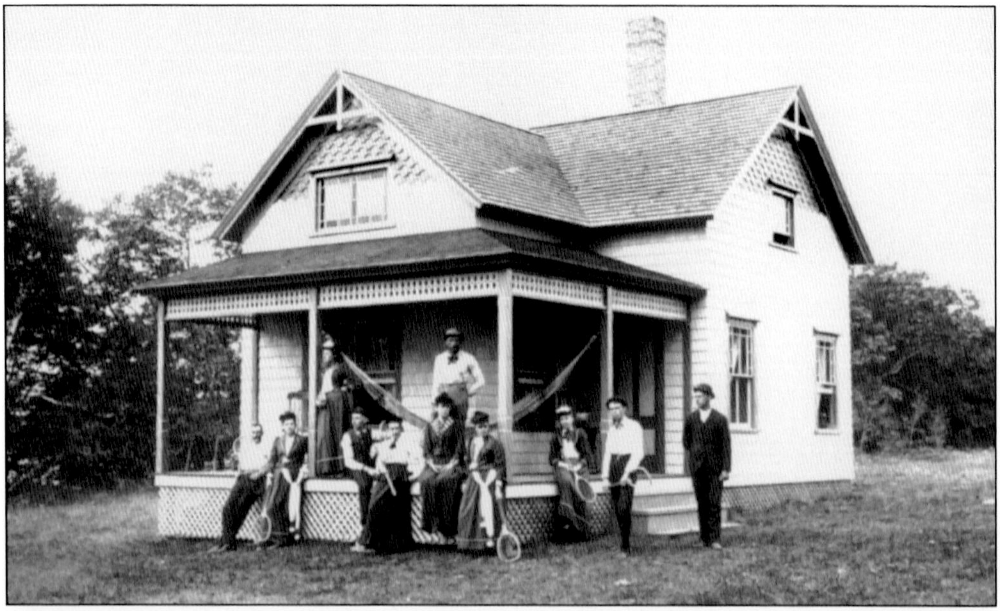

Changes in transportation, such as steamboats and trolleys, made it possible for the inns and boardinghouses on Princes Point to attract distant guests. In the 1880s, the Grand Trunk railway brought an influx of Canadian visitors, including "Mr. D.A. Lewis, the great tennis player from Montreal." Suddenly, lawn tennis became a favorite amusement, leading to an August 1889 tournament at Drinkwater's boardinghouse. (Collection of the Maine Historic Preservation Commission.)

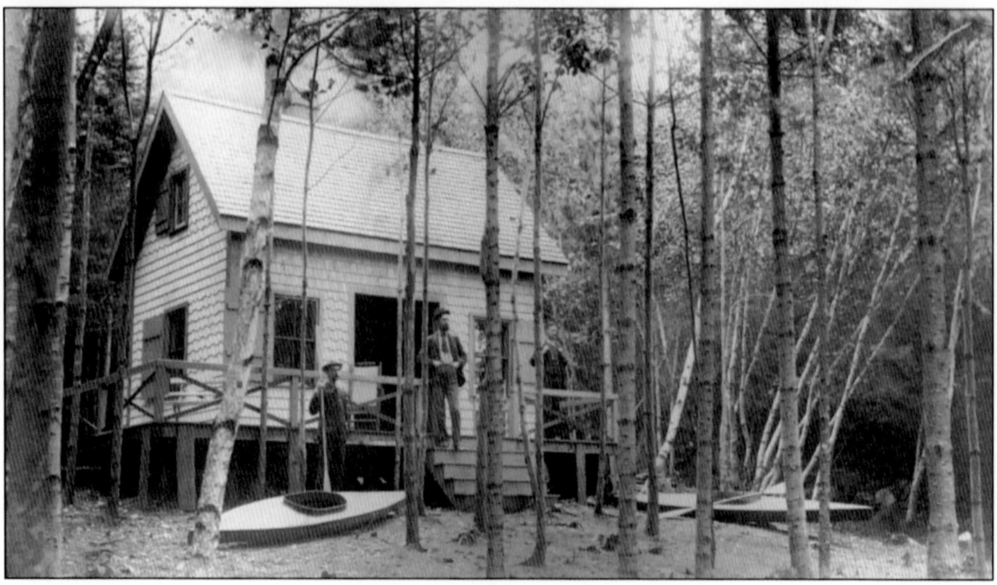

This curious photograph was pasted into an album and labeled "Princes Point." Although the exact location is unknown, the picture was probably taken by Charles Gooding *c*. 1895, possibly near White's Cove. The two boats that strongly resemble kayaks have led to speculation that these men had some connection to Robert Peary's polar expeditions. Although no link has been established, Peary built his own cottage a few miles away on Eagle Island in 1904. (Collection of Lois Rogers Lippincott.)

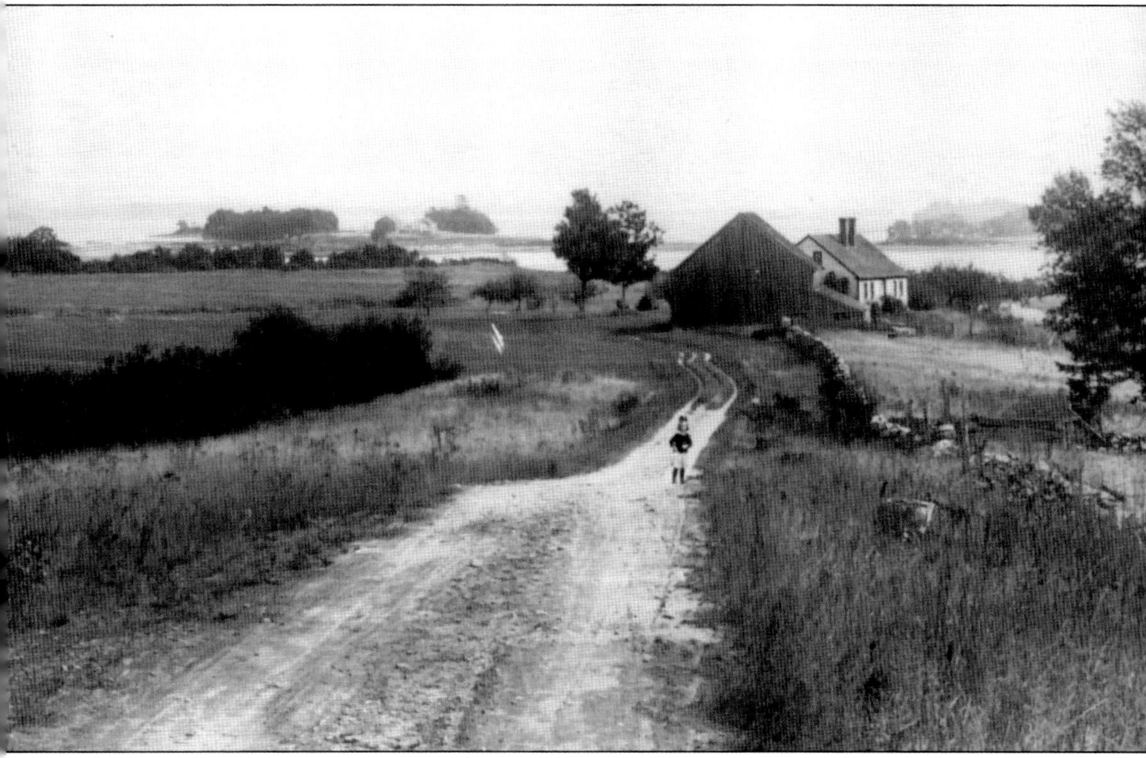

The lifestyle and landscape of Yarmouth's islands were profoundly altered in the 1890s, when investors started to divide the old farms into cottage lots. In 1955, the island was again transformed when a bridge was opened from the mainland to Cousins Island. This photograph from the 1920s looks north toward Harold Sawyer's old farm on Cornfield Point. For much of the 20th century, this beautiful property was owned by the Gibson family. (Collection of Mildred Kenney.)

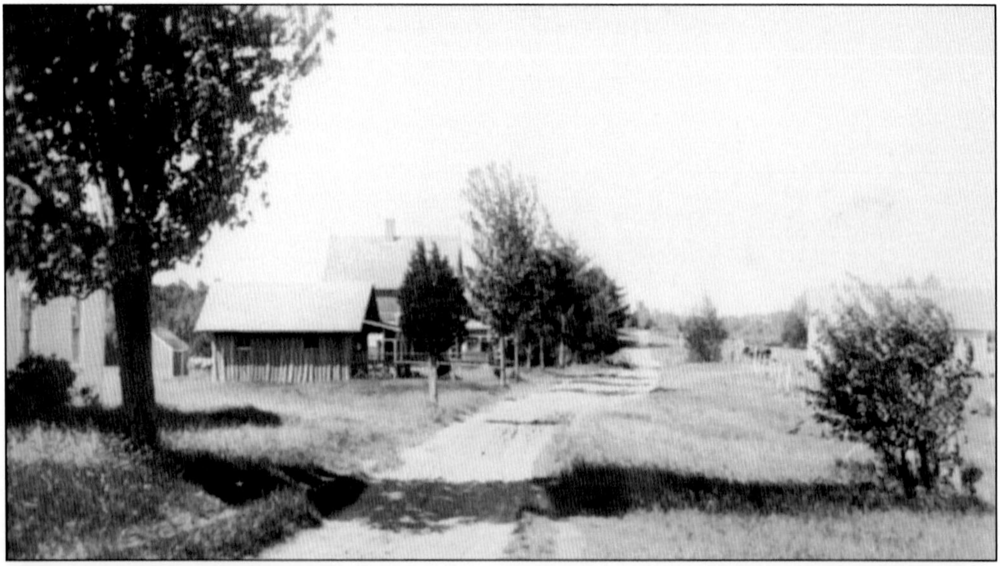

The main road of Cousins Island was still a dirt track *c.* 1917. Joseph Hamilton built the farmhouse on the left in 1848 and faced it toward Chebeague. It burned in 1920. Hamilton's daughter Lizzie built the adjacent log cabin in 1916 as a gift shop and post office. The tall building beyond the cabin was a cottage for Hamilton's daughter Hattie and her husband, Capt. John G. Drinkwater. Across the road on the right was the Rent store, which operated during the summer from 1908 until 1938. (Collection of Mildred Kenney.)

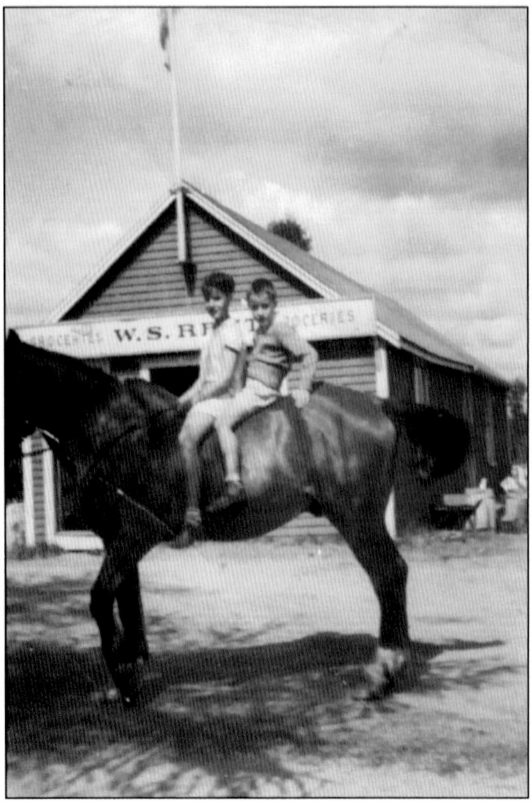

William and Edith Rent set up their store across the street from her parents' cottage. After William's untimely death in 1921, Edith continued to manage the store and also became the island's postmaster. Her daughter Margaret was running the post office in 1936 when Nancy Blanchard and David Kenney showed up one day on horseback. (Collection of Mildred Kenney.)

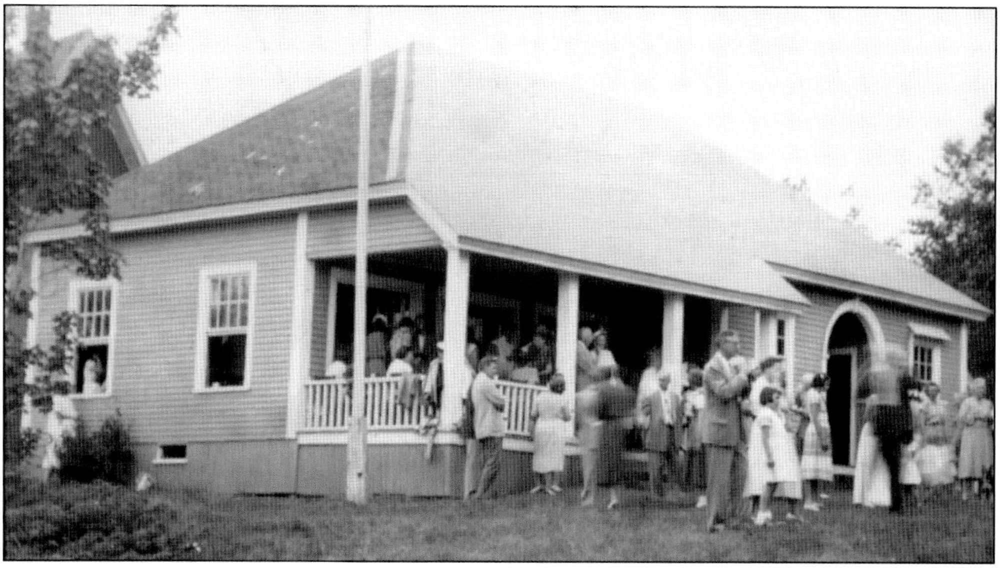

The right side of the Community House began its life in 1898 as a new school for the island's eight children. The committee went $90 over budget, because they figured that no school could be held "without seats or heat." After the school closed c. 1915, the building was expanded to provide a meeting space for islanders. David and Mildred Kenney were celebrating their wedding on July 1, 1950, when someone stopped and took this picture, which soon became a postcard. (Collection of Mildred Kenney.)

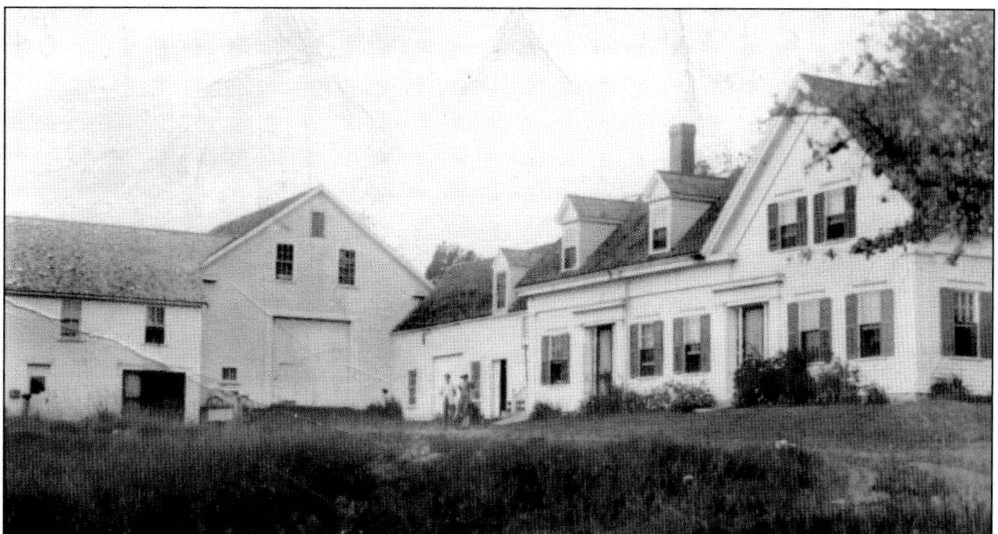

Located near the road to the wharf, the Ridge House was a Cousins Island landmark for more than a century. Capt. Lorenzo Hamilton, who built the farm c. 1859, also owned one of the legendary stone sloops that moved Maine granite along the coast. Between 1938 and 1943, the Ridge House served as the post office and store for Cousins Island. (Collection of Mildred Kenney.)

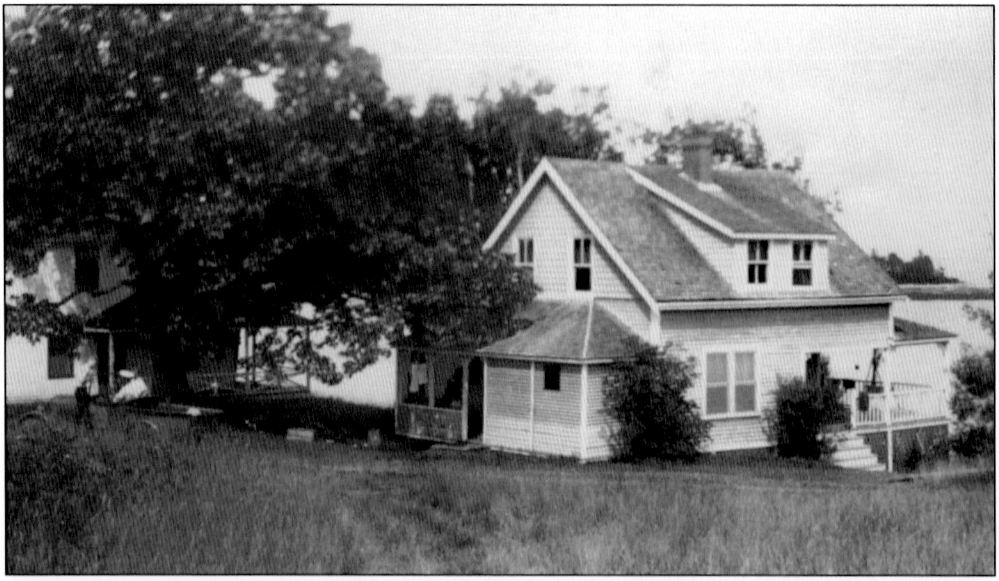

Next to the Cousins Island wharf are two classic summer cottages, Seabreeze (left) and Lingamore. The view from their porches looks across to the islands of Littlejohns and Chebeague. The man who has stopped his truck to chat is probably Raymond Talbot, the mail carrier from the steamer wharf to the post office. In 1886, John F. Hill built a hotel called the Casco House on this site. It was quite popular with Canadian guests until it burned *c.* 1904. (Collection of Mildred Kenney.)

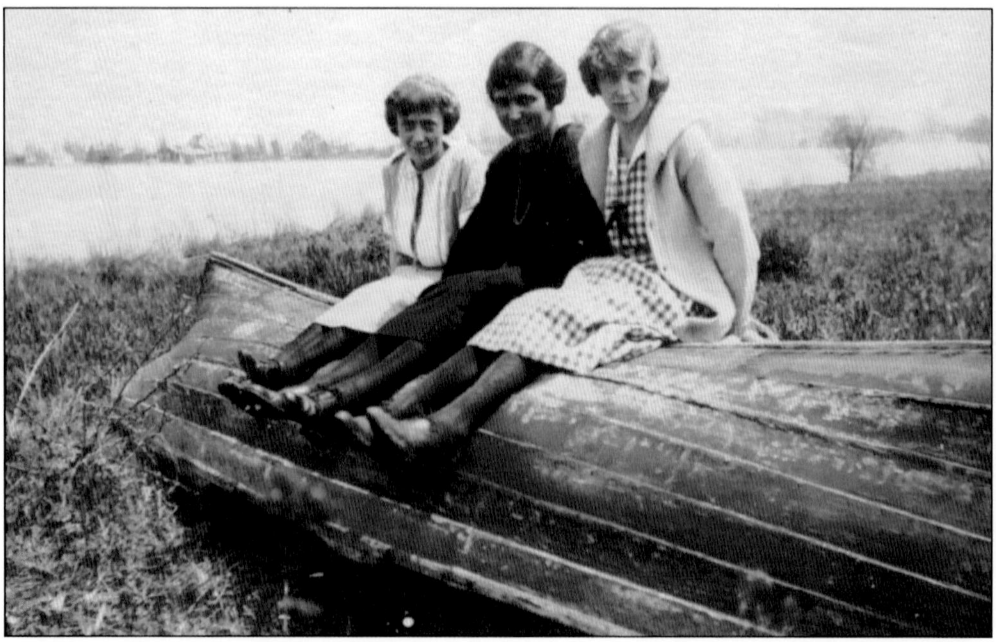

For many years, the Lingamore cottage was associated with Helen Booth, a chemistry teacher from Philadelphia who often invited her teaching friends to spend the summer with her. In this May 19, 1923 view, Booth poses with her sister and Helen Hartman on a rather sway-backed rowboat. (Collection of Alfreda Drinkwater Thurston.)

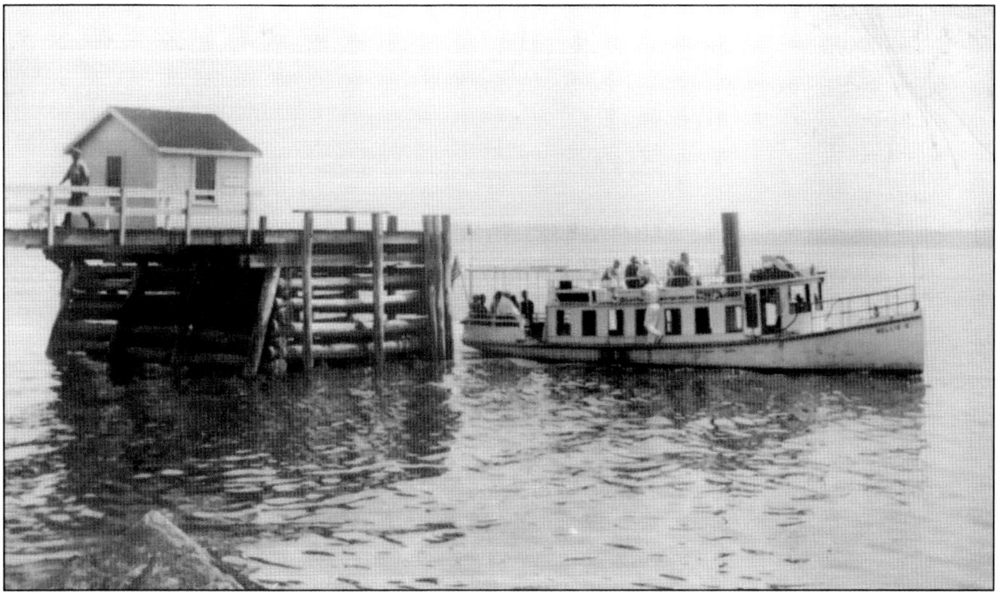

The energetic steamboats of the Casco Bay Lines provided the freight, passenger, and mail services on which island life depended. In an unlikely move, Capt. Orrin Swett of Falmouth began his own passenger service during the Great Depression. His *Nellie* G. was purchased secondhand in Boothbay and provided convenient service from Cousins, Littlejohn's, and Chebeague Islands to the Handy Boat Service in Falmouth. The venture was successful, and various boats with the name *Nellie* G. continued to run until the bridge was built. (Collection of Mildred Kenney.)

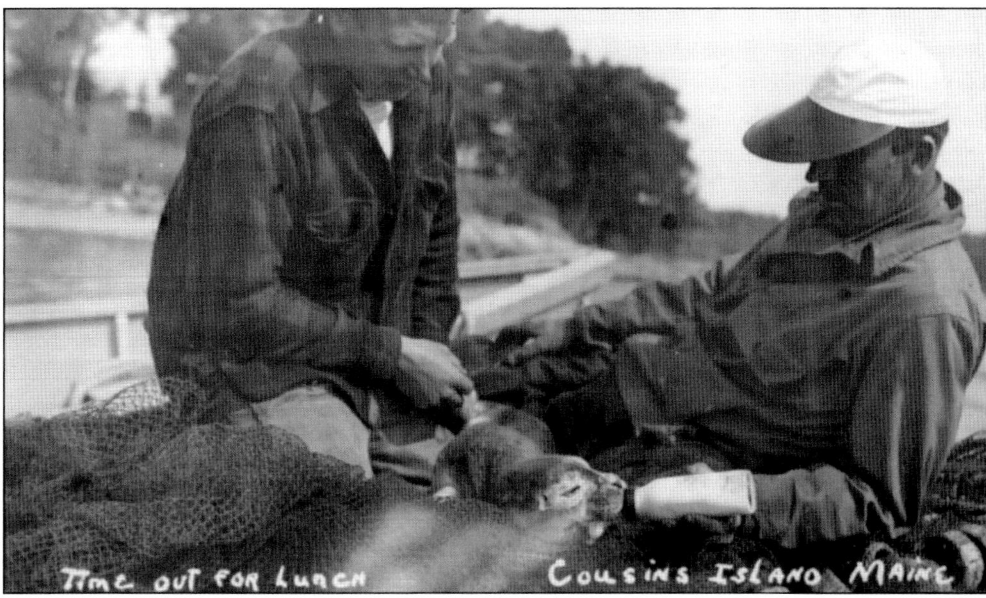

Mildred Kenney recalls seeing these two fishermen feeding a baby seal at the Cousins Island dock in the late 1940s. Although the seal's chances of survival may not have been great, at least the town was no longer paying a bounty to fishermen for killing seals, as it did *c.* 1900. One of these fishermen was Eddie Talbot, whose parents—Carrie and Raymond—handled the island's mail. (Collection of Mildred Kenney.)

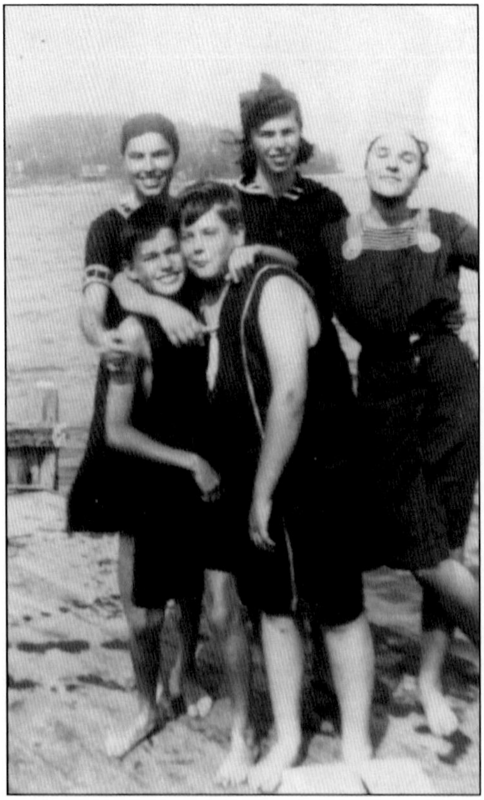

Swimming at the Cousins Island dock was particularly entertaining on a summer day in 1944, after the Luckhardt family discovered a box of old-fashioned bathing suits in Daybreak Cottage. This group includes, from left to right, the following: (front row) Phil Luckhardt and Doug Thompson; (back row) Jean Luckhardt, Mildred Luckhardt, and Nancy Blanchard. While they were posing, the *Nellie* G. unloaded a group of very surprised passengers. During the cottage construction boom of the 1890s, the town passed a bylaw that prohibited swimming in waters adjacent to wharves and bridges "so as to be exposed to the view of spectators." Mildred Luckhardt now owns Daybreak Cottage with her husband, David Kenney. (Collection of Mildred Kenney.)

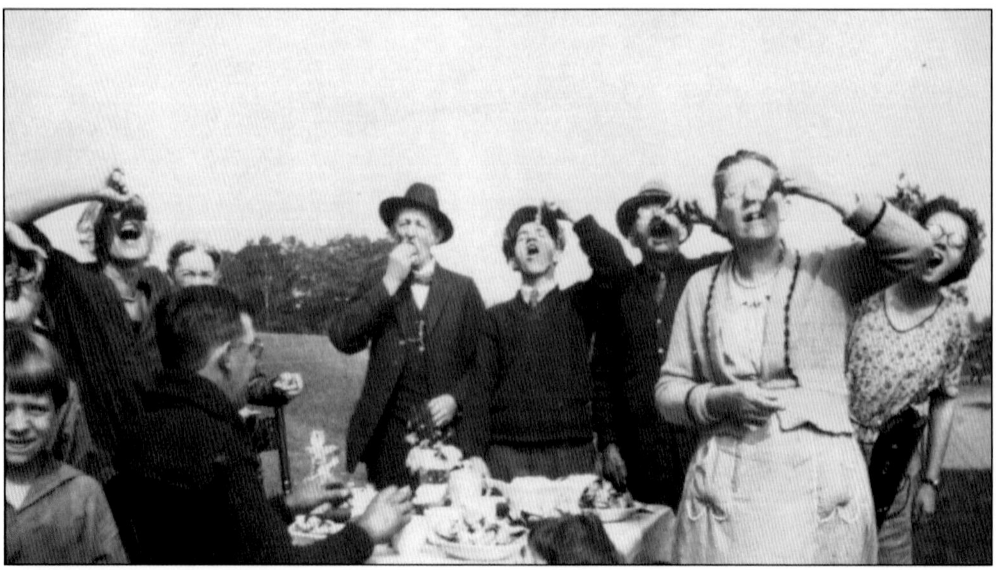

Clambakes are still an important part of summertime along the shore. Although steamed soft-shell clams have a distinctive and delightful flavor, there is nothing attractive about watching people eat them. The Frost family from Dixfield was photographed at this Yarmouth clambake in 1922. (Collection of Alfreda Drinkwater Thurston.)

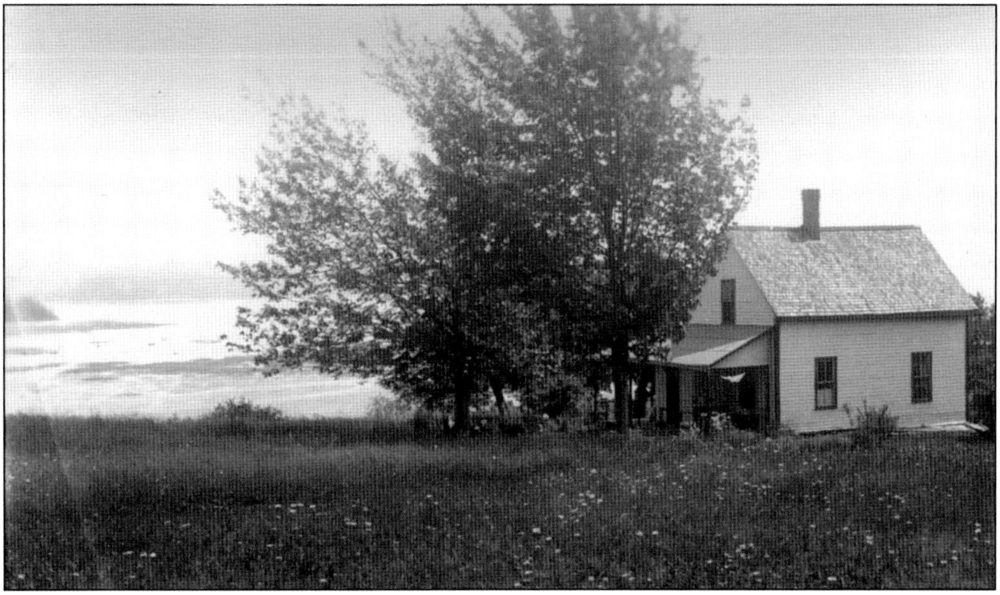

A scenic and twisting road leads from the Cousins Island Community House to the Littlejohn bridge. It was along this road that an artist named Edith Widing Yaffee set up a studio in the cottage on the right. After receiving formal training at several prestigious art schools, she painted such notables as Teddy Roosevelt's daughter, Alice Longworth. When she died in 1961, she was buried in the Cousins Island cemetery. (Collection of Alfreda Drinkwater Thurston.)

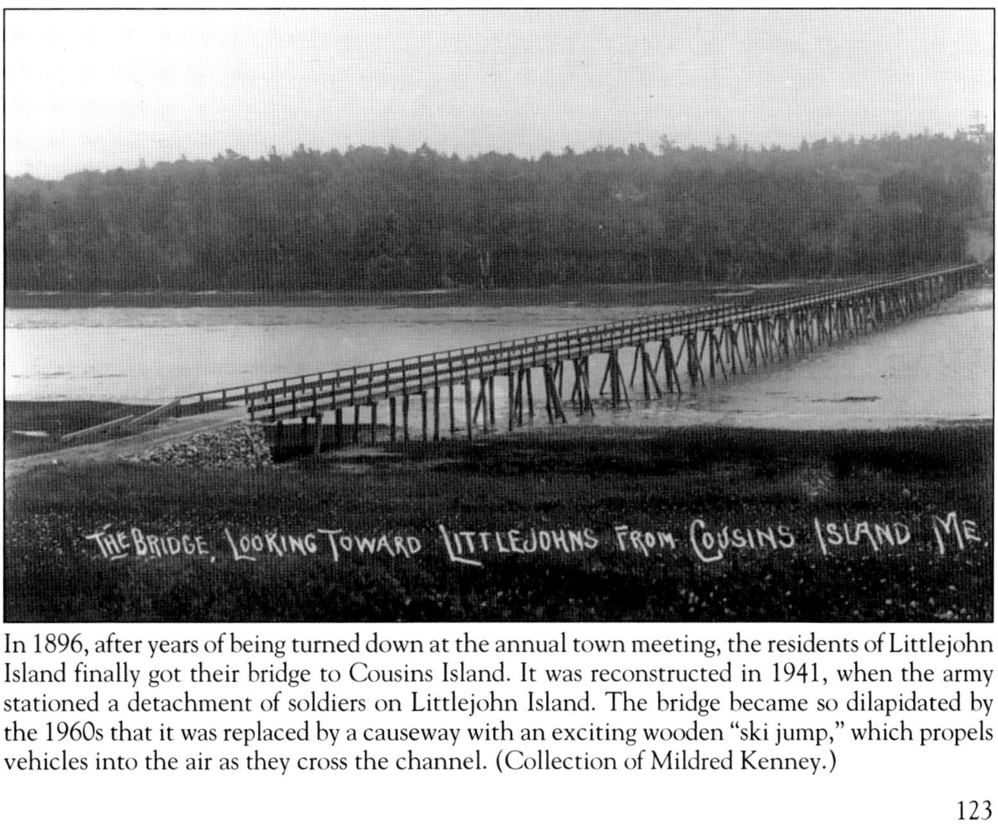

In 1896, after years of being turned down at the annual town meeting, the residents of Littlejohn Island finally got their bridge to Cousins Island. It was reconstructed in 1941, when the army stationed a detachment of soldiers on Littlejohn Island. The bridge became so dilapidated by the 1960s that it was replaced by a causeway with an exciting wooden "ski jump," which propels vehicles into the air as they cross the channel. (Collection of Mildred Kenney.)

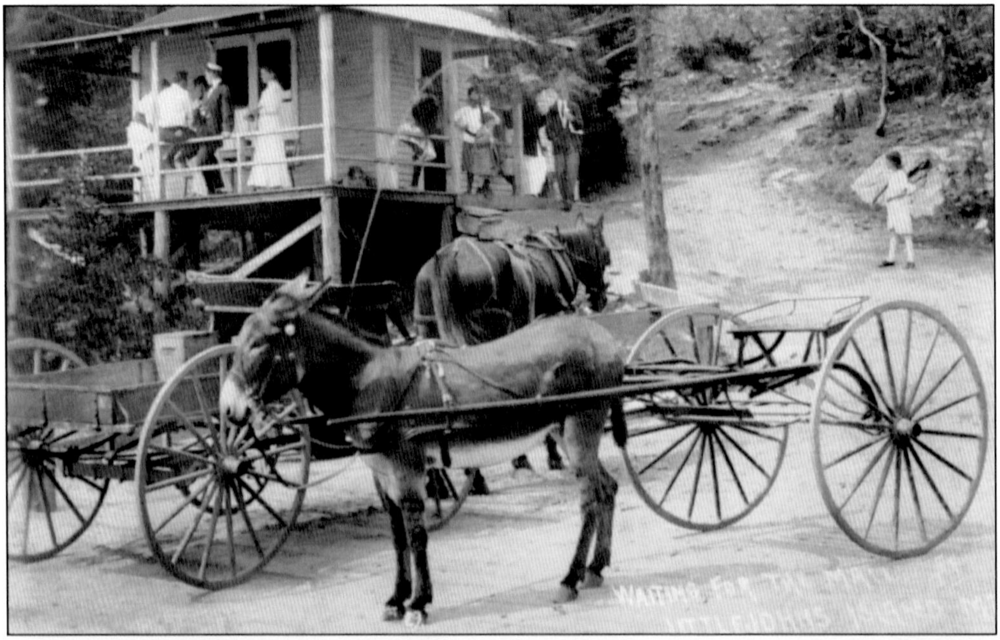

At the head of the Littlejohn Island steamer wharf was a tiny post office where island residents and hotel guests mingled while waiting for their mail to be sorted. Although it looks a bit precarious, the building stood from *c.* 1910 until 1960, with Alice Prescott serving as postmaster for most of that time. In 1907, a burro was shipped from Colorado as a gift to the Prescott children. Two weeks later, it gave birth, doubling the island's herd of burros. (Collection of the Yarmouth Historical Society.)

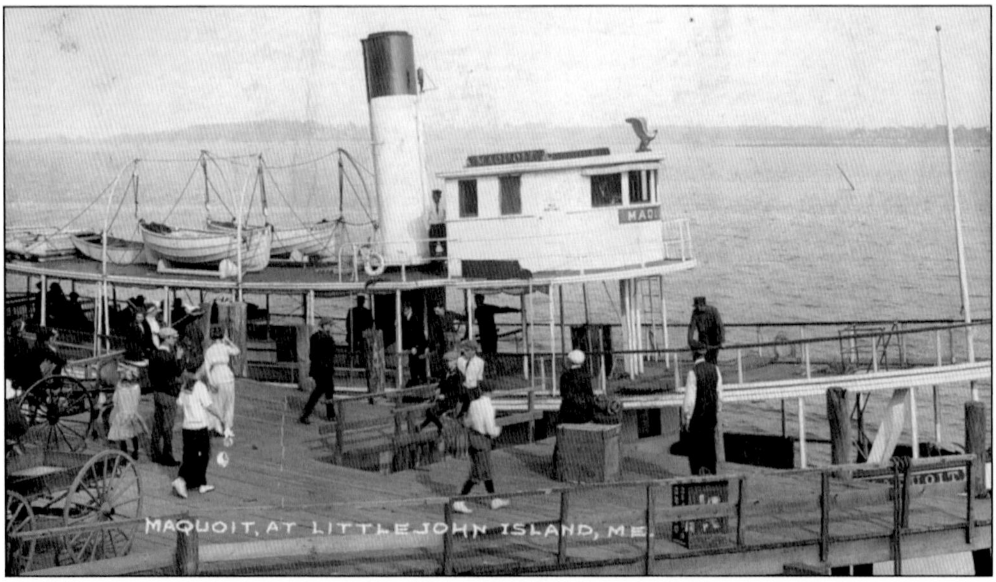

With its steam whistle blowing and a throng of people on the dock, the arrival of a ferry boat was always an exciting part of island life. The 85-foot *Maquoit* was one of the most popular steamboats, with a carved golden eagle perched over Captain Taylor's wheelhouse. Ray Robbins, the quartermaster, stands by the smokestack. On the dock, Katherine Prescott is seated in the donkey cart in this 1909 photograph. (Collection of Mildred Kenney.)

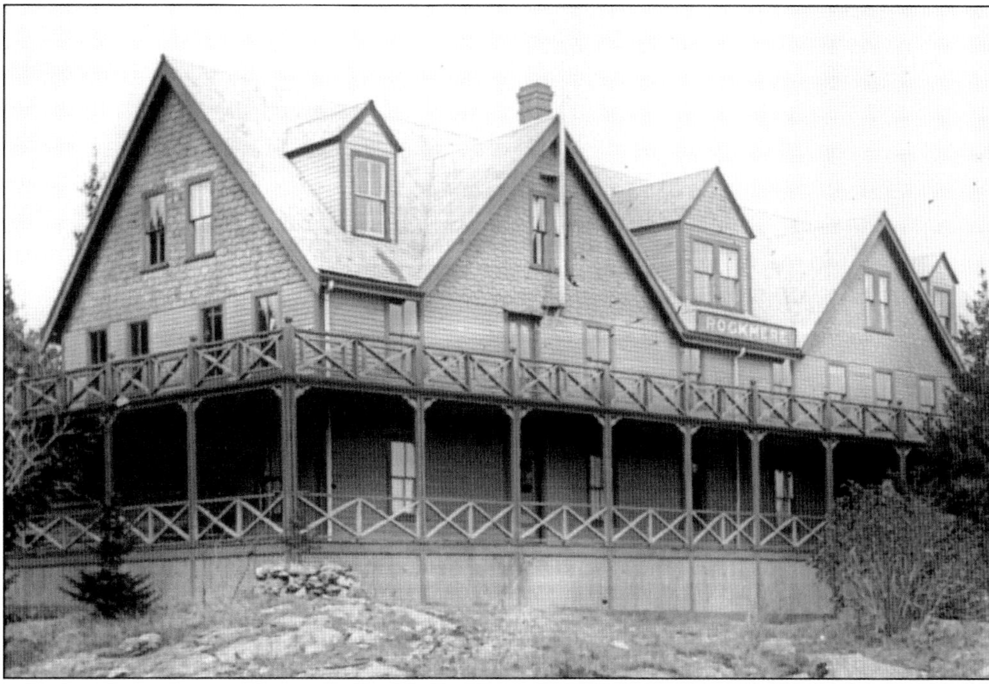

In 1893, the western end of Littlejohn Island was sold to a development company that laid out 325 cottage lots. Since the company was headed by a man from Melrose, Massachusetts, the island's first hotel was named the Melrose House. Later renamed Rockmere, it stood on the hill directly above the wharf. The dances, whist parties, and lobster bakes held in the hotel's dining room made it the social center of island life in the summer. (Collection of the Yarmouth Historical Society.)

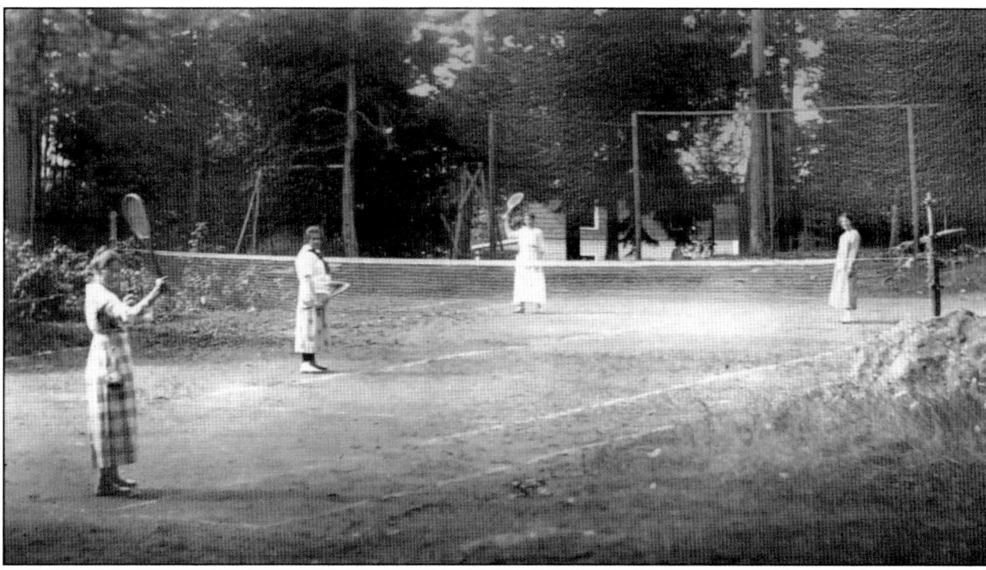

In addition to having a poolroom and a bowling alley, Rockmere had a tennis court. Tournaments were sometimes played against teams from Bustins Island and Cousins Island. This site, overlooking the Littlejohn wharf, is now owned by the Wibby family. (Collection of Peter Moulton.)

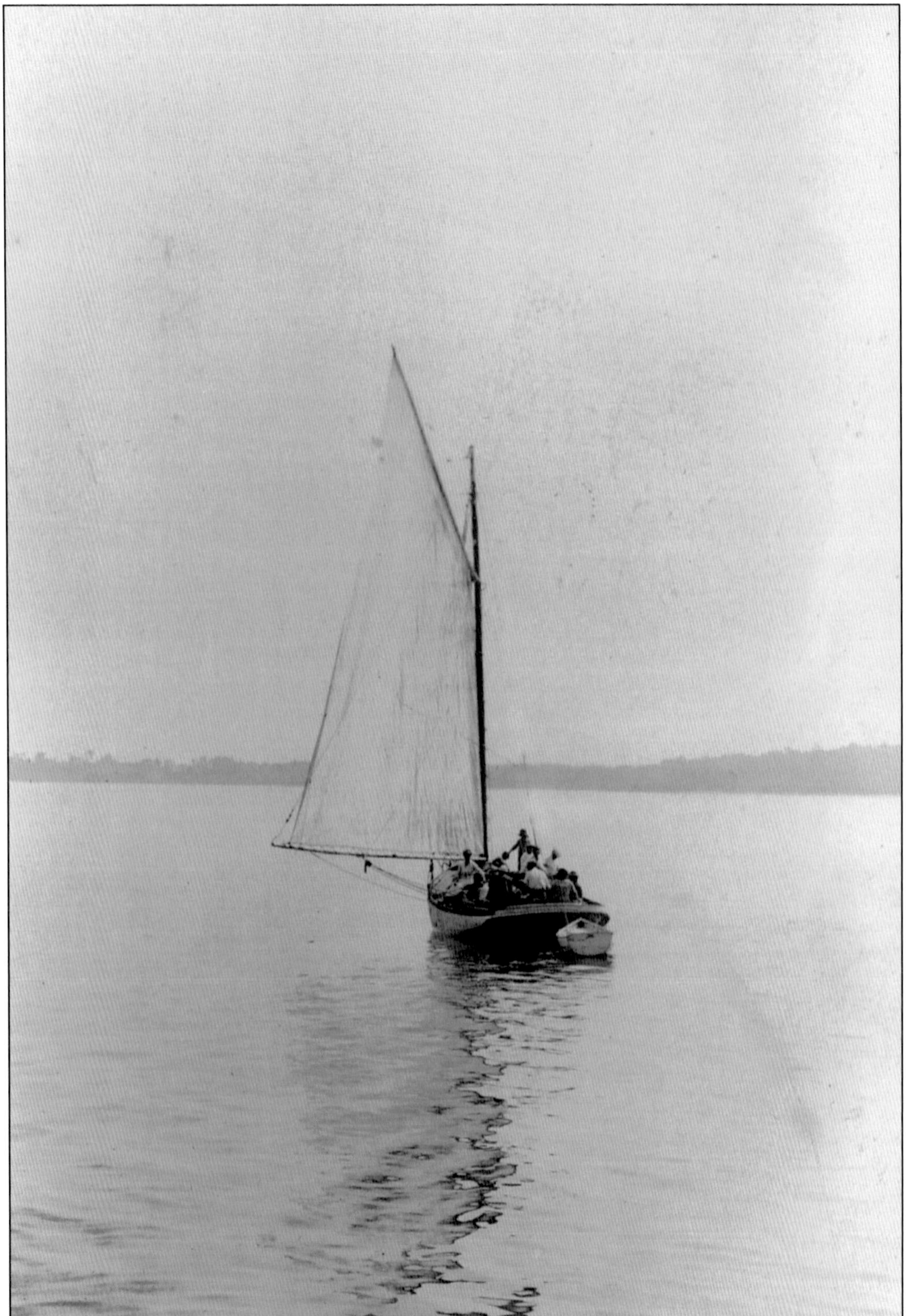

In a tranquil moment c. 1924, the gaff-rigged sloop *Wanderlust* drifts toward the sunset with a party of summer guests. (Collection of Alfreda Drinkwater Thurston.)

ACKNOWLEDGMENTS

After 30 years of doing historical research in libraries, I was delighted that this project gave me the opportunity to learn about the history of Yarmouth from the vantage point of kitchen tables. Many Yarmouth people graciously shared the old photographs and stories that make this book not only possible but interesting. I am particularly grateful for the assistance I received from Alfreda Drinkwater Thurston, Dick and Lois Rogers Lippincott, Mildred and David Kenney, Richard Thoits, Ruth Chaisson, Tom and Alan Dugas, Frank Knight, Virginia Turner, Peter Moulton, Stan Milton, Frank Witkowski, Brenda Roy, and Chris Havey. Bruce Ingraham also deserves special recognition for sending me scanned images of rare Gooding photographs all the way from California. Several other computer wizards politely refrained from laughing while I learned how to scan photographs: Whit Ford, Alison Kenway, Alice Barr, and Gail Sweeney.

I certainly appreciate the fact that the Yarmouth Historical Society made available its extraordinary collection of photographs. The society's director, Marilyn Hinkley, was especially helpful in locating elusive images. Earle Shettleworth of the Maine Historic Preservation Commission provided not only dozens of photos from his extensive collection but also encouraging advice. Chief Fairbanks of the Yarmouth Fire Department generously shared his stories and several historic images from the department's collection of artifacts. I am also indebted to many people who pointed me in the direction of collections of photographs or unusual facts used in this book: Michele Petrucci, Erika Thoits, Ursula Baier, Janice Seabury, Ada Reed, Virginia Ingraham, Ed Ferrell, Gary Ricker, and Carl Winslow. Finally, two people gently prodded me toward the deadlines and away from foolish mistakes: Susie Jaggard from Arcadia Publishing and my irrepressible wife, Martha.

Bibliography

Annual Report of the Bureau of Industrial and Labor Statistics, *Kennebec Journal*. Augusta: 1901–1905.

Annual Report of the Town of Yarmouth, 1894–1948.

Board of Trade Journal. Portland. December 1890, May 1900, January 1916.

Bunting, W.H. *A Day's Work*, Part I. Gardiner: Tilbury House, 1997.

Collins, Robert S. *Wescustogo & Aucocisco*. South Portland: the Pilot Press, 1975.

Corliss, Augustus W., ed. *Old Times of North Yarmouth, Maine*. Somersworth, New Hampshire: New Hampshire Publishing Company, 1977.

Day, Clarence. "A History of Maine Agriculture, 1604–1860," *Bulletin*. University of Maine, April 1954.

Dunn, William. *Casco Bay Steamboat Album*. Camden: Downeast, 1969.

Freehand, Julianna. *A Seafaring Legacy*. New York: Random House, 1981.

Freeport Historical Society. *Six Town Times*.

Holt, Jeff. *The Grand Trunk in New England*. Toronto: Railfare Book, 1986.

Hopkinson, David B. *From Ship to Zip*. Portland and Cousins Island: Privately published, 1987.

Hopkinson, David B. *Joseph and Nancy Hamilton and Their Children's Families*. Portland and Cousins Island: Privately published, 1982.

Jones, Augustus F., ed. *Two Maine Islands*. South Portland: the Pilot Press, 1978.

Plummer, Edward C. *Reminiscences of a Yarmouth Schoolboy*. Portland: Marks Printing House, 1926.

Maine Register. Portland: G.M. Donham, 1880–1933.

Rogers, Orville F. *Grandma's Island and Grandma's Ocean*. Privately published, 1970.

Rowe, William Hutchinson. *Ancient North Yarmouth and Yarmouth, Maine*. Rockport: Picton Press, 2000.

Rowe, William Hutchinson. *The Maritime History of Maine*. Freeport: the Bond Wheelwright Company, 1948.

S.D. Warren Company. *A History of S.D. Warren Company*. Portland: the Anthoensen Press, 1955.

Talk of the Towns 2, No. 10. September 2, 1949.

The Freeport Press 13, No. 8. Freeport, August 5, 1949.

The Sentinel 1–3. Freeport, 1889–1892.

The Hermes. Yarmouth, 1901–1910; 1921–1928.

Vertical files and scrapbooks from the Yarmouth Historical Society archives.